Childless Is Not Less

VICKY LOVE

BETHANY HOUSE PUBLISHERS
MINNEAPOLIS, MINNESOTA 55438
A Division of Bethany Fellowship, Inc.

Published by Bethany House Publishers
A Division of Bethany Fellowship, Inc.
6820 Auto Club Road, Minneapolis, MN 55438

Printed in the United States of America

Library of Congress Cataloging in Publication Data

Love, Vicky.
    Childless is not less.

    Bibliography: p.
    1. Childlessness—Psychological aspects. 2. Infertility—Religious aspects—Christianity. 3. Church work.
I. Title.
HQ734.L757   1984   304.6'6   84–20464
ISBN 0–87123–449–1 (pbk.)

DEDICATION

A Love Gift
to all those
who are searching with us to find,
if not the reasons for,
purpose and fulfillment in the midst of
childlessness.

Other Works Printed or Published by the Author

1968–   *Curriculum Guide for Third Grade Reading Program*
         Seaside Public Schools
         Seaside, Oregon

         Sole authorship

1971–   *Curriculum Guide for Early Childhood Education*
         Prepared for the Head Start Program
         Portland Public Schools
         Portland, Oregon

         Member of a writing team

1975–   *What to Do When There's Nothing to Do It With*
         A guide for International Children's Conference Programs
         Prepared for Operation Mobilisation, Leuven, Belgium

         Sole authorship

1977–Present
         The Covenant Companion
         Monthly Denominational Voice for the Evangelical Covenant Church

         Contributing author

THE AUTHOR

VICKY LOVE graduated Summa Cum Laude from Eastern Oregon College in 1965, earning a B.S. in elementary education. She has also done graduate work in library science at Central Missouri State College. She and her husband are presently involved in a church planting ministry in Mexico City, Mexico.

ACKNOWLEDGMENTS

—My loving partner, Jerry, the best father who never was, who conceived—not a baby—but this book with me. Together we continue to care about its life as it speaks to you.

—Our families who have been committed to us in spite of never receiving what we would most loved to have given.

—Our friends who have so believed it was possible for these words to reach you that they prayed.

—Childless people worldwide who shared their personal journeys.

—Michael Baum, Dr. Edwin A. Hallsten, Jr., Carl Racine, and Daniel Seagren who critiqued without destroying.

—Cena Huston and Sue Mullins who read with their hearts and encouraged with pen and phone.

—Jesus, our Best Friend, who alone gives us reason to believe for ourselves and others that Childless Is Not Less.

FOREWORD

there is no pain i know as crushing and potentially
destructive as infertility, no human experience that every
month, for the rest of a woman's life, reminds her of the grief.
the loss. the shattered dream. the defectiveness. the empty
place. i have been there, and though, as yet, my situation
does not look as hopeless as many others', i know about the
guttural sobs, the tears, the negative pregnancy tests, the
miscarriages . . . and even going to pick up your adopted
newborn and have the mother change her mind while you're
enroute

vicki love has written the story well. she is thorough and
sensitive and creative and Biblical in her presentation. one
identifies with her because she has been there. yet, an
outsider . . . family, friends, business associates . . . needs to
read this, too. it is a very lonely road without much
understanding and support.

the secret of joy lies in these pages of surrender. of a way of
peace. of beautiful, creative, unknown surprises.

i know of no other book like it on the market.

ann kiemel anderson

TABLE OF CONTENTS

SECTION THREE: POINTERS AND PROBLEM-SOLVING

SECTION FOUR: POSSIBILITIES

"Sons are a heritage from the LORD,
children a reward from him.
Like arrows in the hands of a warrior
are sons born in one's youth.
Blessed is the man whose quiver is full of them.
They will not be put to shame
when they contend with their enemies in the gate."

—*Psalm 127:3-5 (NIV)*

SECTION ONE:

PROCESS

CHAPTER ONE

When the Quiver Is Empty

Wearing a blue tropical shirt, my husband escorted the bride through the palm-bedecked doorway of a little stucco church. They passed under garlands of white tissue doilies and clear plastic drinking straws strung like festive beads in jute twine. I played an unadorned version of the wedding march on a small organ as they proceeded with slow, unrehearsed steps down the aisle between the handmade wooden benches. All eyes turned to the lovely bride in her ivory gown. It was much the same as weddings everywhere, except here all the eyes were brown. It was a simple rural wedding in a Third World country.

The bride and groom, our young friends, were now sitting on chairs in front of the minister. Once the music stopped, the burning of incense and the loud engine noises of diesel trucks outside the open doorway seemed all the more audible this dry midday. From the organ bench I looked into the veil-ringed face of that almost breathtakingly beautiful girl. She was thirteen.

My mind wandered to our own wedding almost twenty years before. It could hardly have been more different, having taken place on a cold fall evening in Alaska. But as I considered the two experiences I realized that for all its dissimilarities, today's event was just as significant. Two people were receiving each other as husband and wife. Vows were to be exchanged and a new family formed.

Suddenly I was brought fully into the present. What had the minister just said? "Children are the blessing of marriage. Today you stand before me, but in not too many years your own children will be making this same step. This is the plan of God: life, love, marriage, reproduction, child-rearing, and the children's leaving home to establish their own homes and families. This is God's ordained purpose for man."

The same fleeting thoughts stabbed me as they had so often in the past, "If that is so, where does it leave us? Is our marriage doomed not to be 'blessed'? Are we being left out of God's perfect plan?" Through self-discipline I had learned to trim the time devoted to such questionings down to a slim moment.

The groom's father, a national pastor and district superintendent, reacted in about the same brief time. Nudging my husband, he whispered decidedly in Spanish, "I don't believe that!"

Quite recently during the pre-Mother's day season I happened to open a family magazine to an advertisement for a needlework design. It read something like this:

"Grandchildren complete the circle of love."

Does it capture your notice? For those of you who have or hope to have grandchildren, it probably summons a warm, sentimental response.

For many of us, however, that same verse refuses to lie dormant on the slick paper. It can immediately evoke a rush of sorrow, anger, renewed feelings of inadequacy, or at least relief at being able to turn the page. Such insignificant things can unexpectedly invade our painstakingly constructed walls of emotional control.

We are the childless, the grandchildless, those with the empty quivers. Even though we desire to, we cannot fulfill God's original charge to "be fruitful and multiply" (Gen. 1:28). Significant questions assail our thought life: Have the eternal purposes of God and His rewards and blessings in this world passed us by? Did we somehow miss out? Is that what our childlessness is—*less?*

At times we feel like a youngster losing at Monopoly. If only we had landed on Boardwalk or Park Place! We could have had a real home base, some control over our destiny. Instead, someone else's houses and hotels reduce us to seeking resolutions for our distress from Chance and the Community Chest. We grasp the assorted answers they offer, hope dwindling all the while, as we become aware that they are never quite adequate to meet our needs. So we traverse the board, never sure when we may be at the mercy of those who make up the family groupings of red, yellow, green, and blue while we are left holding the Utilities. On the other hand, we are often relieved not to have to mortgage everything we own to pay taxes on each little house and every hotel!

But who are we, those of us in this growing minority with a distinct sense of childlessness? We are a combination of such separate groups as these:

—people with fertility problems. In the U.S. these account for ten million persons, or fifteen percent of the population of childbearing age.[1]

—couples whose pregnancies spontaneously miscarry resulting in their inability to carry a child full term. This brings the figures to seventeen percent.[2]

—couples, about one out of ten, who perhaps have an only child but have never been able to have another. These are people who feel a sense of childlessness for never having had as many children as they wanted.[3]

—families who have lost one child or more through death.

—parents who have given up a child or children for adoption or have had children taken from them, perhaps through court order or separation proceedings.

—single people, some of whom have been widowed or divorced, who would very much like to be parents but may never have that opportunity.

Although statistics are not available for these final groups, conservatively speaking we may say that at least one out of four people of childbearing age in our nation today is acutely aware that the quiver is not full.

On the encouraging side: medical science is doing a commendable job of research and development to alleviate physical causes which contribute to the problem. Many hospitals now have special units devoted to premature infants and women who are experiencing high-risk pregnancies. Today, according to the American Fertility Society, as many as seventy percent of fertility problems can now be successfully treated by highly-trained specialists.[4] The patient's major obstacles are having the financial resources for and living in proximity to such medical expertise. Even if one qualifies for a specialist's waiting list, some procedures with no guaranteed success cost thousands of dollars.[5] The challenge for the physician is that for every person helped there is at least one other waiting. Doctors are now treating an infertility patient population estimated at five times greater than ten years ago.

Even though childlessness is on the increase, however, the general population often does not recognize the problem. Since adults often interact with their peers on a superficial level, their private struggles remain hidden. People consider it normal that their single acquaintances, perhaps even divorced or widowed, do not have children and they know that some couples decide not to have a family. Few persons pause to consider how their childless acquaintances feel about their circumstances nor do they have a close enough relationship with them to discuss the matter. Many of the childless, therefore, are suffering greatly without anyone even being aware of it. They may be undergoing pain on several levels at once: psychological, emotional, physical, spiritual—even financial! And much of it is silent, personal, lonely.

There certainly are sound reasons for choosing not to have children, physical and hereditary factors being among them. The calling one has is another. For instance, a Christian husband-wife physician team we know have qualified for two medical specialties in order to enter a particular country which is closed to most missionaries. They feel that their ministry requires their remaining childless, but often well-intentioned friends fail to understand their decision. "Oh, you *must* have children," they contend, not understanding the doctors' point of view.

Many adults, such as our doctor friends, face the issue of childlessness and, whether or not they have a choice, arrive at a satisfying personal resolution. These individuals confront being without children as they would any matter of concern and find peace without experiencing crisis. They make a good adjustment and tend to be comfortable with their situation throughout life.[6]

Other men and women, though, have always aspired to be parents and cannot imagine being happy without a family. They may even be exceptionally child-oriented people whose major interests, gifts or specialized training involve children. If against their wills they are denied the "right" to participate in the on-going of the human race, it is almost too great a cruelty to bear psychologically. For these individuals not having a child of their own may be accompanied by a hurt which invades their lives so deeply that this world offers no adequate consolation. Yes, their disappointment can be somewhat compensated for. But although their pain may lessen in its intensity, nothing can truly relieve it. Such sufferers find no help if they do not find it in God.

Parenthood was essential to me as a person. Yet I could not conceive a child. What would life be for me without a family? When we were also unable to adopt, my husband and I reached the conclusion (which I will share later) that we as a couple were not free to insist on getting children just to satisfy our longings for a family. But we had neither the ability nor desire to free ourselves from that yearning which formed so vital a part of our beings. We were caught in a fierce dilemma which we could not humanly resolve.

Medical help had failed us. Very few in the discipline of psychology had addressed the subject. We were forced to look to our God for help. He who first revealed himself as Creator had to be keenly aware of how we felt when the procreation urge within us was thwarted. Surely the Great Communicator, the Word, was interested in expressing himself to us in this vital area.

Before we could explore our specific concern of childlessness and search for personal answers, however, we had to arrive at some general spiritual principles. First, what *was* God's original plan in making man? Was man simply to begin and repeat the reproductive process?

We discovered that God had plainly expressed His intent in Genesis 1:26: "Let us make man in our image, after our likeness. . . ." But when man sinned, didn't God discard that plan? We found the same design in the New Testament: "And we know that in all things God works for the good of those who love him, who have been called according to his purpose. For those God foreknew he also predestined to be conformed to the likeness of his Son, that he might be the firstborn among many brothers" (Rom. 8:28-29, NIV).

This, then, is God's destiny for us: to be conformed to His image, His likeness. And what is He like? The Word of God says He is like Jesus, the One who always did the Father's will; the most balanced Man who ever lived; the perfect Son of God (John 14:6-12).

We became particularly interested in Christ's example as it related to His lifestyle. We knew that He lived an abundant life, experiencing real joy. His person (not His appearance or possessions) had such a positive effect on others that people by the thousands were drawn to Him.[7] Yet, Jesus was single; He led a bachelor's life. And it was this same Jesus who said, "A student is not above his teacher, nor a servant above his master" (Matt. 10:24, NIV). If, then, we followed Christ's path, could it conceivably lead into and through singleness? Apparently so, but with the expectation that He would never leave us alone; He would be working in and through us (Matt. 28.20).

We were hesitant to confront the next, and related, question. Could it be that even married persons walking through His opened doors might find tightly shut the same one He closed to himself: that of having physical children? Indeed, that seemed to be precisely the case (Rev. 3:7-8). He promised, however, that if we were to choose to go His way, His presence would be with us and would ultimately conform us to His likeness.

Of course this matter is only one minute aspect in the great challenge of living the Christ-life. And yet for the childless it is immediate and of great consequence. Our temptation is to protest: "But I shall only *one* day reflect His image perfectly. That will be *then*. It is something I cannot wholly do in the present anyway. I want my will *now*."

In a mundane way we could compare our conflict to that of a kindly, nervous lady of a household in which I once lived. She was a superb cook, but one day she confided, "I can't make an omelet." That didn't seem so difficult to me. Why, it only required pouring beaten eggs into a pan and waiting until they began to solidify. "That's just the point. I can't wait. Every time I put the eggs in and they begin to cook, suddenly I can't stand it any longer. I grab a spoon and start stirring. Pretty soon I end up with scrambled eggs!"

That is our problem, isn't it? Jesus wants to be formed omelet-perfect within us. But because we cannot bear to wait, we take the ingredients of our lives into our own hands. Then we, as well as the world around us, end up with "scrambled eggs." We have to decide whether His recipe for our lives is the only one worth following. If so and if it does not include what we want to add—in this case, a family—we still trust Him with the spoon.

When this depth of confidence develops, our lives no longer revolve around singleness or childlessness. Jesus becomes central. We cease to be embroiled in "Why?" or "Why me?" and begin to be focused on "Who?" and "What is He going to do in and with me?" Although this process isn't automatic, we can choose to turn from railing against God to resting in Him. The purpose of this book is to affirm us in our childlessness and help us move into an ever fuller realization of God's will in our exceptional venture of faith.

Looking afresh at the Scriptures, we may be pleased to discover that the Lord has provided a secure, esteemed place for each of His own, not just for married people with children. Perhaps the first passage we should consider is the one which initially tempted us to frustration or despair:

> Sons are a heritage from the Lord,
>   children a reward from him.
> Like arrows in the hands of a warrior
>   are sons born in one's youth.
> Blessed is the man
>   whose quiver is full of them.
> They will not be put to shame
>   when they contend with their enemies
>   in the gate.
>   —Psalm 127:3–5 (NIV)

If we look at these verses without greeting-card sentimentality, we see that they simply state that one's offspring are "a heritage from the Lord." And further, they are "a reward." Certainly children need to be received as treasured gifts from the Lord. They are, after all, descendants and deserve their parents' best efforts and investment. But natural children are not the only heritage or blessing which God can give. The blessing of salvation, if there were no other, is enough to cause us constant rejoicing.

We read on, "Blessed [happy] is the man whose quiver is full of them [children]." Do we then conclude that the converse of that statement is true? Are we really rendering it: "Parents are blessed, happy; therefore, all others are unhappy and not blessed"? Happiness is not an exclusive quality reserved for those in one station in life anymore than health is. If an expert says, for example, "Eating spinach will help you stay healthy," can we fairly assume that if we don't eat spinach we can't be healthy?

Examining this psalm further we note that individuals with children "will not be put to shame when they contend with their enemies in the gate." But that statement doesn't deny success in difficulties to childless individuals, walking in the will of God and depending on His promises.

Actually, the clue to understanding the psalm is in the first verse:

> Unless the Lord builds the house,
>   its builders labor in vain.
> Unless the Lord watches over the city,
>   the watchmen stand guard in vain.
>
> —Psalm 127:1 (NIV)

At one time or another, haven't most of us contemplated, if not succeeded in, building a home? During a period of time when my husband was a realtor, we became enthusiastic about buying land and having a house built. After touring numerous model homes in our area, we were at last ready to make a commitment. We had seen one we wanted—with a few minor adjustments. Jerry arranged a meeting with the builder to go over the blueprints. Yes, a door could be repositioned and the kitchen could be slightly rearranged. But when Jerry mentioned wooden window frames and an open-beamed ceiling, the contractor stopped him. "You don't want *my* house," he said bluntly. "What you want is a custom-built home."

Whose home are we building in this life? Are we so busy pursuing our made-to-order plans that we miss out on God's design? Is He trying to break through our absorption in our own blueprints to find out, "Is it my home you want with watchman service included, or your own custom-built house on a private lot?"

Let's look at a historical example of someone who built his own house—King Solomon. In all of recorded history he probably had the largest nuclear family: seven hundred wives and three hundred concubines (1 Kings 11:3). It is impossible to estimate the number of children he may have had! But this is what we hear him tell us plainly:

> A man may have a hundred children and live many years; yet no matter how long he lives, if he cannot enjoy his prosperity and does not receive proper burial, I say that a stillborn child is better off than he.
>
> —Ecclesiates 6:3 (NIV)

Poor rich Solomon. He indeed had a heavy quiver—full and overflowing with arrows. For all that, was he happy? His father's counsel had been simple, "Unless the Lord builds the house, its builders labor in vain" (Ps. 127:1a). Yet the son reached his mature years repeating only the last of David's words: *vain*. "Vanity of vanities. . . . All is vanity" (Eccles. 1:2). Sad to say, in pursuing his own idea of blessing, he missed the blessing of God. Eventually his own family detoured him from his God (1 Kings 11:1–11).

So, what does that say to us? Certainly it is not teaching the principle that raising a family will lead us away from God. But it demonstrates that we do not always know what is best for us. Not all of what is truly good shows up on the earthly half of the scale. If we walk according to the will of God, we can expect Him to accomplish the highest good with our lives, and, in the process, conform us to the image of His Son.

We may be standing with an empty quiver for what seems a long time to us. But that's our job: to take a stand. We give Him ourselves unreservedly; He pledges to make good come of us. His creativity in doing just that is His divine option. Yes, God has a plan for us which includes our empty quiver—but it may be He will use it for something besides arrows!

"Now Sarai, Abram's wife,
had borne him no children.
But she had an Egyptian maidservant named Hagar;
So she said to Abram,
'The Lord has kept me from having children.
Go sleep with my maidservant;
Perhaps I can build a family through her.'
Abram agreed to do what Sarai said....
He slept with Hagar, and she conceived."

—Genesis 16:1–2, 4a (NIV)

CHAPTER TWO

Frustration with Infertility

Abraham and Sarah stand out as probably the first and most fascinating infertile couple in all of recorded history. The information the Bible provides about their pilgrimage into parenthood exceeds by far the details given concerning the creation of the world.[1] Rendered in modern clinical records, the data on Abraham and Sarah would immediately identify them as prime candidates to head an infertility support group!

Medical Infertility Workup

Husband: 99 years of age; Wife: 89. This couple has a personal history of about 70 years of marriage without achieving a pregnancy. They have had frequent consultations with their Healer and believe that they have been assured that they will yet conceive. Sarah passed through menopause decades ago.[2] The diagnosis: a case of unexplained infertility.

The prognosis: hopeless.

Adoption Case Study

The husband has initiated steps to explore the possibility of adopting a young man, Eliezar of Damascus, who was born some years ago in Abraham's home and is now steward of that household.[3] Sarah seems not to be in complete harmony with this solution and still has hope for a natural heir for Abraham.[4]

For a number of years they served as parental substitutes for Abraham's nephew, Lot, who lived with them until he became independent.[5] They have proven themselves to be a responsible, if mobile, family and are well able to provide financially for an heir.[6]

New entry: Abraham has announced his intent not to continue with adoption procedures. He now re-voices a religious conviction that he will yet have a natural son.[7]

Legal Brief

Abraham and Sarah are willing to assume personal liability and financial responsibility for a male child, Ishmael, born to Abraham by Hagar, a surrogate mother, of Egyptian nationality. Abraham acknowledges paternity status, claims all rights inherent to being father of the child, and agrees to the continuing support of the surrogate and their son.[8]

Birth Record

Born to Abraham of Ur of the Chaldees, 100 years old, and Sarah, 90 years old, a male child, Isaac Abrahamson, in Gerar, Canaan. The child was circumcised at eight days of age. Comment: the baby's name means *laughter.*[9]

Abraham and Sarah were a determined couple who exhausted the entire array of options in their quest for a child of their own. Today many of us have followed their lead, stepping into one or more of their tracks, depending upon what we feel responds to God's directions for us.

The first, and for some, the only action to take is the natural one. We pray, act, wait, and then repeat the cycle. At first we are slightly puzzled when there are no results. As one friend commented in her journal, "This can't be happening to us! I am a nurse and I know all about anatomy and physiology."

The mystery as to why we are not pregnant brings a slight jolt to our reasoning processes. It is almost unbelievable. Having assumed that conception depends on our action, we are unaccustomed to wrestling with the issue that it is the Creator alone who can bring into existence a human being.[10] We are suddenly aware that we may cooperate with Him, but to coerce Him lies beyond our privileges.

Thus, although many childless people begin their venture toward parenthood with considerable expectation, their success can never be assured. In this day of quality control and "satisfaction or money back" guarantees, we tend to become indignant at the very thought that we, as human beings, do not have the same security. During this early stage of disillusionment we need to have, in addition to medical knowledge, contact with others who have gone through the same discouragement. We may feel that they alone can comprehend our feelings of frustration, and at times, distress. Even if our childlessness is only a temporary condition, it can be personally devastating at the time. During this initial period of *soft shock*, the childless marriage moves from a period of idealism into realism.

My husband and I had the pleasure of enjoying an unusual romance which began where we met, on an island in Alaska. Everything about our early experiences together whispered, "Surprise!" Who could have anticipated that a blind date with someone whose last name was *Love* would have been more than a wry joke? Especially so since he invited me to accompany him that Thursday to the grade-school auditorium to see a Christian film.

As I watched the events of the movie I saw a girl, very much like myself with numerous personal problems, who encountered the revolutionary presence of Christ. Her life began to change. On the screen flashed the reason why: "But to all who received him, who believed in his name, he gave power to become children of God" (John 1:12, RSV).

At last I saw what Jesus had done! He had given His life not only for the world in general, but for me and each one of us in particular. He had completed the first part of a transaction and was waiting for me to close the contract. I could do that; indeed, I wanted to. Later, alone in the privacy of my room, I repented of my sin and rebelliousness and surrendered my life to Him that He might forgive me and live in me.

Through the next four years not only did my relationship with Christ grow more meaningful, but my feelings for Jerry, who helped foster my spiritual growth, deepened as well. During the last two years of our courtship, we attended a Christian college and met for prayer each morning. Along with presenting to God the details of our daily lives, we committed to Him our approaching marriage and future family.

To add performance to prayer, while completing my studies in elementary education and library science I made considerable preparations not only for my career, but also for our own children. I developed files for the various age levels through which they would pass, noting the music and books to which I planned to expose them. Later, I spent years teaching preschoolers, taking graduate work in early childhood education, and developing materials for my classroom and home. I was enthusiastic about being a prepared mother, making certain in advance that our children would receive the best opportunities we could give them.

Going into marriage I devoured such works as *Childbirth Without*

Fear and *Husband-Coached Childbirth*. Birth and child development excited my interest. Eventually, however, I had to divert my attention from La Leche League literature to that which had an immediate and dream-threatening impact: information on infertility. It was a deeply disappointing, almost shattering, step.

I remember as a child that when my mother explained to me where babies came from, she did a most thorough job. She left no doubts in my mind as to how the process would work. She further assured me that any time I had questions, I could come to her and she would be glad to answer them. What questions? I knew it all.

Therein lies the essence of the problem for those of us who will never be able to have our own children. From our earliest years we build our understanding of life on parental role models and "facts" which turn out to be only assumptions. Even the best mothers and biology books seldom mention that reproduction is a fact for some, but for others, pure theory.

Only a careful and concerted medical study is adequate to discover what is factual for a couple having difficulty conceiving. The results of such an investigation can then indicate the pair's particular needs in order to treat and eliminate correctable problems and insure the most favorable conditions for their achieving a pregnancy. Each member of such a partnership has to become a learner, an assimilator, and an experimenter, developing very new understanding about one's self, one's marriage, and the future. To begin such a process demands courage; no one wants to admit to infertility or worse yet: sterility. We rebel against the thought of not having the most basic aspects of humanity in common with the global family.

And so we launch into an infertility workup with our personal confidence somewhat shaken, but trusting that, in return for our efforts, medical science will bring us the answers we need. Thank God that for a growing number of people, it does. To understand the medical processes involved, there are many excellent helps available for the layman today. Some are cited in the Selected Bibliography of this book. These present not only explanations of technical vocabulary but information related to difficulty in conception, causes of miscarriages or stillbirth, and the complexity of feelings and adjustments of the childless.

For the potential infertility patient to make an initial appointment with a physician may be emotionally one of the most difficult steps in the entire medical process. An individual risks exposing to a professional his or her suspicions that there may be a problem. The first time I broached the subject to my Christian doctor, an OB/Gyne specialist, I had already resigned a teaching position to have a child. Six months had passed with no baby and no job.

He replied reassuringly, "Your husband is still in seminary, isn't he?" To an affirmative response he continued, "Well, it's probably just as well, then. Actually, a fertility problem is not assumed until after ceasing to use contraceptive measures for a year, no pregnancy results. I wouldn't be too concerned at this point. You'd be better off waiting, anyway, wouldn't you?" He ended up prescribing birth control pills when what I really wanted was to explore what was involved in infertility! (Besides, my husband did not finish seminary until nearly twenty years later.)

Being relatively young at the time and not very aggressive, I felt intimidated and angry for having acquiesced under the uncomfortable pressure of the moment. I found that I could not return to that doctor. I needed to find someone who would take my doubts seriously and explain what our next step should be. Not every physician is right for every patient. The couple must find someone with whom they can work as a team for what may result in years of medical procedures.

Often the first recommendation that a physician makes is that the wife use a basal thermometer to take her morning temperature, recording it on a graph to the nearest tenth of a degree. A one-half to one-degree jump, often preceded by a slight dip, usually indicates that ovulation has taken place. When intercourse occurs during the several hours before and until a couple of days or so following ovulation, a woman is most likely to conceive.[11] These monthly records are presented to the doctor with indication of when coitus occurred.

Some female patients are instructed to call the doctor's office once or twice a month with the latest readings and information. After giving her medical chart number, she is put on "hold" until her file can be located. The information is then written directly on her medical records for the evaluation and response of her physician. As one woman expressed to her childless friend, "Temperature charts—don't we have enough of them to wallpaper our homes!"

For women there is also at least one monthly appointment which often involves a pelvic examination. Initially, three such exams may be given to coincide with day ten, fourteen and twenty-eight of her cycle. This allows for an on-site determination of the quantity and quality of internal mucus. Later, tests will be performed at specific time intervals following intercourse to ascertain the amount and activity level of the husband's sperm present in the cervical environment at those designated hours.

The male undergoes a genital examination and submits a semen sample which may be one of several required during the process. Once the results of these preliminary tests are known, the direction the infertility study takes differs according to the suspected problems. For either or both of the partners there may be hormone treatments, exploratory or corrective surgery, or other medical procedures.

Initially the investigation does not present much noticeable inconvenience, but as years pass the recommendations become more demanding and the procedures more sophisticated as well as more expensive. Patients begin to tire of the ordeal, but at the same time they realize that their prime reproductive time is running out. The pressure continues to mount. Lovemaking ceases to be spontaneous and becomes calculated. Hormones taken over a long period of time may cause nausea and other side effects, negative emotional changes and, at times, serious secondary physical problems which must then be corrected. The couple is no longer subject only to one another but to what a third party, the doctor or series of doctors, says they must do if they are to comply with the indicated treatment. Most depressing is that throughout the whole process patients often have little, if any, encouragement that progress is being made toward obtaining the goal: a baby. Thus, the couple must contend with increasing levels of stress.

Along the lonely way we begin to look for any hint of levity. One of my specialists had cartoons taped to the ceiling above the examination table to provide comic relief for his patients, and probably for himself.

On rare occasions the unexpected may happen to break the serious medical monotony. During one unforgettable examination, I recall scooting deftly out of my wig on the examining table, not realizing that my hairdo was undone until I saw my entire coiffure poised unceremoniously on the once-sterile paper cover. The doctor must have had his lines rehearsed as he took note of the unhuman addition to his work space. Without interrupting his routine, he commented, "Oh, you wear a wig. My wife has one, too. How do you like yours?" To be honest, at that moment not very well.

During another procedure it was necessary that the patient be positioned at the very edge of the table. To quell my protests that my body was almost certainly not going to maintain such an unpracticed posture, the specialist assured me that he had never yet lost a patient in that position and insisted that I move still further down. His perfect record was broken that day. I fell most awkwardly off the table, landing at the feet of one very startled doctor-nurse team!

For the most part, however, there is little excitement in what may be a long, arduous process. Endless hours are spent in waiting rooms that are well-stocked with *Humpty Dumpty* and *Baby and Childcare* magazines and alive with little children who have accompanied their mothers. For all this effort, infertility patients may spend only a brief time with the physician. They face the prospects of being required to repeat test after test, and sometimes an unsuccessful surgery, in order to continue their treatment. They know, as an integral part of life, the almost unbearable reality of waiting. They wait every day.

Doctors who can meaningfully involve their patients in the adventure of their own study will find that it may be psychologically helpful for them, even though it does not change the results. The tests themselves may prove of real interest to the individuals who must undergo them. My last specialist had just such a patient-involving philosophy. After almost eight years of being a patient, I very much needed the confidence which his approach inspired in me. This doctor did much of his own laboratory work personally, using a microscope set up on a counter at the end of his suite of examining rooms and office space. One day he excitedly called me out of his consultation room.

"Look at this!" he exclaimed, motioning me toward a high stool in front of a microscope. In place was a slide which he had just prepared from a sample of internal mucus. "Do you see it? Can you see that fern-like pattern? That's exactly what the cell arrangement is supposed to look like. It's textbook perfect!" And I *could* see it in all its marvelous ferny excellence. After having suffered the side effects of a hormone treatment in order to eliminate a prevailing problem, I was viewing evidence that it had been conquered! It was a moment of shared victory for my doctor and me. Regardless of other irregularities, I had at least overcome one obstacle. In a long string of disappointments, this one experience encouraged me and gave me just cause to feel good about myself.

Outside this private world of appointments, hope, and disappointments, day-to-day life continues. The couple's marriage, which normally serves as a haven for the partners in their personal struggles and employment pressures, is understandably enduring considerable stress. After undergoing a protracted period of medical study and treatment, a marriage can be in serious trouble.[12] Either or both partners may be expressing feelings of inadequacy, insecurity, guilt, anger, or futility. Individuals who have been for an extended time on certain hormones or fertility drugs, such as Clomid, may find themselves putting on weight, failing to exercise their usual emotional control, suffering the enlargement of various glands or organs—in short, being very unlike the person their partner married. One wife, discouraged by a prolonged period of being depressed and short-tempered, expressed it to her husband this way, "I'm not crabby because of you but because of not having children." She said later, "I felt blessed in having a husband who was not ready to disown me!"

The fact of the matter was that he identified very closely with her struggles. Although he did not often verbalize his inner conflicts as she did, upon reading her personal account of wrestling with the ordeal, he acknowledged, "I probably have had all of the same feelings. I just never would have written them all down."

Most spouses have never had any kind of preparation to help them bear the particular stresses of personal or combined infertility. And they seldom have role models from whom to learn the art of living a satisfying life while coping with such personal distress. To further increase their tension, a couple may find that their only professional resource, their physician, is not able to provide them emotional support in addition to medical treatment. In fact, because of the rigors which an infertility study imposes upon patients, doctors may be major contributors to the immediate problems in the marriage.

At times physicians may force upon their patients responsibilities which they are not equipped medically or emotionally to handle. Most infertility patients can think of various occasions in which they had to be the bearer of unpleasant tidings upon reaching home. I recall waiting as one specialist left the examining room to do an evaluation on a postcoital sperm sample. The test had required an enormous scheduling effort on our part, as I worked full time and my husband was a firefighter with twenty-four hours on duty and forty-eight hours off—assuming a fire was not in progress. The test required that an appointment be made at a specified time during my monthly cycle preceded by a week of sexual abstinence and that I arrive at the doctor's office a prescribed number of hours after intercourse.

The physician at last returned and remarked off-handedly, "Well, sorry to say, although there should have been, there was no evidence of live sperm in the cervical environment." Then he scratched out a new form requesting a further appointment for a repeat performance and said that he would see me the following month. I was slightly stunned. Leaving his office I realized that I would have to explain his findings to my husband when I did not understand the implications myself. Worse yet, we would again have to maneuver through the maze of complex scheduling factors in order to comply with the assignment.

Obviously, there comes a time when a couple must re-evaluate their course of action. Ethical and practical questions begin to assert themselves: Is the potential benefit for the future worth our frustration in the present? How far are we prepared to go? Will we subject our bodies to fertility drugs? What about artificial insemination with the husband's sperm? Should we undergo the risks of elective surgery? How much time, money, and effort can we conscientiously invest in further procedures which may, likewise, end in failure? Is a Christian free to consider surrogate parenting?

Frustration may then take the form of philosophical tension which can develop within the partnership. Perhaps the wife would be willing to take fertility drugs but the husband is opposed. The tendency is for the one who feels restricted to resent and blame the other for refusing to take a step which might result in pregnancy.

One childless couple who has undergone the repeated agony of making hard decisions defined what they felt were the key factors in being able to successfully confront the barrage of treatment-related questions. "We were committed to being honest with each other, meditative when apart, and prayerful that we would really be able to communicate in order to arrive at unity in each matter. At one point they sought the counsel of their pastor who helped them come to a decision about the wife's undergoing a third surgery."

Eventually, either the childless couple or the physician must reach a decision not to continue. Many doctors do not want to state definitively that the couple will never have a child. They have seen seemingly impossible and mysteriously wonderful things happen in other unpromising circumstances. The physician must, however, be honest with his patients and help them close the door on hope when that is called for. At this point they will need to make a realistic adjustment to their present and future.

The doctor who conducts a final session with both partners is in an ideal position to help them with this initial acceptance. In a few minutes the couple will be leaving his direct and extensive care to launch out into the world once again as a childless couple, but this time without the benefit of hope in having natural children. Their goal will no longer be pregnancy, as it has been for the considerable time in which they have been patients. The physician must sensitively guide them toward establishing new goals and avenues of thinking.

This moment may be highly emotional in the lives of the patients, demanding tenderness and support from the physician. The patients feel a double loss: fertility and advocacy. They will now have no one representing them, to whom they may periodically turn in their distress. One doctor has reported the suicide deaths of two of his female patients upon learning that they should not expect to have children.[13] Definitely patients should never be told potentially traumatic information over the telephone.[14]

Many couples, however, will simply experience an overwhelming sense of relief when testing is finally finished. For them it will be a time when once and for all they wearily drop a very heavy burden. At last they can freely face the future with resignation and acceptance instead of living in doubt and half-hope. More than likely they have already considered their alternatives and made some preliminary decisions.

However, any number of initial responses may be anticipated, depending on the couple. The Bible shows us two diverse reactions of people when faced with their inability to conceive. Some infertile couples will relate to the rage expressed by Rachel. She had experienced a beautiful romance with Jacob, but quite abruptly after marriage, everything changed. Rachel was barren, which was further complicated by the fact that her sister, Leah, married to the same man through the deception of the girls' father, had already succeeded in having four sons. The Bible reveals the complex mixture of her emotions, inner motivations, and outward anger:

> When Rachel saw that she was not bearing Jacob any children, she became jealous of her sister. So she said to Jacob, "Give me children, or I'll die!"
> —Genesis 30:1 (NIV)

She was a desperate woman. For her it was all the more infuriating because her husband was not truly sympathetic. He saw the problem as being hers alone instead of a shared difficulty. He unleashed the frustration he felt toward God in anger against Rachel, which is not so different from what commonly happens in many families today:

> Jacob became angry with her and said, "Am I in the place of God who has kept you from having children?"
> —Genesis 30:2 (NIV)

What a contrast to the attitude of Jacob's father, Isaac. During the previous generation his wife, Rebekah, had suffered barrenness for perhaps twenty years. We see Isaac taking an active part in the redemption of their situation.

> Isaac prayed to the Lord on behalf of his wife, because she was barren. The Lord answered his prayer, and his wife Rebekah became pregnant.
> —Genesis 25:21 (NIV)

From our vantage point we can see clearly that both families occupied a unique place in history and that God was well aware of His plan for each one. At the time, though, they had no way of receiving the comfort that their childlessness was only temporary. As one comtemporary wife has expressed, "Maybe in three weeks I'll find out that I'm pregnant and everything will change. But right now I am hurting."

But can God really be leading a couple through a seemingly fruitless infertility study? One childless friend, after she and her husband had both undergone corrective surgery, came to this conclusion:

> I really got a lot out of the book *Joni* [the autobiography of a young woman paralyzed through a swimming accident]. How could anyone feel sorry for himself when he considers what *she* has lost? I couldn't have a baby, but I could run and hike and swim and ride a horse and get on

my knees to pray. That book really inspired me to be content with *me*.

I examined my life. I had a good husband (that in itself is enough to rejoice about), a strong faith, and a loving Father.

Now, I must add that this peace of mind came only after I had had all of the testing for infertility there was to be had.

What a contrast between this mindset and that of many infertile persons who, after years of treatment with no result, allow a defeatist attitude to crowd its way into their mind and heart. "What's the use? What did it all accomplish? Nothing. While I was involved in the medical processes, I missed out on many of the prime years of my life and my marriage. Was it worth it? Should we have tried years ago to adopt?"

The same courageous woman passed on the following advice to couples considering the value of an infertility study: "I'm not trying to tell you that this is a formula for success or anything, but if I were you I'd go as far having testing as you can go."

Perhaps it will not change your ability to have natural children, but having engaged in a fertility study can ultimately allow you to come to a settled peace in your own heart. You have prayed, committing your desires to the Lord. You have cooperated in every way to see the fruition of that prayer, trying as perfectly as you knew how to give God the freedom in your life to bless you as He has purposed. There is nothing more you can do to obtain natural children. That knowledge in itself is reassuring.

One further advantage of having gone through an infertility work-up is that it forms a bridge into adoption proceedings. Although most adoption agencies will not process couples currently involved in an infertility study, many of them require a doctor's statement, based upon evidence, that the couple cannot have natural children. Perhaps, unknowingly, you will have completed a requirement for your future fulfillment as an adoptive family.

Regardless of the ultimate meanings of infertility for you and your marriage, upon learning your prognosis what you most need is personal assurance. You yearn for the comfort that you are accepted as you are and that you matter to people who are significant to you. Remind yourself that those who love you have always known you as a non-parent and have never based their relationship with you on something you were not or did not have. That will not change now that you are more informed about yourself. People like you because you are *you*. Gather strength from recalling that the Lord knows who you are and exactly what your situation is.[15] Turn to Him in your fury or frustrations; He's big enough to handle them.[16]

Receive your child-free status from Him as His will for you in the present. You did not put yourself in your circumstances. Since God already knew, and now you also know, that you are not going to have your own children, should you feel frustrated about not being fertile? If you have been obedient to Him, is there any cause to feel bad about yourself?

If He, as head of your family, has not designed for your having natural children, then He, not you, is responsible for the results of His leading. One shut door does not mean all doors are shut. Anticipate what He *will* give you the opportunity to be and do. Move from frustration to a new sense of freedom. Join those of us who refuse to stay bound by our former presuppositions. Let's look forward to the interesting realities behind the new door the Lord is waiting to open for us.

We are involved with Him on an exceptional adventure with unique possibilities instead of foregone conclusions. Our answer will not be identical to Abraham's. But we have every right to join him in asking—not only the God of Abraham, Isaac, and Jacob—but of Sarah, Rebekah, and Rachel: "O Sovereign Lord, what can you give me since I remain childless?" (Gen. 15:2a, NIV).

"There are three things that are never satisfied,
four that never say, 'Enough!':
the grave,
the barren womb,
land, which is never satisfied with water,
and fire, which never says,
'Enough!' "

—Proverbs 30:15b, 16 (NIV)

CHAPTER THREE

Coping with Hoping

A spiritual retreat—just what I needed! Since it would last an entire weekend, and in the five years of our marriage my husband had never been on his own that long, I made certain that he wouldn't starve. After planning a Friday-through-Sunday menu, I sectioned off the two bottom refrigerator shelves and taped tags along the racks to label the day and the meal. Then, I left final instructions on the table and a love note on his pillow.

I was off! I would have two days to get alone with the Lord. The secret desire of my heart was that I would have a chance to thoroughly plead my case before God and receive some word from Him.

The weekend began less enjoyably than I had hoped. A school-teacher friend of mine, happy to get away from her husband, had eagerly agreed to go with me. She had even offered to drive. As we rode the sixty-five miles she talked; she complained; she expressed her frustration; she constantly asked my advice for solving the complex problems of her marriage. Since she was a young Christian, it was invigorating to see her struggle to put her new life with Him into perspective. But I was drained. To be expected to produce instant answers to help resolve years of their marital conflict was too demanding.

What a relief to at last crawl out of the small foreign car, get away from the chatter, and set foot on the moist grounds of the Cannon Beach Christian Retreat Center. For me it was a sentimental moment, a homecoming; I had once taught school in the community when my husband had pastored a nearby church. The time we had spent in this coastal area of northern Oregon had been the most fulfilling, exhilarating period in our married life.

I was back home—back to the kind of wet ocean-side naturalness to which I had become accustomed as a teenager in southeast Alaska.

Surely here I could do business with God. Jerry had never quite understood why I had to pull aside and battle my way through a spiritual issue in order to come to peace with it. There were times, however, when I felt a great need to do so, and at that I moment I could hardly wait to get together with Jesus for a good heart-to-heart talk.

We entered the wooden registration building and were handed the weekend schedule. I began to realize that a ladies' retreat did *not* give one much chance for retreating: Friday—supper, evening meeting, and an afterglow time with coffee in the main lodge. The next two days were filled as well. While waiting to pay the registration fee, and in between greeting friends who had begun to arrive, I studied the program more thoroughly. Everything was programmed! There was even an extra meeting Saturday following the evening service: a former Miss Oregon would be giving her testimony in the fireside room.

The only open space of time seemed to be the hour after Saturday's lunch which was reserved for rest and relaxation. I silently drew that to God's attention: He would have to be prepared to retreat with me then or never that weekend.

The next day was an intensified repeat of the evening before: delicious food, the rustic environs of the retreat center, two sessions in the varnished-log chapel, and good conversation with other women. At last the time arrived. While my friend enjoyed the company of some mutual acquaintances, I left them to make my special date. Rushing back to our cabin, I grabbed my Bible and blanket. I chose what turned out to be a moderately soggy spot on the grounds, where a hopeful streak of early afternoon sunlight filtered through a crevice between two buildings. Most important, it seemed that no one else wanted to be there but God and I.

First, I prayed and cried, not giving the Lord a chance to do anything but listen. I had complaints—but not about my husband: about having followed His prescription in everything and still not having received a child. I voiced my frustrations and my lack of understanding as to why He would deny us children. Next, I expressed my confusion about unanswered prayer. It was understandable that He could not respond to *our* prayers because perhaps they were adulterated by some wrong motivation. But why, when we requested the prayers of people whom we knew to have sincere faith, did He not respond to them, either?

Then, I asked His blessings on the fertility workup in which we were engaged. He knew perfectly well that at present there were many areas in which I could not be effective in His service. Caring for infants in the church nursery or even presenting a baby gift on behalf of the congregation was proving too much for me to do without losing emotional control. Expectant mothers both attracted me because of my strong desire to participate in their experiences and repelled me because I was excluded from their club.

Instead of being helpful around most young families, inwardly I was critical. Their inconsistency with their children, their lack of appreciation for and verbal abuse of their offspring, and their marital disharmony expressed in front of these youngsters distressed me. Why, we would never do such things! How, then, could God be so unfair as to give them children who might end up the products of broken homes while we, a solid Christian family, were left without? God had some things to answer for.

So, at last, I gave Him a chance to respond. He did not choose to do so.

"Lord," I pleaded, "if you give us children, I promise that we will dedicate them to you from the moment we know of their expected arrival. We will bring them up as if they were your very own children." That was the strongest card in my bargaining hand. Surely God wanted sons and daughters reared from their earliest years to put Him first.

"We will give you all the honor and glory possible for blessing us in such a way." He seemed content with the honor and glory He already had.

"Well, *what* then? What do you want from us?"

He did not tell me, and the hour was almost up. Already I could hear more distinctly the soprano-pitched laughter of my companions who were once again making their way back to the chapel.

"I can't go home from this retreat and take back nothing. God, I need you. I need you to provide for me now." That seemed to be something to which He could respond. If it were He that I wanted, instead of immediate answers on demand, He was pleased to share himself with me.

How had I been expecting Him to speak to me? I realized that what I needed to do was reach for my Bible which was, by then, considerably damp on the underside. But where was I to look for comfort? The most natural place seemed to be the Psalms. "All right, Lord. I will begin to read the Psalms until you speak to me. If I never get to chapel, even if my friend comes to find me, I will continue on until you give me comfort."

And so I began with Psalm One, not knowing how long the reading would continue. Psalm Two was short; Psalm Three, even shorter. And then, I reached Psalm Four.

> Answer me when I call to you,
>   O my righteous God.
> Give me relief from my distress;
>   be merciful to me and hear my prayer.

How long, O men, will you turn my glory into shame?
    How long will you love delusions and seek false gods?

Know that the Lord has set apart the godly for himself;
    the Lord will hear when I call to him.

In your anger do not sin;
    when you are on your beds,
    search your hearts and be silent.

Offer right sacrifices
    and trust in the Lord.

Many are asking, "Who can show us any good?"
    Let the light of your face shine upon us, O Lord.

You have filled my heart with greater joy
    than when their grain and new wine abound.

I will lie down and sleep in peace,
    for you alone, O Lord,
    make me dwell in safety.

—Psalm 4 (NIV)

That was it. Peace came to my heart. But what did it mean? I understood very little of what He was using to comfort me. Were we going to have a child or not? That was what I wanted to know.

The Lord will hear when I call to him. . . .
When you are on your beds, search your hearts
and be still. . . .
Trust in the Lord. . . .

Those were the simple, direct things which I could comprehend immediately, and there arose a new hope within me as I read: "You have filled my heart with greater joy than when their grain and new wine abound." At the moment I saw only everyone else's abundance, but I would trust the Lord as He had directed and wait for joy to come.

During the following years, God has been faithful to continue to open up my understanding of that psalm. At first I quoted it by faith alone, stressing the part which referred to my act of will in choosing to do so: "I *will* lie me down and sleep in peace." Later, I learned about spiritual rest as I concentrated on: "You, alone, O Lord. . . ."

Through the passing of time God has woven our experiences and understanding through the warp and woof of that psalm until we, and even others, have begun to see a pattern emerge. It has been wonderfully reassuring to have a solid loom of support behind the moving threads of our life. Repeatedly, when I have had no other comfort or place to seek refuge, I have been able to lean back on the assurance which that psalm gives me.

"The Lord will hear when I call to him" gave us the courage to continue in prayer, trusting God for appropriate answers for ourselves and others. Two of those "others" were a delightful international couple who once shared sincerely with us their longing to have children although they lived an extremely mobile life. They were in their middle thirties and she and I were patients of the same doctor. She asked us to pray that they would have a baby. My husband replied, "I can't do that because I don't know if it's God's will. I'll pray that God will give you a conviction as to whether you ought to have children or whether you should have peace about not having them. When you know which it is, let me know, and I will pray specifically to that end." In response to prayer they did reach a conclusion, and they now have two children.

We tend to *assume* that our own way is surely God's path. One basic lesson which childlessness teaches us is that we are not self-sufficient. I realized that afresh one day while meditating on the phrase: "For you alone, O Lord, make me dwell in safety." I had always taken for granted that my pregnancy would be normal, my delivery uncomplicated, and my child perfect. But what if God knew that for me pregnancy and childbirth were not places where I or a baby would dwell in safety? I would have no way of knowing that. Only the God who created me and knew me from before the foundation of the world[1] would be able to protect me from myself.

Whether it is a psalm or some other passage of Scripture, the Lord wants to give you His bedrock assurance of His presence in your circumstances. The Apostle Paul states that one of the principal purposes of Scripture is to comfort us:

> For everything that was written in the past was written to teach us, so that through endurance and the encouragement [comfort] of the Scriptures we might have hope. —Romans 15:4 (NIV)

Ask your Comforter to cause something from His Word to bring you consolation and peace. Childless persons have shared with me the significance to them of such passages as Isaiah 54, John 14, Acts 16:16–40 (speaking of the importance of praise in all circumstances), Philippians 4:11–13, 1 Timothy 6:5–8, and Hebrews 13:5. Perhaps you have never before felt so much the need for God's presence. Let some scriptural reassurance become a living reality to which you can cling.

COPING WHILE HOPING

Although the problems and feelings one confronts in being a nonparent may seem unique and immediate to each of us, they are really quite universal. Someone once jested, "Half of the women in the world (and, we might add, their husbands) are hoping they are *not* pregnant, and the other half are hoping they *are*." Those of us who continue hoping we *are*, month after month and year after year, eventually run into a problem. How do we handle our unfulfilled hope?

The mere thought that we may live our entire lives without children does not initially strike us as revelation but rather, as impenetrable darkness. We crave the friendship of another human being who has experienced what we are facing. We want to know: What has served to illumine the path of someone else? We desire such a relationship just as art students seek out an artist rather than having to discover everything personally by trial and error. The practiced painter may unlock for them a whole world by saying, "To understand Rembrandt's work, you must search out the light. Where did he put it in each painting? Where is its source? What does it reveal?"

The first shaft of light to penetrate our personal darkness of childlessness exposes our manner of responding to circumstances: it spotlights our attitudes. Are we facing up to and living in reality? Or do we still permit ourselves the unproductive luxury of imagining ourselves surrounded by the family we have always envisioned?[2] Are we living by our preconceptions of what our home should be like? Perhaps our thinking is based on our own childhood experiences or what friends' and relatives' families have. Maybe we have been influenced by movies, books, and soap operas.

Hollywood has convinced a lot of us that we can cut, splice, and edit our story until it results in a "happy ending." When, at times, our part in the script appears to be that of supporting actor or actress, we long for the really important roles. The life of those with children gets top billing, and our own existence, by comparison, appears only lackluster.

So adept do some of us become at idealizing what family life would be like that the actuality of becoming pregnant or being a parent would be a terrible disappointment! A childless friend recently stated that for her it helps to realize that "dreams are dreams. Everyone has at least one unfulfilled dream. I'll never be a size five." You and I are not alone in battling lifetime frustrations. Everyone else is struggling with limitations as well.

Recognizing our specific needs and unresolved tensions is the first step in letting God help us overcome them. I used to experience what could have been called a frustration cycle, but which since has become an acceptance cycle. For a number of years I didn't realize what my mind and spirit were feeding on when I felt dejected about not having children. My thoughts actually followed a pattern somewhat like this:

1. Why can *they* have children and *we* cannot?
2. It is not fair.
3. Others have children and grandchildren—real families. We have no one.
4. I am getting older and, as an adult, I have missed out on almost all of the really important things in life.

Obviously, my set of "grievances" sprang from self-pity and envy. It was helpful for me to identify the crux of my problem. Perhaps your inner protests stem from anger, self-depreciation, or bitterness. Write down the things you feel as you recognize them. Then, go back and find biblical truths to counteract the false notions with which you have been besieged. My parallel list looks like this:

1. I am unique in God's kingdom and have my own worth and place of usefulness. Others are serving Him in their appointed places.
2. Earthly life may not be fair, but God is just and righteous.
3. Jesus did not have a family either; He is my example.
4. My hope is not an earthly one alone, but a future one as well. I am in the center of God's will and moving forward with Him.

As a twinge of self-pity or envy strikes, I strike back. I have determined that, immediately upon becoming aware that I am feeling sorry for myself, I will respond with something more powerful than my own pettiness: the reality of God's truth. Usually I can move through an acceptance cycle quickly and emerge feeling strengthened by recognizing and accepting who God says I am.

But resolution doesn't come without struggle. As one pastor friend often comments, "There are no permanent victories." That doesn't mean our overcoming is not real; it simply means that we cannot expect a one-time action to suffice. I find this particularly true if I am in close contact with children from pitiful home situations or with successful parents of admirable families. I must then wage a major skirmish against my unpredictable foes—my jealous feelings. Through me Jesus has to actively serve and care for the very ones who received the blessing I wanted.

But though it's a fight, it's a worthwhile fight—a fight of faith.[3] And most of the time I win. I encourage you in your personal contest to use your spiritual battle gear: truth, God's righteousness (not your own "goodness"), readiness to share testimony about Christ, faith, the Word of God, prayer. In a word: reliance on your salvation—that God will undertake for you, not only eternally, but *now*.[4]

You and I cannot afford to lose our spiritual footing in what may be our most fundamental lifelong spiritual, emotional, intellectual, and physical struggle. If Christianity does not work in this life issue, it will not work at all. Christ's Spirit and His Word must live in us in our trial. One advantage for those of us grappling with childlessness is that our life with Christ remains practical because our tribulation is so basic. Abstract spirituality is not enough. We are forced to learn how Jesus meets the real needs of people like us who hurt. And because we continue to discover how a living Christ helps us, we always have something fresh to share with others.

Jesus often strengthens us while under fire by reminding us of our basic security. One such foundation for me was knowing that my mate was God's choice for me as I was for him. Granted, many couples have not had the benefit of receiving such confidence through prayer during courtship. But spouses can rely on the clear statement of Scripture that when a man and woman make a marriage commitment, the Lord ratifies that transaction. According to Scripture He, along with society, is honor-bound to respect the unit which man has formed.[5]

We are not at liberty, therefore, to consider "what might have been" with another partner, or entertain the thought of ending one fruitless marriage to engage in a more promising opportunity. Further, between spouses neither blame nor disappointment is appropriate. We received what we chose: each other. We made a lifelong commitment to our mate on unconditional conditions; the growth of love is not dependent upon marriage fulfilling all of our dreams.

Inscribed on my wedding band is a simple statement: "Each for the other; both for God." Isn't that the essence of a Christian marriage? Be encouraged: the childless marriage can be strong. Much of the energy which we do not invest in children, we can direct toward each other. Let's build up our marriage and make it one which functions happily. By so doing we will be preparing ourselves to confront together the various obstacles which any couple faces and the specific ones which we will meet.

Some of our challenges will come in the guise of pregnant women (perhaps good friends, or even relatives) and sweet, innocent babies. They certainly don't mean to threaten our sense of well-being. Being aware of this fact intellectually, however, is not enough. God's goal for us is not information, but formation. We are to become persons who can accept others lovingly.

Being around expectant women and babies has its ups and downs for those of us who would like to be parents. That hardest part is never knowing when we are likely to feel up, and when down. Walking outdoors on a splendid April day, we may be caught by surprise to discover that all pregnant women seem to bloom in the spring! Coming babies were not so obvious while winter wraps covered their expectant mothers. Suddenly, we feel surrounded. Mothers-to-be are everywhere: coming out of our favorite fast-food chain, watching a parade, shopping at the grocery store—literally every place *except* standing in our shoes.

Sometimes the present is difficult to endure, no matter what preparations we have made. One woman recalls attending a send-off party for a young missionary family about to depart for Africa. Everyone brought children's clothing and other gifts appropriate for packing in the family's missionary barrels. In itself there was nothing personally threatening about the event, but my friend had to leave when she couldn't keep back her tears. It was an unexpected personal defeat.

It is often helpful to explain in advance to our relatives and close friends how our sorrow sometimes prevents us from responding as we would like. Regardless of our sex, our emotions may betray us at the most inopportune moments when we are least able, or it would be most unfitting, to verbalize the inner upheaval we are experiencing. We should make it clear that occasionally we may feel more comfortable serving in the background rather than being directly with the guests. Sometimes we may simply have to excuse ourselves. Our growing at such a time needs to be in private, not public.

We will usually find our families and friends to be very empathetic and considerate, but we must bring up the subject. Having done so, however, we may experience an interesting phenomenon: once we feel the psychological freedom to express our negative emotions, we may not have to do so. From time to time my husband has assured me: "It's all right to weep. You can cry all you want. You have a right to cry." And simply because I know I can, from that moment I no longer want to!

A common psychological temptation which we face is that of over-compensation, perhaps to cover our true feelings or to make up for embarrassment which we feel about some past inappropriate action. One childless woman, for instance, devotes excessive time and attention to her dogs. Another, who has a small house, continues to buy homey "things" which have to be packed away because of lack of space. One lady became known in her circle as the Baby Shower Queen because of her obsession to plan elaborate parties for every new arrival.[6] Some of us disguise our true feelings at showers by giving expensive gifts or creating intricate, handmade items. Of course, all such actions may be undertaken independent of any relation to one's childlessness. We alone must question our own motives if we note such a behavior pattern, to see what it really indicates.

At certain stages, the continuing inner conflict may become so intense that we are tempted to deny our inner nature. It would be easier to hate babies or simply be delivered of our parenting desires. When this happens our partner is the one most likely to point out that either of these options would be an inadequate, if not impossible, solution.

My husband once put his arm around me and gently reassured me:

"It's part of a woman's nature to want children. The nature of kitties is to use their claws. Birds fly. Horses don't. Why, you would be an exception if you didn't have this desire which could be frustrated. You might question whether you really were a woman. If God just took away your desire for such a thing, would that be grace? . . ."

Until now we may have experienced God's provision when He has given us strength, which wasn't ours naturally, to confront the minor challenges of life. Or, He may have supplied one-time deliverance from some dreaded end, perhaps financial ruin. But because of the depth and extent of this personal trial, we will begin to experience some new forms of grace: the grace not to have to know the future; grace not to be self-sufficient; grace to live heartily under pressure in the present.

COPING BEYOND HOPING

"I remember the day," commented an open-hearted pastor's wife, "when we received letters of rejection from five adoption agencies. It was the hardest day of my life. I felt like I wasn't worth anything to anybody."

Because she had had a hysterectomy before marriage, she and her husband had always planned to adopt. What adoption agency would refuse to place a baby with such a deserving family? Those agencies with few babies and hundreds of potentially ideal homes would. Of course, their decision is not a personal act against the families *not* selected. And yet, their rejection feels heartlessly, excruciatingly personal.

Many of us can be thankful that our process of dying to the hope of having children has been much more gentle, even if more protracted. At last we know—or are almost certain—that we will never be parents. That knowledge, though, forces us into a new and dangerous state. Hope must be displaced. At this point one of two major changes occurs: our life becomes either bitter or better.

Ultimately, our making a positive response often hinges on our taking the initiative to seek out people who are willing to listen to, dialogue with, or struggle in prayer with us—our mate, friends, a counselor, our family or church members, or an infertility support group. With them we may safely vent our anger, frustrations, bewilderment, and hurt, knowing that they want our best and are committed to helping us find peace.

We've now come midway in a journey we never expected to take.

With the security of land far behind, we find ourselves re-evaluating our present state and determining where God is heading with us. Some of us recall that when we were launched involuntarily into our unpredictable sea, we were vulnerable to almost every minor adversity. We now find that our little vessel has been scraped, patched, and repaired so often that our hull is thicker and more resistent than ever before. Others of us—formerly independent, sure craft plying the surface waters of life with ideal weather and full sail—have been unexpectedly rammed broadside by the most destructive storm of our lives. We've taken in water and have needed to be bailed out. No longer sporting the same self-assurance, we are considerably weathered by the blast we have endured.

What has happened? Although we've had neither identical preparations for, nor confrontations with, this tremendous force against our personal will, our ships have suffered the same assault. Like a tropical storm it has a name: childless. Very little of our trial has been agreeable to us, and yet, in reflection we see that even the scarring and struggling have strengthened our spiritual fiber and given us a horizon-goal approach to life. More important, we have learned that God has been faithful to keep us afloat and is with us still!

We start to comprehend God's creativity in working with His children. Just as He promised in Romans 5:3–5, suffering begins to be expressed positively in our lives in the form of patience, endurance, perseverance, and the kind of hope that does not disappoint us. We may often have prayed for some of those qualities, but we never expected Him to use such a life experience to help form them into our character!

We may be surprised to recognize some atypical, but nearly automatic, responses which He has developed in us. To mention one: praise. Praise is undoubtedly one of the best depression-fighters, but have we ever *had* to put it into practice in other aspects of life? In order to survive childlessness without bitterness, we have to cultivate a thankful spirit.

What do we have for which we *can* genuinely praise God? Aside from common blessings, we may recall various strengths from our childhood or youth which have helped us move through the strains of adulthood. You and I can also praise God for our mate or other loved ones—for God himself—who have encouraged us in this, our most significant trial. Only we can offer God this unique praise.

Moreover, we may gain incentive for heartfelt praise by reviewing answers to past requests. We may be amazed at the many times God *has* responded positively to our private needs in daily life and the multiplied other concerns which we have brought Him. Our personal focus must never be concentrated on one denied request, but on the Savior. As we exercise praise throughout our lifetime, we begin to realize how little that attitude need be connected to particular, visible reasons for thanksgiving. We can eventually praise God for being Lord, and Lord of *our* life, apart from any tangible benefit of that relationship.

Sometimes the Savior does provide specific and obvious answers in the midst of our plight. One friend who underwent major surgery in her unsuccessful quest for fertility shared afterward: "I am thankful that I was led to agree to surgery. In the process the doctor found and corrected two potentially dangerous physical problems which we didn't even know I had." Left untreated, her conditions could possibly have claimed her life. Being a nurse she could understand the deliverance that the Lord had provided. Yes, "you alone, O Lord, make me dwell in safety" (Ps. 4:8).

Unquestionably, those who have known the greatest anguish are you who have miscarried or suffered the death of a child. Your pain is very private and intense. Only you as a family fully appreciated the significance of your child. You, alone, experienced that little one's life and anticipated with hope your child's future. But ah! There is, indeed, One other who shared your baby's brief hours. He sees a child's embryonic development in its mother's womb when, out of sight from the world, an individual begins to exist. God has fashioned and recorded forever the uniqueness of each human being. He has put great thought into the formation and development of every person. Nothing is hidden from Him (Ps.139:11–18). Your baby is likewise important to the Creator and, although perhaps you have never known your child, God does. The Lord speaks about knowing people before they were born or even conceived![7] He who experienced the prenatal state and remained God is not bound by, nor does He restrict others to, developmental stages. He sees the perfected end of all of His creation.[8]

In Matthew 18:10 Jesus tells us His concern for and the value He places on "the little ones." He says: "See that you do not look down on one of these little ones. For I tell you that their angels always see the face of my Father in heaven" (NIV). Who is more defenseless and in greater need of the watchcare of the heavenly Father than an unborn child? God loves and appreciates innocence. Praise Him for His ability to redeem and preserve that which is His forever.

Can we thank God yet? Counting as good in themselves those monthly disappointments, the misunderstandings of other people, the heartbreak of miscarriage, the shattering agony of a stillborn baby amounts to no more than futile rationalization. Probably only after a period of adjustment can we honestly see God's gracious hand producing a work of art in our lives. God uses strange tools in His crafts-manship. If we look at a statue carved by an artist we see only the finished work. We can't tell what the stone originally was like, nor how the large sections were removed, nor what hard, sharp instru-ments chipped away at delicate features. Similarly, we may be una-ware of what is being shaped in us through the painful processes we are undergoing. Our confidence rests in the conviction that the Sculp-tor's work serves not to destroy but to create.

If we can't praise God that we don't have children, we can praise Him in spite of that fact, trusting that someday we will understand and be able to thank Him for what He gave us in place of our first desire. Perhaps we deeply regret not having experienced the miracle (which it *would* be for us) of birth. But have we considered how many miracles the Lord may have performed to prevent us from having children?! Have we ever expressed our thanks for having been spared experiences worse than being childless? Do we appreciate the joy of participating in His highest ministry for us? We may spontaneously offer Him whatever praise comes to our heart. And remember: incred-ible as it may seem, in a marvelous way God inhabits the praises of His people (Ps. 22:3).

The acts of self-evaluation and praise help us realize that we are no longer at the mercy of others in our grief-to-grace process. Ob-viously, no one, including our doctor, mate, or pastor, is going to be able to provide all of the personal emotional support we need. Under-standing that ultimately we are responsible for our own progress, we begin to see that our journey, although seemingly slow-moving, is not at a standstill. It is getting better. We are able to identify various expressions of grief that we have successfully (maybe repeatedly) passed through: shock, denial, anger, hope, bargaining, loss of hope, accep-tance, and resolution.[9]

Then, quite unexpectedly, we may feel a burst of vigor—even as a teacher after spring break may redouble efforts to crowd into the re-mainder of the year many experiences the class has not yet had. We have a renewed capacity to read, learn, and make personal adjust-ments.[10]

We have finally emerged from hibernation! Our outlook broadens, no longer confined to factual and practical matters related to our sin-gleness, infertility, sorrow, or grief. We begin to focus on hobbies, career-related information and experiences, spiritual gifts and min-istries, self-realization ventures, or any number of things which revive our zest for living.

There was a time when I expressed to my husband, "It seems so long since I've laughed." Fatigue was partly to blame, but I recognize now that I was in one of the final stages in my journey through personal despair. Just at that time we spent almost a week's vacation with my husband's parents. On the last night before arriving home, we played a game together in our little camp trailer. For some reason we all felt silly and I laughed uproariously. It was not until I was ready to fall asleep that I was aware of how good I felt. It had taken almost a week's relaxation and a long period of inner metamorphosis—but at last I could laugh again!

Eventually we begin to bear our heartache more easily. Our emotions no longer seem to be presiding over us, swayed by changing circumstances, rather than obeying our inner determination. An amazing practicality may accompany this final phase. As one couple put it: "You realize that it's not so bad to have time to spend with your nephews and nieces and then go home to fall in bed without all the responsibility."

My husband and I are now able to say, "If we had had a family when we planned, they would be in college by now, and we still wouldn't have a child around." That is not a sour grapes attitude; it is reality. Instead of having an empty nest at this time of life, our nest is as full and as empty as it ever was. Besides, it's a good nest.

Childless individuals have given me a variety of responses when asked what has brought them comfort in their most trying moments. They often mention words from such hymns as "Day by Day, and with Each Passing Moment," "Great Is Thy Faithfulness," and "Like a River Glorious" have upheld them.

Before my husband and I married we chose a family theme song, little suspecting that there would be days when the message of that hymn alone would encourage my faith:

IN HEAVENLY LOVE ABIDING
(To the Tune of: "The Church's One Foundation")

In heav'nly love abiding, No change my heart shall fear;
And safe is such confiding, For nothing changes here.
The storm may roar without me, My heart may low be laid,
But God is round about me, And can I be dismayed?

Wherever He may guide me, No want shall turn me back;
My Shepherd is beside me, And nothing can I lack.
His wisdom ever waketh, His sight is never dim,
He knows the way He taketh, And I will walk with Him.

Green pastures are before me, Which yet I have not seen;
Bright skies will soon be o'er me, Where darkest clouds have been.
My hope I cannot measure, My path to life is free,
My Savior has my treasure, And He will walk with me.[11]

I never tire of the sound and message of that song. It lifts my eyes off myself and places them once again on the Great King who has committed himself to taking me all the way through this life and into the next.

Should it surprise us that the last thing Jesus did formally with His disciples was to sing with them? "When they had sung a hymn, they went out to the Mount of Olives" (Matt. 26:30, NIV). Evidently the song they chose had special meaning to Jesus. Perhaps it was a traditional Passover hymn which would have encouraged Him as He stepped out into His night as a lamb, soon to fulfill His redemptive calling. Jesus will place music in your mind and heart as you face your lonely places, too. Ask Him for it, and enjoy His song in the night for you (Ps. 42:8).

He knows how badly we need Him near. The scripture at the beginning of this chapter, Proverbs 30:15, expresses His keen awareness of our crying out. He in no way belittles our sense of loss; rather, He elevates it to the level of other cataclysmic events:

grave—with its death and corruption
barren womb—with its unspeakable emptiness
drought—with its killing dryness
fire—with its power to consume

God really understands the intensity of our agony. He recognizes our desperate need for satisfaction. Death, drought, fire, and childlessness are terrible realities. Not only is God aware of such personal devastation, He seeks to bring to the attention of the whole world the magnitude of what we experience daily.

Yes, He knows. Have you ever considered that God is allowing us to discover what He alone knew through the eons of eternity past? In the midst of our desire to impart life to someone else, He extends us an invitation to a holy place. He welcomes us, as it were, into the very bedchamber of God. What He shares with us is a gift of himself: a knowledge of how it was before anything was, before anyone else existed. As the God of love, the One with the Father-Mother heart, existing in trinity, He had no one who could freely respond to Him and on whom to bestow His love. Although mystery still surrounds our understanding, we know that He experienced a sense of childlessness. We are not meaning to bring God to our level of experience, but we know that there was within the heart of God an unfulfilled desire to share His love in a personal relationship with someone like himself.

When at last the time was right to fulfill His deepest desire, He burst forth with: "Let us make man in our image, in our likeness; and let them rule over . . . all the earth. . . . So God created man in his own image, in the image of God he created him; male and female he created them. God saw everything that he had made, and it was very good" (Gen. 1:26a, 27, 31a, NIV).

To some is given the close association with God, the Creator, in childbearing. Considering eternity, however, the Fatherhood of God has only been tangibly expressed for one brief hour. But by entrusting to us the experience of childlessness, He is sharing with you and me, in part, an understanding of the mainspring of all His creative acts. He is—do we see it?—imprinting us with the very image of himself.

Therein lies the fundamental possibility for our coping with childlessness: *we identify with Him*.

Our second source of fulfillment comes from responding to this One who, not having children, yearned for us to be His as we long for children of our own. We, physically barren, understand this intense desire of God which moved Him to come in person to establish His family. Not that He was to leave a natural heritage, for "who can speak of His descendants?" (Isa. 53:8a). But His body and soul were to enter into a labor unto death to bring us newness of life. He tells us a small part about that experience through Isaiah:

> . . .when he makes himself an offering for sin, he shall see his off-spring, he shall prolong his days; the will of the Lord shall prosper in his hand; he shall see the fruit of the travail of his soul and be satisfied.
> —Isaiah 53:10b, 11 (RSV)

What He went through to create us physically and then to gain us eternally wins us because we know that we would do the same for our own children. We are eager to bring *Him* long-overdue satisfaction, to become part of His family at last.

Being "family" to God takes us beyond the confines of our single state or couplehood. We become part of an international and eternal body with a relationship not only to the Father but also to every other member of that same great entity. We begin to participate with our larger family, experiencing life in a dimension beyond the borders of our own home. We further discover that every son and daughter of the King of Kings and Lord of Lords has the high privilege of sharing this gift of everlasting life with others. Our spiritual capacity to reproduce is not hindered—in fact, it may even be enhanced—by our not having natural children.

My husband and I have had the joy of seeing a child take his first steps to the delight of a whole household. Afterward, however, we had to agree that as rewarding a moment as that was, it cannot compare to the overwhelming joy of seeing people—children, teenagers, and adults—step into new life in Christ, learning to walk, and at last, run!

What is even more satisfying is to see them speed right past us, greater and stronger than we are in many respects, and more able themselves to become producers in the kingdom of God.

We *can* reproduce ourselves—many times over. And our offspring are just as real, only infinitely more varied, than had they come from us physically. Each of them has a living, never-dying spirit which has received through us that same spark which brought us to spiritual life through someone else.

We are links in an eternal family chain. When history is laid open to the view of all, the important question will be: What lives has Jesus joined to himself through us?

Let us look forward in hope to Him who may one day say to us:

> Sing, O barren one, who did not bear, break forth into singing and cry aloud, you who have not been in travail! For the children of the desolate one will be more than the children of her that is married, says the Lord. —Isaiah 54:1 (RSV)

"He was despised and rejected by men;
a man of sorrows,
and acquainted with grief. . . .
Surely he has borne our griefs
and carried our sorrows. . . .
But he was wounded for our transgressions,
he was bruised for our iniquities;
upon him was the chastisement that made us whole,
and with his stripes we are healed.

"Yet it was the will of the Lord to bruise him;
he has put him to grief;
when he makes himself an offering for sin,
he shall see his offspring,
he shall prolong his days;
the will of the Lord shall prosper in his hand;
he shall see the fruit of the travail of his soul
and be satisfied. . . ."

—Isaiah 53:3, 4, 5, 10, 11 (RSV)

CHAPTER FOUR

Good Grief

Sixteen childless years had passed while I searched for inner spiritual satisfaction, a final resolution. I yearned for a book or series of articles which would present a biblically sound basis for putting my life into perspective at last. Not only was that not forthcoming, but we had been outside the United States for five years with little access to recent scientific research.

To make our personal pilgrimage more lonely, we had no intimate friends who were locked into the same struggle. My only resource was God himself. Even being able to read His Word in two different languages, however, did not bring me to the "Eureka!" point.

God *had* satisfied our inner need to know that being without children was somehow right for us. He had revealed glimpses of growth in the personal process through which we had been passing—He had even shown us some reasons! But there was yet something missing. I couldn't understand my turmoil about not being a mother. Why couldn't I just drop the terrible burden and walk away free?

There was still the monthly sobbing into the night and red eyes in the morning. How my husband managed to remain creatively consoling I don't know. But although he never *seemed* to tire of ministering to me, we both knew he did not have the answer we so desperately sought. Time after time he listened as I tried to express my bewilderment: "Jerry, did you ever know there was such a dichotomy? It's settled in my spirit, but my emotions won't always submit." In fact, they almost never submitted!

Oh, I knew the necessity and process of dying to one's self and coming alive to Christ.[1] A turning point in my experience with Jesus came after a year of unstable and inconsistent Christian behavior when I made a conscious decision to make Christ Lord of my life.

Permanently. No paragon of human flawlessness resulted, you may be sure. But by foregoing my right to say no to God and committing myself to be in agreement with Him, the yo-yo quality of my spiritual life and outward testimony smoothed out.

I learned that, although it caused some very real pain at times, I could align my will and spirit with the will and Spirit of God. Feelings of inner peace always followed; it never failed. Our toughest test had been giving up everything: home, cars, business, furniture, money, friends, my teaching position and master's degree program to end up with only forty-four pounds of luggage apiece and the opportunity to serve as missionaries. There had been a marked peace during the process and following it.

That's why I was so mystified when, having gone through the same process of inner relinquishment in this trial, I received no lasting peace! Hadn't I surrendered everything to God? Was there anything I was afraid to face? Was I angry? Was the enemy of my soul deluging me with opportunities for self-pity, and was I drowning in them? Was I not appropriating the peace God was providing? Every probe I sent into my inner being returned *negative*. There was something dreadfully wrong but I didn't know what it was.

One bright Mother's Day arrived in our adopted sub-tropical country. My husband and I had bought flowers for all of the ladies in the congregation and I was wearing one myself. The Sunday service began with joyful singing. However, as the moment for testimonies arrived and thanksgiving was expressed for the mothers in our congregation, tears suddenly exploded from my eyes. By the time Jerry began the sermon, my hanky supply was already sodden. I could not stop weeping. People's attention would focus on the preaching and then, it would shift to me. The jubilant occasion, the whole service—everything was ruined! It was all my fault. And yet, it was not my fault; I honestly could not help it.

I would have absented myself from the group, but there was no place to go. We were meeting in an open patio under a tarp supported by four poles and a metal framework. A national sister beside me felt so sympathetic that at last she could restrain herself no longer. Nudging me she said, "I'm hungry, aren't you?"

"No!" I blubbered.

After the morning worship hour it was worse. Little children were giving me Mother's Day gifts. "Don't cry, Sister Veeky, we love you. You are a mother to all of us." Even the ladies were hugging me, repeating the same sentiments. I could no longer stand it. They followed us to the car and kept touching and patting me, assuring me of their love through the open window while Jerry packed the trunk with everything necessary for the next two-hour service. At last we could drive away.

My husband knew I could not endure a second Mother's Day service; he also decided he would not leave me alone. Depositing me under a tree, he delivered the chairs to the midday meeting and returned, taking us to a refreshment stand where he bought two bottles of pop. We drank our pop in the car. One of us was wearing dark glasses; neither of us was talking.

Really, after so many years, what was there to say? I was not yet healed. Would I ever be? It had been such an awful, crushing defeat in front of the new believers in our infant congregation. And we were their spiritual leaders!

After a subdued dinner at home, Jerry went upstairs to read. I could at last be alone in the study where no one would hand me packages or construction-paper greeting cards. "God, oh, God! I cannot bear this any longer. You must tell me. What is this?!"

"Grief."

"Grief? But nobody died!"

"But nobody lived."

What? How could that be? I had never experienced grief. Could one grieve without a death? No one in my immediate family had ever died; I didn't know what it was like to lose a loved one. Neither had I ever died, spiritually speaking, to another person. Always before I had relinquished tangible things or real desires. Now was I to die to someone I would never have the opportunity to love?

"But, Father, why does it hurt so much?"

"Because it is a living sacrifice."

I knew Romans 12:1 by heart—in two languages, "Therefore, I urge you, brothers, in view of God's mercy, to offer your bodies as living sacrifices, holy and pleasing to God—which is your spiritual worship" (NIV). For years I had heard, taught, and purposed to live that concept. As a love offering, I had willingly surrendered my life wholly to Him who is Lord. I was committed to following Him no matter what the cost.

But it was no longer just *giving* Him a sacrifice; it was *being* one. Part of my person—my strong desire to impart life to another human being and share in the parenting process with my husband—was literally being sacrificed. I then became aware that I would not be able to die to this reality once and for all. It was and would be an on-going, living sacrifice, not a dead one.

I could not fulfill the ministry I was purposed to have in the Body of Christ if He simply took these strong child-caring urges from me.

They formed part of my natural person as well as my spiritual gift. He had to leave them, but I could not exercise them for myself. I had presented Him my body as a living sacrifice, and He had taken me at my word.

Before me is a small paper dated Mother's Day of that year. Beneath the date was the revelation: "It is a living sacrifice." Below that are my immediate and understated reactions:

"Oh, that is awful.
That is terrible.
Now, I know what that *is!*"

The full impact of what it meant to be a living sacrifice had dawned upon my spirit.

I still did not understand, however, why it was that sometimes I would be completely unaware of my state and at other times I would be stabbed by its reality. A word, a look, the appearance of a pregnant woman, mothers comparing notes, a man playing with his son—I never knew at what moment there might come a great inner sting to my spirit, and sometimes, to my eyes as well.

A year and a half passed and one Sunday morning found us thousands of miles away from Latin America, at a modern church in Wheaton, Illinois. My husband was to bring a missionary message in the 8:30 and 11:00 services. I sat at the front of the church while the morning texts were read in the first service and my husband preached. The second hour of worship arrived and again, the same Scripture was read. I was mentally preparing to hear the identical sermon, when all of a sudden one of the verses I had heard earlier leaped out at my heart:

> For every one shall be salted with fire, and every sacrifice shall be salted with salt.   —Mark 9:49 (KJV)

Salt! That was what it was—the random landing of salt in the wound! That is why it stung so much, why I never knew when it was coming or was quite prepared when it struck.

At home I searched the Old Testament passages on the use of salt for sacrifice. Leviticus 2:13 (KJV) spoke most clearly:

> And every oblation of thy meat-offering shalt thou season with salt; neither shalt thou suffer the salt of the covenant of thy God to be lacking from thy meat-offering: with all thine offerings thou shalt offer salt.

Unger's Bible Dictionary explained further, ". . . salt was the symbol of covenant. The meaning which the salt, with its power to strengthen food and preserve it from putrifaction and corruption, imparted to the sacrifice was the unbending truthfulness of that self-surrender to the Lord embodied in the sacrifice, by which all impurity and hypocrisy were repelled."[2]

Until then I had at times doubted whether I had completely given my offering to the Lord because I still felt such pain. I had thought that, once surrendered, an offering belonged to Him and should no longer touch me. Most of the time I didn't ache and felt quite assured of the transaction. But when unexpectedly overwhelmed with grief, I mistakenly thought that the living sacrifice had succeeded in crawling down off the altar.

I had never considered that the sting of the purifying salt is evidence that, indeed, the sacrifice still lives before God according to our agreement. The dead sacrifices in the Old Testament never felt the salt. We who are living sacrifices can depend on experiencing it.

This "salt" can actually aid in the process of our healing. Once we comprehend that we are in harmony with our God and His Word, and that we can expect momentary anguish, then we can rest spiritually. The inner confusion disappears. We understand that separate elements are intertwined in our facing childlessness, but we can separate them. Having dealt with the physical and spiritual strands, we can now recognize that the remaining trauma is emotional. We are experiencing something very normal, the grief process. We can even verbalize it: "I am not crying because I feel sorry for myself for not having children. I am weeping because I feel afresh the pangs of grief."

I remember how excited I was when I finally had an opportunity to investigate the latest scientific findings in the area of infertility. I rushed home from the library to tell my husband that researchers have discovered that very frequently, but not always, persons coming to grips with being childless undergo profound grief.[3] They may even go through the acknowledged stages of grief: denial, rage and anger, bargaining, depression and acceptance.[4]

Not always do both partners in a childless marriage suffer such a sense of loss. Sometimes neither will. In other cases only one of the spouses will have such a reaction. More lonely and frustrating may be the instance of one partner passing through a time of grieving while the other experiences wholeness only to have the situation reversed later on. With infertile couples it is usually the partner who has lost hope of his or her reproductive ability who is more likely to respond with grief. But there is no way to ascertain in advance who may react more intensely since men and women may grieve with equal feeling as if a loved one had died.[5]

If only I had previously had access to such findings! Perhaps my heart would have been brought to a place of peace much more quickly. It was a relief just to learn that I wasn't the only one who had suffered a severe sense of loss. This information served as external confirmation of an inner process of grace which the Lord had worked directly in my spirit when I was without other resource.

The childless can be comforted by God directly, but because this particular suffering is only in part spiritual, we may benefit from help available to us from various quarters: medical personnel, social and counseling services, scientific research, and peer support. Let's be perceptive about our problem areas and move toward finding answers which are adequate to satisfy us.

One of the ways God ministers to us is by using experiences which we have already had. You, the reader, may note something in your background which has served you in your present struggle. A personal acquaintance put it this way:

> I feel that the Lord has given me "protected feelings." My mama died giving birth to my little sister when I was 13. I knew the Lord before then, but at that time I resented God and everybody. But once I came to terms with the big loss the other was easier. You come to a place of realizing that it is God's will.

She shared that her mother entered the hospital showing no alarming symptoms upon going into labor. The mother's death in childbirth was an inconceivable shock to the father and daughter. Suddenly, she was forced to care for the baby that came home from that hospital alone. In a very real sense she reared her little sister. As the child grew up, graduating from high school and going on for further studies, she brought our friend a deep sense of joy and accomplishment, almost as if the girl had been her very own daughter.

If we allow Him to, God will turn that awful grief to good—His and ours. Sometimes it happens without our being aware of it. A couple of years before I understood what I had been experiencing spiritually and emotionally, I found myself engaged in a most peculiar activity. As I heard of friends who had lost a loved one, I would wait a couple of weeks and then seek an opportunity to be with them, perhaps at a restaurant. After talking about their experience and the person they had lost, we would explore together what the Scriptures say about death and the resurrection.

I didn't understand why the Lord had opened the doors to this particular ministry. Why, I had never suffered the loss of a loved one. And very often I had never known personally the relative who had passed away! But I felt so right about being with the people who had suffered such a personal loss, listening to them, crying with them, and sharing with them from the Word of God. We always ended up feeling mutually edified, although I did not then recognize that God was ministering to my own grief. Just so perhaps you don't know how the Lord purposes to use your sorrow, but I encourage you to give Him the opportunity to use it positively. He will not waste what is His.

What did He consider valuable in His own life? Earlier in this book we looked briefly at Jesus. Were your initial thoughts about Him that: He was full of joy, taught with great authority, showed compassion, healed the sick, raised the dead? These aspects are all strong, positive truths about His character and ministry.

But so often we forget that Christ was, as well, "a man of sorrows and acquainted with grief" as we read in Isaiah 53:3. He knew grief intimately. It is very probable that before He began His ministry, He may have had to watch one or more of His own loved ones die, knowing He was not yet free to exercise His resurrection power to save them. Could it be that His own stepfather had passed away? Joseph is not seen after the last childhood reference to Jesus,[6] nor is his presence alluded to at the cross when Christ placed Mary in the care of John.[7]

Perhaps Jesus could minister with compassion precisely because He knew through experience how much in need the people were. We see His own reaction after hearing of the beheading death of John the Baptist, Jesus' cousin who had baptized Him, the one person who probably most clearly understood the significance of His life and ministry. Matthew (14:13–14, NIV) tells us:

> When Jesus heard what had happened, he withdrew by boat privately to a solitary place. Hearing of this, the crowds followed him on foot from the towns. When Jesus landed and saw a large crowd, he had compassion on them and healed their sick.

One might think that He would react with holy indignation and vent His wrath against Herod. Instead, He took His grief personally to the heavenly Father, and then allowed the wells of compassion within Him to overflow to those who needed what He could do for them in that moment to relieve them in their suffering.

There is something about grief which profoundly affects the sufferer. Many times a person is more spiritually open at the moment of personal loss than ever before. For those who have known the grief of childlessness, there is the side benefit that it is *not* an experience bound to a person and moment in the past. It serves as a springboard for compassion because its immediacy and freshness can be drawn upon whenever ministering to someone who is hurting.

Previously I mentioned that those suffering such loss may not find in this world any real consolation. God is, after all, its ultimate source. As we find His comfort to us valid we will be able to recommend it to others. The Apostle Paul puts it this way:

> Praise be to the God and Father of our Lord Jesus Christ, the Father of compassion and the God of all comfort, who comforts us in all our

troubles, so that we can comfort those in any trouble with the comfort
we ourselves have received from God.   —2 Corinthians 1:3–4 (NIV)

Did you catch one of the delightful surprises of this passage? To
whom does it say the comforted will be able to minister? To those who
are in "any trouble." Unexpectedly, the doors of ministry for me, for
you, have swung open! We are no longer just receivers; we are givers.
And we may give not only to those acquaintances who share our particular grief. Suffering becomes a context for ministry. Our ability in
Christ to console knows no bounds; we may comfort people in any kind
of trouble whatsoever. When we ourselves have been to the depths
with Christ, we know that others may pass through safely as well. We
can be conductors, encouragers recommending "the God of all comfort."

The world and the church are crying out for someone who has the
right kind of ears to hear. You do if you have heard Him speak to you.
The work that sorrow and grief does is not finished, however, if it stops
with you. It will equip you, in turn, to minister in matters of the spirit.
Do not be afraid to care about people enough to cry with them in their
agony. Spanish speakers express it marvelously when they say, "We,
the beautiful people, weep." You may be one of the beautiful people to
someone.

As a young teenager I had a piano teacher who tried desperately
to get us students to play with real feeling, expressing emotions through
our fingers. One day she exasperatedly complained, "I wish you girls
would fall in love so you could play these love songs!"

Jesus must wish to echo the same sentiments at times. How He
must long for us to know, in part, what He experienced so that in those
depths His tenderness and compassion will sing out through us. Then
we will not be reticent to play His love song to others throughout our
lives. Grief in the hands of God works its own beauty deeply into our
beings. It emerges at last through the outward actions and voices of
our inmost souls, not as its former melancholy dirge, but as a victorious
rendition of living testimony to Him who alone can orchestrate *good*
grief.

"And let not any eunuch complain,
'I am only a dry tree.'
For this is what the Lord says:
'To the eunuchs who keep my Sabbaths,
who choose what pleases me
and hold fast to my covenant—
to them I will give within my temple and its walls
a memorial and a name
better than sons and daughters;
I will give them an everlasting name
that will not be cut off.'"

—Isaiah 56:3b–5 (NIV)

SECTION TWO:

PEOPLE

CHAPTER FIVE

The Single Non-Parent

I was surprised. The young woman at whose dining room table I was sitting stated flatly, "For me the biggest battle is *not* not being married; it is not having a family."

Was she expressing only a momentary thought, or could it be true? She explained, "Some singles enjoy adult company and find real fulfillment doing things together—not that I don't like my single friends. But given a choice of going out with friends or being home with some kids, I'd choose the kids."

We were looking through her photo album at the latest snapshots she had inserted. "This is what I call fun," she remarked, pointing to pictures taken the night before Easter. She and a family of four had been invited to have dinner with mutual friends and their two children. Afterward the guest family decided to leave early so as to bathe their children in preparation for Easter morning.

"Why not give all of them their baths here?" someone suggested. Before long the tub and floor were being sloshed by warm water, bubbles, shampoo, and several preschoolers. The proof of their fun was in the prints she had taken.

A memorable occasion for her consisted of four little kids messing up a well-ordered bathroom and running on wet feet across the floor. It was a simple thing, but one that she seldom experienced in her singleness. "Some of my friends say they get lonely for a man's voice and footsteps in the house. But I miss the sound of children."

Being married, I realized that I did not fully comprehend the first-mentioned loss. But I certainly understood the latter. There was an affinity between us: a shared emptiness. Childlessness sensitizes the people who undergo its pain and creates within us a mutual transparency, a peephole of sorts into our common suffering. It is as if we were walking beside Hester Prynne, of *The Scarlet Letter*, who was able to recognize those she passed whose experience paralleled her own. Although we aren't wearing a letter *C*, our very lack of identifying marks sets us apart. Many of us continue a lifetime without a wedding band, and none of us carry telltale baby pictures, birth certificates, immunization records, or crayoned hugs and kisses on folded tablet paper in our wallets.

A similar loss seems poignant even in the animal kingdom! One morning newscasters announced the sad tidings that the newborn baby of Ling-Ling the panda had died. A week later the Washington Zoo keepers reported finding the grief-stricken panda sitting, hunched up by herself, cradling an apple in her arms. If Ling-Ling, who knew nothing of hopes and dreams, could so miss having her own baby— how much more human beings?

Upon being asked what made being without children difficult for her, one single friend responded simply:

> The feeling of empty arms. I love to hold babies and small children. I like to amuse and play with younger children. Often I find myself listening to the child instead of the parents when they are present.

The contrast between life as it is versus life as it "should be" can be an awful reality for those who are single and childless but who have never desired to be either.

The singles camp, of course, includes a lot of territory. There is the "confirmed" bachelor or career woman, the divorced person, the older single who never married (sometimes because of war or other tragedy), the celibate by religious choice, the widowed, the disabled, the person who would like to marry but has yet to meet the right mate, and the younger single who is not ready for the responsibility of lifelong commitment, as well as those in various other categories.

For some, the mere idea of longing for children is foreign. One person made this quite clear when asked whether adapting to single life without a family was difficult:

> No, because I am working with kids all day. When I come home I am ready for some adult companionship. Also, I have enjoyed the freedom and flexibility of living alone.

A single male acknowledged that in the future he wouldn't mind parenting. But for the present:

> I do *not* feel any special urge to have children and would feel perfectly happy if I never did have any [children]. Wifelessness is a bigger problem for me.

Authors of books for singles, aware that matelessness is the immediate concern of the unmarried, discuss and explore in depth adult life without a partner. Your local Christian bookstore can refer you to a number of excellent titles. These resources are most adequate for any single who isn't experiencing the accompanying struggle of childlessness.

Sometimes I have forgotten how separate these two issues may be. I once made the mistake of glibly remarking to a single acquaintance in her late thirties, "After all, at some time every adult is childless."

Used to confrontation in her profession, she vehemently disagreed: "No, they aren't. They still have either a dream or real children. I haven't yet given up my dream, and I therefore don't feel childless."

She certainly had a valid point: as long as one's dream child or real children live, childlessness in its fullest sense cannot be realized by an individual. She herself was presently in the throes of deciding whether to marry a widower with two children.

And so it is for the single. One such decision can drastically affect a person's dream-state and present reality. The option of finding a mate with a built-in family, grown children, or even grandchildren always remains a possibility. Further, in many states singles can adopt children; indeed, it may even be easier for them to do so! They do not have to meet the same requirements that a couple has to; for instance: providing medical proof of not being able to conceive a child, having the family's financial status reflected only through the prospective adoptive father's salary and length of time on the job, or having an ideal husband-wife relationship.

For many singles, therefore, hope for parenthood remains very much alive throughout the greater part of their lives. Since there is no moment of ultimate verdict for the single, the grief point may come much later than for the married. And very possibly, it may never arrive at all.

While on assignment in England and Western Europe, we discovered that European young people tend to marry later on than their American counterparts. Many didn't consider themselves eligible to enter into a lifetime commitment until their late twenties. Our Christian friends were very comfortable and unhurried in their adventure through singleness, considering it a positive time in which to give the Lord undivided attention and service. Some, already in their thirties, had never had a serious relationship with anyone of the opposite sex—nor were they worried about that fact.

I remember visiting a Dutch couple in their seventies who were parents of one of the over-thirty girls on our team. Surrounded by his daughter and photos of his two sons and grandchildren, the hulky gray-haired father declared quite adamantly, as he was evidently accustomed to do: "No marriage is any good if the partners aren't at least forty. We didn't marry until I was forty-one and look how happy we are!" Their daughter has since married and she and her Dutch husband have produced two children to further delight her parents' hearts.

My husband and I had been the exception on the team: the married couple, obviously the most likely to become a family replete with children. But ten years later almost all of our long-time single friends have subsequently married and are parenting children. Waiting does not necessarily mean denial.

Just as the Dutch parents set the stage positively for their daughter's feeling at ease with her circumstances, so the families of any single person can increase or decrease the pressure their relatives' experience. Sad to say, family members often make it *more* difficult for the ones they love. Sometimes the teasing and jibes can be laughed off, but sometimes the barb isn't as stingless. And what's worse, family members are often oblivious to the hurt.

Our friend Melanie is the private secretary to an executive of an international organization and as such she bears great responsibility for worldwide communication. Recently she flew to her parents' ranch for a well-earned vacation. Her brothers and sisters and their families were all at home for a big dinner. Afterward her mother pointed to a wall with a few family photographs: "I'd like some up-to-date pictures of everyone. You (she indicated her married children) can have photos taken with your families. And you, Mel, can have a picture taken with . . . your desk."

Initially, Melanie was stunned: first, that her mother would even make such an unfeeling statement, and second, that no one seemed to think it in the least unfitting that she had. Upon later reflection, it struck her as side-splittingly humorous. Soon it became an office joke as to how she should best pose with the desk. A number of the office secretaries were convulsed with laughter as she tenderly embraced her desk, ready for the all-important shot!

But not every deep hurt can be so easily assuaged. Sue, a young woman doing innovative cancer research in a large hospital, had been looking forward to returning home instead of being alone in the city for the Christmas holiday. During her stay, however, not once did anyone ask her about her job or about the potential breakthroughs with which she was uniquely acquainted. Everyone was taken up with the babies of her brother and sister. The cute things the youngsters said and did were the main topics of conversation. Sue returned to her apartment so put-down that she later expressed her intent not to go home for future holidays.

Family members are often unaware how important their relationships with their childless relatives are. A single uncle or aunt who lovingly invests time in the youngsters of family members may find that these kids become almost substitute children. And yet both single and child are in a vulnerable position because ultimately the decision as to the quality of their relationship is determined by the children's parents. In ideal circumstances, everyone may benefit from this extended family unit. But in an age of easily severed relationships and divorce, both the children and the childless may suffer the pain of involuntary separation.

Such was the experience of a single friend who deeply loved her niece and nephew. Fran was hurt almost beyond words when presents she sent to them after her brother and sister-in-law divorced were returned unopened. She has not been allowed to regain contact with the children.

Similarly, a bachelor from our home church had been telling us that he could hardly wait for the Father-Son breakfast. Bob came that morning . . . alone. His request to take his nephew to the breakfast had been denied at the last minute. He felt terribly defeated in his effort to establish meaningful ties with the only little boy in his life.

There are such risks, but fortunately, they are the exceptions. Many singles have rich, lifelong relationships with their younger relatives. A widowed mother with her two single daughters were one such family. They received great comfort after the father's death when a third daughter and her two small children stayed with them during the husband's term of military service abroad. The toddlers bestowed names of endearment on the grandmother and aunties which have survived to this day. Through the years the aunts have had the pleasure of hanging the children's art work and school photographs on the walls as if their sister's children were their very own.

They have now become significant persons to their grandnieces and nephew, as well. For vacations they fly halfway across the United States to be with these youngsters for piano recitals, graduations, and other important events. They are a close family, although the miles on a map might make one think such a relationship to be impossible. Since they are not perceived as "parents," but single persons to whom teenagers can relate, they have never experienced a communication gap with their "kids."

How a single invests in the lives of others depends on who one is and what opportunities present themselves. A high school teacher who had been conducting a home Bible study in her apartment was overjoyed when a young woman in her group made a commitment to the Lord. However, since the woman was barely literate and did not have any marketable job skills with which to support her four children, she was on public assistance. Our friend decided to dedicate as much time as necessary to help the family succeed, not only in their newfound relationship with Christ, but in society.

She taught the woman to read and write, waited in food-stamp lines with her, and frequently stayed in the family's home—in reality, she undertook a discipleship relationship with the whole family! She spent a summer working without pay beside the woman to teach her a marketable skill. Gradually she began to influence not only their household management, but their treatment of one another. That family is now able to operate as an independent unit; the children are affectionately known as Judy's "godkids."

Divorced, Lee is unable to live near his grown children, but having worked for an airline he is able to visit them frequently. In addition, he has become "family friend" to many who need him. He takes particular pleasure in encouraging young people who are going into Christian service. Half-spanning the continent three times and flying to Europe on another occasion, he has been with us at crucial times in our own ministry. Closer to home, if he notices that a ministerial student's study or work load is getting heavy, he invites him for a weekend retreat. Or he will accompany a young preacher to investigate a potential field of service. Although Lee will never be a professional minister himself, he is a support to many who will be, by his presence and personal interest.

Clearly, a single person has a constant choice to make: self-centeredness or other-centeredness. Persons with families, whether they care to be or not, are constantly put in touch with the larger community through their children. But only through decision and determination do most singles direct their lives outward. As they age, singles may lose sight of their importance in the Body of Christ. One such person confided, "I find it more difficult to reach out to new people as I get older."

It was refreshing, therefore, to hear a widow's response after attending a presentation in which seminary wives were interviewed. When asked what made each seminary family feel at home in this particular church, one young wife answered that they were attracted by the families and singles who had invited them into their homes for fellowship or a meal. "I had no idea that anyone would want to come to *my* place. I'm old and live alone. I'm so surprised to find that it really makes a difference." It may make *all* the difference! You have undivided love to lavish on people.

While talking with singles about their struggle with aging and blurred spiritual vision, I hear another common tale. See if it has found its way into your thought depository, too: "This summer was one of the worst in my life. Two of my best friends got married and asked me to be a bridesmaid. I should have been thrilled for them because I know how long they have waited. But all I could think about was me. When would it ever be my turn? It was terrible. I fought back tears through each wedding and reception. Here I am almost thirty and I want to get married and have kids. The only thing that encourages me is that my parents didn't marry until they were in their thirties."

Jealousy, our treacherous "old friend," is back and we can't seem to avoid meeting up with him. Although we recognize him immediately and know him to be unhealthy, unbiblical, and immature, we tend to invite him along for the ride, anyway. Then soon, we find ourselves being driven by him. Our thoughts continue in the malicious route he takes us, even while our will is slamming on the foot brake and eventually yanking on the emergency brake!

We *will not* become jealous. But the fact of the matter is that we already *are*. How do I know? . . .

There were eight hundred of us in a conference. My mind was suspended between two worlds as I heard the muffled tones of the speaker in English, while taking in the Spanish version through earphones to check out the accuracy of the translation. A Christian psychiatrist was asking us to identify the person with whom we were experiencing a strained or broken relationship. Perhaps it would be someone no longer living. Giving instructions as to what we should do, the speaker paused in prayer at the close of the morning session to give us a few moments of reflection.

"I can't think of anybody living or dead with whom I have a poor relationship," I determined immediately.

The speaker continued in silence.

"Really, there doesn't seem to be a soul. . . ."

Evidently there were *some* people in the audience who were having to make things right with a lot of individuals. I adjusted my earphones and the dial of my hand-held receiver.

Although the headset really wasn't uncomfortable, *I* soon was. What if it were true that my relationships with others were all right, but my inner attitude toward countless people was imperfect? What, in fact, if basically I had some unresolved jealousy? What, indeed!

The doctor was still waiting, head bowed, at the lectern.

"There have been so many people through the years for whom I have felt a twinge of jealousy. I wouldn't be able to think of them all."

The message that morning had been pointed: get things right between specific individuals. "Besides, envy is basically a problem of the past. I have matured a lot. I swiftly defeat that onslaught now."

But had I entirely eliminated it?

". . . No, Jesus, I haven't. I still get jealous, don't I?"

He didn't seem at all surprised. In my inner person it was as if a great teacher had walked into a classroom of distracted students and purposed to set the stage for a lesson which would live as long as his pupils.

"Vicky, are you ever jealous of Me?"

"Of *you*, Jesus?" That was ridiculous. No one could ever be jealous of Jesus. He had had no money, no worldly possessions, no prominent positions in society, no wife, no children, nothing that anyone would have desired—not even good looks![1] Furthermore, He died young in a most horrible manner.

"Would you be jealous if I'd have had children, something that you could never have?" No, honestly not. He was Lord. I would have trusted as right anything He had chosen to do.

"And if I give permission to someone else to have or be what you can't or aren't, does that mean I don't love you?"

Just at that moment—why the rush?—the conference speaker chose to issue the final statement before being seated.

"Listen to Jesus' answer." And then abruptly a voice blared into my ear, "¡ESCUCHA LA RESPUESTA DE JESUS!" It was a direct translation, all right.

As I hastily turned down the volume control, I had the feeling He was still waiting to hear my response.

"Jesus, if you give them permission . . . then, I give them my permission, too."

The session was quickly finished. Hundreds of people arose from their seats and headed toward the back of the auditorium where I was sitting in the last row. The lady in the aisle seat across from me got up with her infant son. "You have *my* permission. . ." I smiled. I felt liberated to have something to offer her in place of my jealousy.

We who are childless are involved in a lifetime process full of possibilities for growth. Included in the singles' venture through childlessness are the inevitable mini-crises.

> Up to this point I haven't felt a strong desire to have children. My career has been important to me.
>
> But recently I have felt a sense of urgency. If I'm going to have a family, I'd better get started. It's part of turning thirty.

And well it may be, too. I listened to a single in her mid-thirties who had sought out a women's advisor in an international volunteer organization comprised of thousands of young people. I was not surprised at the counselor's response to my friend's sense of loss and panic. "I don't know a woman who hasn't wrestled with it . . . if not before, then around the age of thirty." Much has been said of the mid-life crisis of men and women; the unmarried may experience a "mid-single" crisis as well.

This growing desperation evokes a willingness to consider new alternatives to alleviate one's sense of childlessness even if matelessness cannot be remedied. Two friends describe their groping:

> I guess I've thought that marriage could happen at any time, but there's a definite time for giving birth to a child.
> I've thought about the possibility of adopting as a single or taking in welfare children if I could have a job that would keep me in one place.

> I had a great sense of loss when I realized I was going into menopause and would never have a baby of my own. I feel sadder for a childless couple than for myself. In reality I have chosen singleness and childlessness and they haven't. I'm toying with the idea of possibly taking on a welfare child.

The single non-parent may feel locked into a series of life events over which he or she has little control. This trapped feeling may be accompanied by a sense of hopelessnes, especially if a search for biblical encouragement ends fruitlessly. After all, even Jesus had rights, although He decided to forego them to fulfill Scripture and complete His calling.[2] But at least He had a choice. Many singles have never had this option.

Jesus knows that. He is fully aware of the tremendous suffering which the permanently mateless and childless may undergo.[3] Even so, He views not only the disadvantages of such a state but the opportunity it presents:

> Jesus replied, "Not everyone can accept this teaching, but only those to whom it has been given. For some are eunuchs because they were born that way; others were made that way by men; and others have renounced marriage because of the kingdom of heaven. The one who can accept this should accept it."   —Matthew 19:11 (NIV)

He accepted it.

Paul the Apostle did the same: "Don't we have the right to take a believing wife along with us, as do the other apostles and the Lord's brother and Cephas [Peter]?" (2 Cor. 9:5, NIV).

Obviously it was his human, even apostolic, "right" to be a family man. But there were two essential other considerations: (1) Was it the will of God for him to claim that right? (2) Had God given him a gift of continence which he could exercise to enhance his ministry?

He came to some conclusions about both of those matters and shared his understanding in 1 Corinthians 7. The chapter must be read in the context of some "present crisis" (v. 26) which they were facing (perhaps local persecution) and advised accordingly. Nevertheless, we do see an overshadowing desire of the Apostle Paul for the fullest possible Christian service (vv. 32–35). Verse 7 may serve as a summary of his thoughts: "I wish that all men were as I am. But each man has his own gift from God; one has this gift, another has that" (NIV).

There is great interest these days in the gifts of the Spirit. No doubt one of the least-sought biblical gifts is this one: continence. If you are single, whether you ever purposed to be or not, present yourself as a candidate to receive God's special provision of grace to be able to abide contentedly in your solitary state—whether it is to be temporary or permanent.

As one young man concluded after having studied this seventh chapter:

> Paul says for Christians to serve the Lord in the state they are in. This means that children (or even a wife) are not essential to my purpose and existence as a human being, which is to love God and enjoy Him forever.[4]

A middle-aged woman found her earliest consolation for her singleness in the Psalms and her later answer from the words of Jesus himself:

> My time of lashing out at God zeroed in on my husbandlessness rather than my childlessness. My cries for fulfillment were for a friend and lover. The cries of the Psalmist helped me to recognize and accept my own hurts.
>
> Underneath the turbulent waves was always the assurance that "all these things" (Matt. 6:33) would be mine. Even if my "all these things" did not include a husband and children, my "all things" would be sufficient.

But practically, what does that mean? Someone has described it like this:

> A friend asked why God would allow such a waste. She was single and strongly desired marriage and children. I told her of my experience.
>
> I had had such a strong desire to marry and have children that I prayed to God to either give me a husband or take away all desire and help me be content to be single and childless. He made me content with my singleness and childlessness. I still yearn, but it doesn't hurt like it did.

Daniel was ivy-league quality. No expectation was too high to hold out for him. Not only was he from one of the noble families of the kingdom, but he was handsome. It was his keen-mindedness, though, which set him apart. He had an unusual ability to concentrate, quickly gaining insight and assimilating practical knowledge.

And then came conquering Nebuchadnezzar, the Babylonian king who overcame the king of Judah. With total disregard for everything sacred, the barbarian swept away even the holy articles of the temple of Jehovah to deposit in the shrine of his base god.

Great Nebuchadnezzar then sent Ashpenaz, chief of the eunuchs, on a mission to this defeated land. His mission was to select just such men as Daniel to be subjected to his king, to become steeped in the language and culture of the Babylonians, and to serve in the palace for life. Daniel was an ideal candidate for such an "honor." Thus ended his freedom of choice.[5]

During the following 70 years, Daniel rendered public service to a series of at least eight rulers, including Darius the Mede and Cyrus the Persian. And what can we say of the scene of his lifetime ministry? It was near the idolatrous site of the infamous Tower of Babel.[6]

Except for his three friends, we see him *alone* throughout the book which bears his name. When sought by men intent on having him put to death, apparently *alone* "he went home to his upstairs room where the windows opened toward Jerusalem. Three times a day he got down on his knees and prayed, giving thanks to his God, just as he had done before" (Dan. 6:10b, NIV).

He was found to be "guilty" of not worshiping the king and thrown into a den of lions, again *by himself.* When Daniel was removed, justified, from the den, his false accusers, along with all of their wives and children, were tossed in to take his place![7] The Medes and Persians were rough. Would they have originally spared Daniel's family for his seemingly greater "crime"?

Throughout the book of Daniel God communicates with the prophet as if he were *a solitary figure.* But what a man he was! Successive kings recognized his wisdom and spiritual ability. They knew he spoke the truth and lived unimpeachably, in line with his convictions.[8]

So what does the example of ancient Daniel have to do with our being childless? Everything. Forced to forego his own will, he nevertheless chose to do so. Freed from the gall of his circumstances, he was released to reach the goal of them.

But how do we strip off our blinders which restrict our sight to the old, fixed goal and receive our unrestrained peripheral vision?

Centuries of valuable experience by thousands of celibate Christians may help us in our modern search for answers. Donald Goergen explains in *The Sexual Celibate* that those who, out of Christian conviction, lay aside a sexually intimate lifetime relationship with one person, customarily exchange it for multiple intimate, non-sexual relationships, often with both sexes. Historically such a person has belonged to a religious community. Outside that context the celibate also develops deep friendships through his professional and personal contacts. These relationships may be even more satisfying than a one-on-one or one-with-a-family lifestyle.[9]

For singles outside the context of a religious order, the same principle for success may very well apply. The single, instead of being bound to a family, has the advantage of choosing the company (individuals and groups) he or she wishes to keep. Finding one's self alone, at other times, a person can as easily experience the pleasure of solitude as the emptiness of loneliness.

Singles who have lived fulfilling lives tell us:

> You substitute other things: your profession, church functions. . . .

> Since college my interests have extended beyond my backyard. Perhaps I would have been restless as a mother. My professional accolades have increased my feeling of self-worth as a person.

> I've been able to comfort many women who do not have children and others who are not yet married. I would not have had the time to spend with my students if I had had children. I have had more time for those who are lonely.

> I've had more time to study to become a better teacher and a better witness for our Lord.

> I find it easier to extend hospitality. I can be more spontaneous and don't have to coordinate with others' schedules. Probably I have more people in [for hospitality] than most families.

> Some of the sadness has been lifted by having animals to enjoy. Also, teaching preschool children for twenty years has given pleasure.

> I feel that my ministry has been enlarged because I have more time for counseling teens and college/career people. I don't feel as removed from their problems as parents sometimes do.

> If I'd had a family, I couldn't have done most of the things I've done: travel, summer volunteer work, sports, etc.

There are some drawbacks. One single mentioned that she saw her ministry as diminished in the area of helping parents with problems since she had never passed through the growth stages inherent in marriage and child-raising. There is the potential for loneliness and dependence on others in order to be included in family and social events. And there is the inevitable facing of old age:

> Sometimes I realize that there will be more loneliness later because I won't ever be a grandparent.

Joan, a career woman, shared that the most difficult matter for her to resolve was what her responsibility should be toward her aging parents. Her married brothers and sisters expected her, since she had no family of her own, to stay at home caring for her ailing mother and father until death. Eventually she had to make a career advancement and ministry decision: should she move halfway across the country, leaving her mother alone, or should she pass up the opportunity and remain at home? With great inner conflict she finally agreed to take the new position. Shortly afterward, her mother passed away without Joan's being able to be present. Her immediate reaction was remorse. However, in the intervening years, the leading of the Lord in her life has been obvious to all who know her, and she continues working in an educational institution dedicated to preparing young people for ministry.

In spite of crisis times, Joan has been able to see God's provision throughout her life. She puts it this way:

When I was a teenager and supervising some primary-aged children on a summer outing, one of the girls asked me, "Are you a mommy?"
"No," I answered.
"Will you ever be a mommy?"
In one of those God-inspired moments, I responded, "If God wants me to be."
The answer satisfied the child . . . and has somehow satisfied me throughout my life.

"And let not any eunuch complain,
'I am only a dry tree.'

"For this is what the Lord says:
'To the eunuchs who keep my Sabbaths,
who choose what pleases me
and hold fast my covenant—

"To them I will give within my temple and its walls
a memorial and a name
better than sons and daughters;
I will give them an everlasting name
that will not be cut off."
—Isaiah 56:3b–5 (NIV)

"The one who can accept this should accept it."
—Jesus, Matthew 19:12 (NIV)

"Elkanah her husband would say to her,
'Hannah, why are you weeping?
Why don't you eat?
Why are you downhearted?
Don't I mean more to you than ten sons?'"

—*1 Samuel 1:8 (NIV)*

CHAPTER SIX

Partnership in Process

Ten sons! Who would want ten sons? All Hannah ever asked for was one. Didn't Elkanah understand that?

This passage from 1 Samuel—particularly in some translations—gives the impression that Elkanah was short and unfeeling with his wife, machine-gunning her with piercing questions, making her burden of barrenness seem even heavier. At such a fragile moment, would he crush her already broken spirit with an accusatory, "After all, don't I treat you better than any ten sons would?"

From other references, though, we see that Elkanah and Hannah were a very loving couple, despite years of childlessness (1 Sam. 1:5, 19–25; 2:11, 19–21). More than likely this conversation is not an account of a single scene in the couple's life, but rather a summary of years of family drama centered around their basic problem of infertility.

Amid the dreadful struggle of being tormented about her infertility by Elkanah's second wife (1 Sam. 1:6–7), Elkanah would engage his beloved wife in a private comfort conversation. Recorded are the kinds of things that Elkanah frequently said to Hannah. They must have shared many such intimate discussions. After all, this was the most important matter in the world to her, and probably to him, as well. Elkanah appears as a good man, willing to talk with his wife, gently ask questions of her, and encourage her to speak. He was an active listener, able to voice the very things which she found difficult to say. He cared, and he loved her just the way she was.

Considering the complexity of any human relationship, have you ever in awe reflected on the partnership process? Those of us who enter into marriage receive a treasure: our mate is meant to be our closest, dearest human resource throughout life. We may not truly be able to evaluate the greatness of that gift until a crisis arrives in which we need to call upon each other for mutual or personal support.

Of course, no spouse can ever become a Department of Human Resources. That is where the church comes in. Here we find a multiplication of strength which exceeds the individual efforts of two separate people. We see it poetically expressed by Solomon:

> Two are better than one, because they have a good reward for their toil. For if they fall, one will lift up his fellow. . . . Again, if two lie together, they are warm; but how can one be warm alone? And though a man might prevail against one who is alone, two will withstand him. A threefold cord is not quickly broken.   —Ecclesiastes 4:9–12 (RSV)

Today the bond of marriage is seldom highly esteemed. People talk of marriage as merely a "piece of paper" or a "contract." What it really is, or ought to be, is a commitment—a total commitment. God purposed marriage to have a respected place in society. Being the greatest expression of human unity, it illustrates our integral, lasting oneness with Christ.[1]

Since, in capsule form, we represent to ourselves and the world the relationship of Christ to the church, it behooves us to give our best effort to our marriage and get the fullest blessing from it. From this basic unit *may* come offspring. But regardless, marriages make children; children do not make marriages.

We may never complete our dream of leaving partnerhood to becoming a family with children. If not, let us become the finest couple we can be. Instead of languishing in disillusionment, let us live courageously and build a new dream that we can fulfill. Thinking realistically, even families who have children must eventually live without them. Babies do not stay little very long. But the married couple— ah, yes, in any event "couplehood" should be very good. If you and your mate are among those who will never be *procreative*, then be *pro-couple*.

A couple, after all, can freely be best friends, confidants, lovers, workers and planners together. Unencumbered, it is easier to follow through on God's directions for our lives, whether it means to pursue higher education, change careers, move, travel, etc. Very often we can afford to do much together precisely because we do not have children. The Lord has, indeed, given us some wonderful, accompanying blessings in life. Because of the time and energy which we can invest in each other, we are also in a unique position to develop a deep level of intimacy and communication in our marriage.

This is not to say that married people with families cannot have the same depth, but they have to work harder to achieve it during child-rearing years. For them to squeeze out time to talk over a cup of coffee at a local cafe may involve locating a baby-sitter, arranging the sitter's transportation, and paying a fee. Besides, after an exhausting day with the children, a young mother may prefer a relaxing soak in the tub to an in-depth conversation.

People experiencing the pressures of parenthood are not necessarily trying to be comforting when they tell childless couples how "lucky" we are. They may actually envy the time and independence we who are childfree enjoy. How lamentable that many parents genuinely yearn for that kind of freedom almost as if they do not value the great gift that God has given *them* in having their own children.

The best way to appreciate each other's mode of life may be to commit ourselves to pray for one another. During our daily time of prayer, my husband and I often find ourselves lifting up before God our single friends; at other times we will be burdened for certain married people who are having serious problems with their children. One of the personal results is that we remain freshly thankful for our own family status.

If you will be sharing your life with only your chosen partner, you may find yourselves unexpectedly amazed at the delightful oneness you were meant to have. There can be a certain serendipitous quality to your lifelong romance. Allow yourself to enjoy it!

I recall the day, required of all our denomination's missionary candidates, that we spent in a psychiatrist's office. We were ushered in and given a series of marital inventories with parallel questions for husband and wife. To our surprise, the more questions we answered, the more humorously inappropriate some began to appear. I would nudge Jerry and whisper, "Have you reached number 76 yet?" which on my sheet read:

When your husband drinks too much, how would you describe his behavior? He becomes
   a. sullen.
   b. flirtatious.
   c. belligerent.
   d. loud and embarrassing.

He was just as stumped as I as to how to answer number 91, which appeared on my copy as:

When your husband pays attention to other women, you react by
   a. becoming angry.
   b. getting jealous.
   c. retaliating in kind.
   d. pretending not to notice.

Later, we presented ourselves to the psychiatrist who was going over the results of our tests. At last he remarked, "This is very unusual. You ribboned out on the tests!"

He slid the results around so that we could see the two sets of lines running across the page indicating the battery of tests. "The black line shows your scores, Jerry. The red line indicates Vicky's. They follow each other right across the sheet." Sure enough, they were nearly identical. We had similarly answered the entire questionnaire!

Certainly no one should place undue emphasis on such test results. They do tend to indicate, however, that when two very different individuals are committed to each other and have a good base of communication over a period of time, there will be a unique blending of thought processes and responses, an almost imperceptible development of unity. A couple is not merely two people who live together. They have life together. This is the essence of "family."

Fortunately, because of your own marriage, you are not alone in your pilgrimage through childlessness. The quality of communication which the two of you share will hopefully be one of your particular lifelines to emotional survival. Ideally, most of the time your mate will be able to sense your pain and help meet your need. Often that will be in the form of reassurance that you are accepted just as you are, not for what you can or cannot produce.

Researchers have discovered that if only one partner is infertile, that individual tends to suffer emotionally more than the fertile mate.[2] Particularly if that partner grieves alone, he or she may feel terribly isolated from the mate who is adjusting to the same facts but relatively painlessly. Thus, it is often necessary for one spouse to be continuously reaffirming.

Above all, we as partners must in no way reject each other in our shared need. If we feel angry, that anger should never be directed at our beloved. Our reaction should be comparable to what it would be if one of us were to develop, let us say, diabetes. Yes, such a thing could change our lifestyle, cause inconveniences, raise doubts, result in medications and visits to the doctor, and mean a sizable and unexpected financial outlay. But the sufferer least of all should be the object of anger or resentment. The shock and sorrow of adjusting to a new life package is traumatic enough. When one partner discovers an absolute limitation, both must express the confidence that they can and will continue facing life together. That is the unconditional commitment of on-going love.

The height of rejection for a barren individual would be, of course, to be abandoned by one's mate. In many societies this is quite acceptable (or at least tolerable) behavior. During a visit to the dentist in the nation we serve as missionaries, my husband was asked if he was married and then, how many children he had. When the dentist heard that we had none, he questioned Jerry a little further, and then suggested matter-of-factly, "Well, why don't you do what we do? Find another woman who *can* give you children."

Our own society is not immune, however, to similar types of justification. The other day I read about a movie star who had recently passed away. The account of her life mentioned that after having had children by previous marriages, she wed her last husband when she was in her mid-forties. Twenty years later he divorced her because of a "need" to have his own child![3]

I thank the Lord that never once in our particular struggle has my husband ever used my physical limitation as a weapon. That is one rule couples must keep absolutely. We may be grappling to overcome difficulties and scientific odds, but we are fighting together, never against each other. Even if only one of us has a fertility problem, we must remember that it is our combined infertility as a couple that matters. No one should be blamed for that which cannot be helped.

If in some manner an individual is culpable for having lost his or her reproduction capacity, repentance before God and one's partner is necessary. But what if the offending partner never seeks forgiveness? Then the party who has been hurt must take the initiative, by choice and by the grace of God, to forgive from the heart. The door to reconciliation is thus swung upon from the inside. It frees the forgiver and may make it possible for the other to face his or her responsibility.[4] Either way, accusation or self-incrimination must simply cease. Forever.

Sometimes it is harder to forgive ourselves than to forgive someone we love. Many people spend their lives plagued by a sense of guilt about some foolish or sinful act committed in the past and never find personal liberty. I remember a man in my husband's Sunday School class who insisted that God could forgive sin, but that He kept reminding us of it. No one in that group will ever forget the look on that man's face when he finally realized that it was not God who kept bringing it back up to him.

If the enemy continues to badger us, we must recognize that he is a liar.[5] The Psalmist expresses the truth about God's treatment of our forgiven sin: "As far as the east is from the west, so far has he removed our transgressions from us" (Ps. 103:12, NIV). If we, ourselves, have felt trapped into dwelling on confessed sin, then we have cause to rejoice with John the Apostle who says, "For if our heart condemn us, God is greater than our heart, and knoweth all things" (1 John 3:20, KJV). We have been freed from being victimized by our forgiven past.

Scripture and our spouse are our twin comforters. And we shouldn't be surprised to need one or another of them at any time. Occasionally a major responsibility for our partner's sense of well-being falls to the human part of that team. Having been the one in our own marriage to have suffered the most emotional distress, I consider myself very fortunate to have a husband to whom nurturing others comes easily. This has permitted him to untiringly minister to me with tender, spontaneous reassurance.

For many people, however, giving verbal affirmation and sustaining a mutually supportive relationship do not come naturally. Take courage; you can learn. Even if you have established habit patterns which tend to undermine your partner, by making a conscious decision to act according to the Word of God through the Spirit of God, you can begin to put down the "put-down." The destructive part of our old way of behaving can be changed. We are designed to be good to and do good for each other during all of life.[6] What more personalized opportunity to begin!

Become aware of what effect your words and actions have on your partner. You probably already know your mate's areas of particular vulnerability. Discipline yourself never to say anything which may hurt, not even in jest, and especially not while in the presence of others. Substitute affirmations which will be planted solidly within the growing being of the one you love. Your spouse is still learning to love him or her self, perhaps on ever-new levels of recognition of imperfection. Now is when the nutrient of your high regard can revitalize your partner's own self-esteem.

Some spouses wonder what they can do, what they can say, to help. My suggestion is to free yourself to creative abandonment in your efforts to encourage or console your partner. Many of the loving things which my husband has said to me restored my feeling of self-worth at the time. And because I wrote them down, I can look up my "Jerry Personal" file any time I am discouraged about myself. I invariably end up feeling better and laughing over what otherwise would have been a vague memory. Your "sweet nothings" have the power to pass from the ear to the heart of your hurting partner, too.

Let some of the following fragments of conversation prime your own pump of praise. They are not literary gems, just real-life examples of supportive statements which some partners have made. Notice how often the expression of negative self-doubt is returned positively.

Husband: You're my woman.
Wife: But I'm not pregnant.
Husband: But . . . you're lots of other things.

Husband: You ought to listen to me and stop telling yourself how imperfect you are. You are the perfect wife for me. Don't go telling yourself otherwise or else you are casting doubt on my word and calling me a liar.

H.: (In response to wife's expressed disappointment about her behavior while taking hormone medication): You weren't all that crabby. Your expectations for yourself are just too high.

W.: I'm sorry I have been such an awful wife for you lately.

H.: Stop knocking yourself. When you're feeling great you don't go around saying, "Wasn't I super today?!" Why should you always be making negative comparisons when you don't think you're so good?

H. or W.: I didn't marry children. I married you.

You get the picture. More than anyone else you know your own mate and will be able to apply consoling comments when they will do the most good. That may be frequently for a number of years. Those of us with a fertility problem tend to get "temporary amnesia" when it comes to remembering that we were chosen because we were adequate to satisfy our partner. Having assured your beloved of that a month ago doesn't insure that he or she will not need fresh reassurance today.

Husbands, you perhaps feel that you have to stretch yourselves to understand the female psyche. Unlike the proverbial, "I'll never understand a woman," my husband claims it is not so difficult. After all, you are not called upon to comprehend womanhood in general; you are expected to learn to love and cherish just one woman. If you are puzzled by why your wife acts or reacts as she does, ask her. Most women like to verbalize their feelings, and your partner may be waiting for the opportunity to share these matters with you. Observe your wife; attend a family conference or a couple's seminar with her. Read what psychology or medical science has to say. You may find that she is not so complicated after all. A farmer friend on his twenty-fifth wedding anniversary shared with us what he had discovered through the years: "I've found there are three things my wife needs: someone to love her, someone to love, and something to do."

And wives, at times we may feel that the inner-life workings of our husband seem quite implausible, too—particularly if he is not very communicative. He is, though, our best source of information about himself.

Other support is close at hand as well. One of the personal goals I set for myself as a young wife was to read at least one book about marriage or the family each year to keep my perspective fresh and growing. With good literature, recorded tapes on marriage, retreats, films and other information available today, if there is something about our husband which still baffles us, let's search out this specialized help instead of complaining to our friends . . . or worse yet: to our mother!

For those of us facing a major life crisis such as infertility, sterility, miscarriage, or the death of a child, however, more than just a general understanding of ourselves and our mate will be necessary. We need to dedicate study to the particular issue at hand to understand what is happening to us in the present and what we may anticipate for the future. The more you face your challenge together the stronger and more prepared you will feel. My husband and I have found that one of the best ways to assimilate information is to read material aloud to one another. He reads to me while I iron or wash dishes; I read to him as he drives. If we come across something we want to comment on, we cease reading and begin talking. It helps us to grow together on our journey.

Physically and psychologically the male and female psyche may react somewhat differently to infertility and childlessness. But one encouraging finding is that regardless of sex, if a person generally confronts difficulties realistically and copes effectively, he or she will succeed in overcoming this hurdle, too. Even though there may be suffering involved with the impact of the facts, an emotionally healthy person will move toward acceptance of the situation and a new and positive life orientation.[7]

A male faced with his own reproductive incapacity will often experience an initial anger or shock followed by a long period of deep, inner pain. Being able to father a child is part of his mental picture of manhood. The man who cannot do so must remove that image by an act of will, though it involve a great wrenching-free process, and replace it with a new concept of masculinity. It will take time for him to determine what *does* constitute maleness. Is it largely what someone can produce or is it who that someone is? Does impregnation in any way prove one to be a "real man"? Where did Jesus get His sense of self-worth? Or John the Baptist? Or Paul?

I would encourage any of you struggling through this process that just as God knew the strength, courage, and principles of those aforementioned men, He knows what kind of a man you are as well. He knows, too, exactly how good a job of parenting you would do. Before Isaac was born, the Lord said of Abraham: "For I know him, that he will command his children and his household after him, and they shall keep the way of the Lord, to do justice and judgment; that the Lord may bring upon Abraham that which he hath spoken of him" (Gen. 18:19).

You don't need to prove anything to God. If you never have a family, but you feel you would have been a good father, then receive God's assurance that He concurs. He knows you would have been delighted to have held your own infants and that you would have prayerfully guided your children. Further, you would have set them a good example and would have been the father that they'd have needed at each stage of growth.

Then consider this: could it also be just as true that for you, as for Jesus, there awaits an even greater lifetime challenge? What if the Lord has chosen a unique way for you to invest your manhood for Him—one which will cause you to exercise greater faith, and see Him accomplish more lasting results through you than would have been possible had you been occupied with your own children? Do you dare allow God's personal evaluation of true manhood to slip into your frame?

As husband and wife we form a team in this process of discovering the truth about ourselves and our life together. Scripture says that a wife is a "help meet" for her husband.[8] Could there be a more crucial time for us as wives to be that particular helper, adequate to meet the needs of our mate? Wives, let's set ourselves to promote healing. Later we will see how the Lord has used us to help encourage our special Elkanah and stimulate growth in our relationship.

The most important contribution we can make to our husband's regaining spiritual perspective and emotional integration is to pray for him—silently. We may not entirely understand the inner upheaval he experiences, and he may not be able to describe it to us. But we can remain open to talk about it as he desires. This may be one phase of our married life in which we must hear with our heart. Let's allow our intuition to be guided by the loving impulses of the Lord Jesus.

During this critical time we can take several helpful steps:

—Lay aside all unnecessary demands on our husband.
—Give him legitimate praise.
—Make it easy for him to express himself in areas which affirm him as a person whether they be hunting, fishing, cooking, carpentry, music, or mechanics.

His self-esteem is being partially reconstructed, this time with a more realistic understanding of what, for him, constitutes manhood.

If facing infertility is your husband's first encounter with a shattering emotional experience, and more especially, if it came unexpectedly, he may not be equipped to deal with it successfully as he has with other things in his past.[9] Even if he should evidence a temporary impotence, don't despair. He is in a period of recuperation much as one might experience after a grave shock, accident, hospital stay or loss of a family member. Be supportive and understanding during this brief interlude in your life together. Only if the problem persists do you need professional help. Meanwhile, physical expressions of love may be continued at a different level: a loving touch, hugging, a well-deserved kiss, caressing, massaging, playing. You may wish to explore some interest or activity you have long wanted to do together, such as playing tennis. Now is a good time to use some vacation days purely for fun or to attend a couple's retreat.

At this point the two of you would find additional support by sharing your feelings with your pastor, a counselor, a trusted friend, or another couple. You may find that the very person or persons you seek out have been wanting to share in your special trial, but they have not known how to let you know that. You do not need to be as "alone" as you may have been feeling.

Earlier we briefly observed the intimacy between Hannah and Elkanah. Throughout their married life, they tried to please the other. We need to do the same. Sometimes this means doing a job that is particularly *displeasing* to the other. My husband and I apply this love law quite faithfully. For instance, knowing that my physical problem often involves severe discomfort, my husband makes certain that I have remembered to pocket my painkillers on that day. At night, there is no question: if I am uncomfortable he gets up for my medication and juice (since water tastes insipid with the pills). That is love in action. I lie there, often in tears from the pain, trying to think of something kind I can do for him in return.

For a barren woman, not only is there the monthly crushing disappointment of again not conceiving, but if she is suffering physically as well, she can easily feel as though she is a dismal failure as a woman. In a very marked way, pain tends to aggravate feelings of depression and one's sense of loss. Beyond that, as a couple you may have to face the issue of pain as really as the family of a cancer patient. If a woman lives with severe menstrual discomfort two days a month, or twenty-four days a year, that means she will spend over two years during her lifetime in pain. This suffering will definitely affect you as a couple and should cease to be "her" problem and become your problem together.

During the eleven years I spent as a teacher, there were times when, after suffering all night, I was very little better in the morning. My husband simply insisted on my not working that day. Over my protests he has gone to the phone and matter-of-factly called in my being sick. I was certain that my children at school would not survive without me. He was even more convinced that I would not endure the day *with* them. He was right! I lacked the courage to acknowledge my weakness.

Only you as a sensitive spouse are going to be able to determine what will be an act of love toward your mate. Interfering in your partner's professional life might not at all be the thing to do. Remember, love acts appropriately. But it *does* act!

Perhaps you will decide as a couple that the wife should be in the home with less strain than if she were responsible for a full-time job. Maybe the wrong place for her is to be sitting at home—waiting. There are no absolute guidelines. Only you together can determine what brings health to your home. No one else has to understand, and others certainly do not have to lend their agreement to your decisions.

One of the strengths of Hannah and Elkanah's relationship was the mutual confidence and freedom they enjoyed. We see examples of that trust after Samuel was born. Elkanah allowed his wife to name the miracle child and keep her promise to dedicate him to God's service as soon as he was weaned. During that historical period what other couple demonstrated so much democracy in their decision-making?

> And the man Elkanah and all his house went to offer to the Lord the yearly sacrifice and pay his vow. But Hannah did not go up, for she said to her husband, "As soon as the child is weaned, I will bring him, that he may appear in the presence of the Lord, and abide there for ever." Elkanah her husband said to her, "Do what seems best to you, wait until you have weaned him; only may the Lord establish his word."
> —1 Samuel 1:21–23a (RSV)

You are going to be living a life for which there is no mold. It is an invigorating challenge. Encourage each other to do what seems good in your situation. And may the Lord establish His Word in the midst of your home.

"In bitterness of soul Hannah wept much
and prayed to the Lord.
And she made a vow, saying, 'O Lord Almighty,
if you will only look upon your servant's misery and . . .
give her a son,
then I will give him to the Lord for all the days of his life. . . .'
Hannah was praying in her heart, and her lips were moving
but her voice was not heard.
Eli [the high priest] thought she was drunk. . . .
'Not so, my lord,' Hannah replied, 'I am a woman who is
deeply troubled.
I have not been drinking wine or beer;
I was pouring out my soul to the Lord. . . .
I have been praying here out of my great anguish and grief.' "

—1 Samuel 1:10–16 (NIV)

CHAPTER SEVEN

Couples in Crisis

Hannah was desperate. We find her in this account pleading fervently, almost frantically, with God. So alone was she, and in such need, that her emotions spilled to the surface flooding through her veil-thin protection of restraint.

Her final crash came at the very temple door where she did not even have the freedom to sob aloud. Hannah's whole being ached from her overwhelming anguish. With her last vestige of control she managed to smother her screams and push her hurt and sorrow out through a straining, quivering lower jaw as she pled her case before the Lord.

Whatever was wrong with this woman? Eli, observing her, could see that she appeared perfectly normal. She certainly was beautifully dressed. In fact, she had come just that day with a rich caravan. Looking outside he could see neither a funeral procession nor a drunken brawl. So, what was all the fuss?

The fuss was really *fusion*. Hannah had internalized every negative experience: her incapacity to reproduce, the misunderstanding of others, and the prosperity of the rest of the family while her hopes for fulfillment declined. In one fierce moment their combined impact left her without sufficient inner reserve to match such compressed grief. Her inability to cope with being a barren woman unleashed a powerful fusion of frustration which exploded at the very gates of God.

Fortunately, God is never taken by surprise. He does not have to gear up for the worst we can hurl at Him; He has already maneuvered through the greatest and least of evils. The Wailing Wall is erected in His own city and He can receive us there.

Hannah, in her moment of extremity, had only Eli, the high priest, available to help her. Imperfect as he was and burdened by his own problems, he at least listened to and recognized her need. She opened her whole heart and shared with him her anguish. For years no one had heard from God directly, but fresh hope broke through that very day. The Lord responded to Eli's intercession and shortly thereafter gave Hannah and Elkanah a very special child, Samuel, destined for a long life of service to God as judge, priest, and prophet for His people.[1]

Well, then, isn't the point of this story that God grants the heart's desires of all of His trusting children? No, at least that is not the *full* truth. Hannah's aim in life was to fit in with the purposes of God. She considered herself a maidservant to the Lord and to those ministering in His name. God knew the sincerity of her servant-heart. She was not a manipulator; she was a woman of her word. After vowing lifetime service and sacrifice to the Lord, Hannah was prepared for one of two demanding responses. A *no* would leave her as she was, simply a maidservant of the Lord continuing to perform the task He had given her to do, that of being a wife to Elkanah. A *yes* would give her a mission for the King which would cost her everything, including the very gift she asked of Him.[2]

Clearly, Hannah did not get a miracle baby just so she could have what she wanted, and neither did Sarah, Rebekah, Rachel, the wife of Manoah, or Elisabeth. These women and their husbands were people especially equipped to raise specific men to spiritual usefulness in God's historical plan. Somehow their experiencing a period of childlessness was part of their preparation to give to the world: Isaac, Jacob, Joseph, Samson, Samuel, and John the Baptist.[3] God was forming a unique physical family through which, as He explained to Abraham, all the families of the earth would be blessed.[4] Until that time there was no family line which respected the one, true God. The Lord himself had to bring into being such a people from whom would come His Son. He, the Christ, would then provide everyone the possibility of spiritual, eternal life.

For a Jew not to have participated in such a venture of faith and family would have been more than just a personal trial; it would have become a matter of community concern. At some point in her experience, a barren woman would have suffered public reproach, perhaps even censure.[5] A man with physically imperfect genitals was not even permitted to enter the congregation of the Lord, let alone perform priestly duties associated with Jewish manhood.[6] To remain childless was a punishment for certain crimes and in itself was commonly considered to be a curse.[7] How dismal their state must have seemed to those who lived without physical hope. They were acutely aware of the "curse of the law."[8]

At last, Christ came forth from that intricate family network, burdened as it was by laws. He it was who fulfilled all religious requirements and set individuals free from such restrictive legalism. No longer were people to be accepted or rejected based on their sex, physical perfection, offspring, heritage, or multiplied other distinctions. Now all of us were equal: we were simply sinners who could stand on the same level spot beneath the cross. Almost more remarkable: instead of considering us according to what we were before, He newly instated us in places of honor as kings and priests to God, His earthly representatives.[9]

In audiences with our King we have confidence that not a single concern entrusted to Him will ever be misunderstood, misrepresented, or answered mistakenly. Thus, if we see our being parents serving His good as well as our own, then we should boldly present Him this request. He, in turn, has the right to make the choice.

Most of us, like Hannah, could spontaneously rejoice in God if His answer to us were in the affirmative.[10] But if it isn't? As an envoy of our Lord we may undertake a rash of shuttle diplomacy tactics before we accept our no compromise orders. Our finiteness may struggle upon receiving the plan of the Infinite.

Since childless individuals are just as varied as the population in general, none of us will have identical experiences or reactions, only a common reality to confront. If facing a life without children has never been a perplexing issue for you, then don't let anyone keep you from continuing on in that peace. The integration of your life in this area serves as a blessing to you and a positive example for others.

Our God, however, is perfectly capable of incorporating more reactionary mortals into His scheme of things, too. Somehow I qualified in this category. Because no one ever told us that many couples experience life crisis in their process of adjusting to childlessness, however, we never knew that such a possibility existed for us.[11]

How could we have suspected such a thing? After all, we were well-educated, happily married, independent people. Neither of us was very sentimental: even birthdays and holidays passed with very little notice. Nor were we explosive: in fact, we had never had an argument. As a couple we were usually able to confront our problems in a reasonably logical way, openly discussing our differences and communicating in depth about decisions which had to be made. We had never encountered any situation with which we had been emotionally unable to cope, nor did we ever expect to. We were uncomplicated, practical people with a realistic outlook on life and a faith firmly planted in a God who had proved himself trustworthy to us.

Although we were strangers to depression, we quite often experienced cause for rejoicing. We frequently anticipated with pleasure the imminent excitements of young adulthood; these were the milestones of life about which we conversed and wrote home. So it was that on a particular spring day I was ready for one of the most significant events of my life.

Checking into my specialist's office, I felt absolutely buoyant. What was routine to his receptionist-nurse was a joyful, proud moment for me. My doctor's treatment had been successful, and we had achieved the long-awaited goal: a pregnancy. After having waited the pre-scribed number of days, I had come for a confirmative lab test.

While awaiting the results, I went to the basement cafeteria and splurged on an ice cream soda. I was so excited that I drank the liquid through the straw too fast and had to pry loose the solidly-packed ice cream on the bottom.

Think of it! At last we were going to be parents. The marvelous wonder of carrying a human being on its journey to independent life caused me to smile and almost imperceptibly shake my head in awe. Long ago I had planned exactly how we would announce the occasion. I had prepared a telegram to send to our parents in Alaska. Would the telegraph office deliver the message to them that evening? If so, we could expect two jubilant phone calls by midnight.

The most fun of all was going to be sharing the news with Jerry. I had bought him a humorous plaque about expecting a baby which I had been saving for this day. Dinner would be prepared by the time he arrived, and without saying a word, I would let him discover the little sign propped up just beyond his plate. How would he react?

The lab work was probably completed by now. Taking the elevator to the fifth floor, I entered my doctor's office once again and chose the empty seat nearest the reception window. I picked up one of the mag-azines on baby and child care, read a couple of the short articles and relished the thought that soon I would be devouring all the informative literature available about babies.

"Mrs. Love." I abandoned the magazine and took the few steps to the counter-topped window.

"The results of that lab test were negative."

I tried to think for a moment what, in medical jargon, *negative* meant. Usually when doctors said "negative" that meant "good; every-thing turned out all right." But in this case . . . I decided that it meant that everything *wasn't* good, not good at all!

"Are you sure? Should I wait another week and return?"

After asking for details and checking calendar dates, she replied, "No, this should be definitive." Of course, I could come back at another time if there were further symptoms. . . .

A "Thank you," stumbled from my lips.

Suddenly I just wanted to escape! It was all so clinical, so sterile.

My whole future clung to that printed slip of paper which would now be neatly filed away in a tall gray cabinet.

Tears were already forming in my eyes as I managed to get through the door and into the hall. I had failed to notice before how institutional it was with its high celings and cold, beige walls. Starting toward the 1940s-style elevator, I realized that at this hour it would be crowded with people. I opted for the stairs; it would give me time to dry my eyes.

But I could keep back neither the tears nor the self-incrimination: Why didn't I wait longer before coming in? Why had I driven all the way into the city for that "definitive test"? I should have known better. Of course I wasn't pregnant. I never would be. It was silly to think that we would ever have a baby! Only other people could have that experience. I resolved never, never to suffer such a blow again. No stranger would ever deliver me another negative verdict.

Worst of all, I realized that I had done it all willingly, happily. I had set myself up for a come-down I was not equipped to handle. Blithely I had thought I was prepared for what that wonderful day would bring forth!

A hope that I had lived with all my life died that spring day.

But it did not die quietly. I was powerless to stop the ever-present tears and jerking sobs on the way home. Even as I followed the old scenic Oregon route, winding through a forest of mature Douglas firs with their fresh pea-green fringe, the tangled naturalness of a bird sanctuary, and moss-encrusted tunnels—nothing spoke to my sliced-open spirit.

Upon entering the house I snatched up the sign and the telegraph messages which I had so elatedly left spread out on the table. I tore into our little guest room, which in my mind had already been decorated as a nursery, and buried them deep in the drawer of a white dresser where no one would ever find them.

By the time my husband came home from work, entirely unsuspecting of what he was to encounter, I was at a convulsive level of sobbing. I couldn't voice, except with some airy and gulpy words, what had happened. Instead of giving him the best surprise of his life, I dumped on him the greatest disappointment of both our lives.

He held me closely that night while I let out stifled sobs and screechy little noises until my stomach almost rejected the ice cream from earlier that afternoon, Then, for hours in bed he let me curl up in his arms where I continued sobbing a wretched little cry, occasionally spitting out an unintelligible word. Eventually I was able to hear him as he began to tell me again and again that he understood. I didn't have to tell him all the details. It was all right to cry. He loved me.

It was the only time in the whole process that I couldn't verbally share with him. I wanted to, but the hurt of that crushing disappointment went so far beyond anything I could communicate with words that nothing emerged but repetitive animal-like sounds and whimperings between convulsive crying.

Finally, the sounds were gone and only my shuddering frame, heaving shoulders, and dry sobs were present. He had kissed my sweaty, salty face again and again. Only then did he begin to audibly pray for me—for us. I could only tremble an assenting response.

But I knew there were three of us in this together.

For every childless family the circumstances will be different, but there may well come a final crisis point. Perhaps it will be after one or more miscarriages, a diagnosis of sterility, a doctor's advice that for any of a number of reasons a couple should not have children, or knowledge of impending surgery which will destroy one's reproductive capacity. We cannot deny our feelings. Nor can we diminish the reality of what this means in our lives.

Usually we receive the news in a quiet way; nothing catastrophic takes place. It may even seem inappropriate to react strongly to what may be so matter-of-fact. To us, however, one sentence may fall as a death knell to all our dreams, to our former understanding of ourself as a sexual human being. Even the kindness with which the information is shared with us may be a special type of cruelty. If the doctor hadn't shown such concern, perhaps we could have expressed our own feelings instead of trying to console him, letting him know that we appreciate all that he did to help us. There is, really, no one to blame, no action the doctor or anyone else can take to change the situation. We know we have to accept the facts. And yet, we don't even know what all "the facts" of childlessness are.

If we search the stress-factor charts, which may list everything from going to jail to selling the family car, we fail to find *barrenness* listed. It is as though we are trying to confront something invisible. Problems we can resolve. Accidents we can accept. Concerns can be addressed; misunderstandings, clarified. Doctors can set broken bones, and we can live with a cast. But what can we do with childlessness?

The first thing which we must understand is that what may be only a simple fact represents a grave loss to us. The intensity of that felt loss will vary with the person's customary emotional reactions as well as the circumstances and the people in one's environment.[12] Our sense of loss may be as real as though we had suffered the amputation of a limb. What has been a part of us throughout life is now gone. It may be as grievous as the death of a loved one. The child we were to present to the world is dead. It may be as shocking as a kidnapping. Our spouse's baby, our parents' grandchild, our own offspring has been snatched away and no one can make any sense of it. That is what we are really reacting to.

Mourn, cry, talk it out, become angry, pound a pillow, write poetry, scream—do whatever you must do initially in the face of your personal tragedy. My only suggestion for you in your shattering experience is not to be alone. Have someone you trust by your side.

It will be, in part, through strengthening the relationships you already have that you will begin to experience inner healing. If for no other reason, you can express gratitude to God for those who faithfully stand by you now. Be thankful for your partner, grateful you are not alone. When one of you is low there is at least the possibility that the other can listen and hold and help. As one friend discovered, "When I'd be most depressed, he'd be most stable." At other times it would be she who would encourage him.

But how will you handle it if your mate's emotional reserve crumbles? You probably are not an expert at dealing with distraught persons. You may feel like escaping from the crisis. This is what you must *not* do. Neither should you absent yourself emotionally from the person who is hurting. Avoid making the response of one young husband whose wife broke down in his presence. She remembers that he stood off to one side of the room, looking up at the ceiling, and screaming, "God, do something!"

You do something. Of course it is not easy, but in that moment you represent Jesus to your loved one. You are not a psychiatrist; you are a loving person through whom the Spirit of God can work. What would Jesus do to comfort him or her? At times Jesus listened to, touched, talked to, prayed for, provided rest for, or prepared food for the ones He loved. Sometimes He took them for a walk or a boat ride. Jesus spent time with those with whom He was intimate, walking in the countryside, sitting on a hill, relaxing by a shore. He went into the sickroom of some who were in need; He made a compress for one man whom He healed. During His final hours He ate and conversed with His friends and bathed their feet. He then took them with Him to a garden to spend time in God's presence together.[13]

Surely, you can do some of those very things with and for the one who means more than anyone else in all the world to you. Accept the responsibility from the Lord of your ministry to your mate in these moments; you are His personal representative. Hold your loved one in your arms when you can. Listen; try to understand even what cannot be verbalized. Express your empathy and confidence in your spouse and in the two of you as a couple. Stay with the person as long as he or she may need you, or as long as you can. Call a trusted, affirmative friend or pastor if you need help or if you should have to leave.

Your partner will always remember your tender mercy. No one will ever have been able to love him or her so much. In these moments you will have become a great lover. Your spouse will never lack security in you as a mate—yourselves as a couple. Nothing can destroy the relationship which stands in spite of everything hoped for being dashed. There will be no other time in all your lives when you need each other—must have the comfort of the other—more than at the moment of personal crisis.

As you come through this you will have reason to rejoice. How many couples have survived that rock-bottom experience of at least one of them being completely devastated? Your mutual confidence that, in moments beyond your worst, your spouse still loves you and accepts you exactly as you are, brings lifelong strength. You are indeed an exceptional couple.

Hopefully, you will also have a loving extended family and church body to help see you through these days. If not, you as a couple will have to take a stand together for the sake of your family wholeness. It may be that the stronger of the two will have to make some difficult decisions for both of you. You may have to pare down some activities and temporarily limit your expenditure of time and energy in serving others or doing favors for them. Before this crisis you could easily take care of your nieces and nephews for several days or plan a baby shower for a good friend. Later you will again be able to do such things; just now you cannot. Be patient with God's schedule for your healing.

This is a good time for the two of you to share your burden with your pastor and certain relatives so that they may be supportive. You may enjoy spending some informal times with understanding friends. Or you may choose to join a good peer-support group in your community.

Begin to evaluate, perhaps by keeping a journal, your progress through this personal pain. Note any encouragement you receive, any new understanding at which you arrive. The wife of one childless professional couple expressed their discovery this way:

> We have never had any financial need, and both of us have been very fulfilled in our careers. We're self-sufficient people who would never have had need of anyone. I guess the most valuable thing we have learned through our experience is: it's all right to be weak. We shouldn't expect to be giving all the time. We need to be on the receiving end sometimes. After all, we are in the body of Christ.

If your circumstances are at crisis level right now, do not judge yourself harshly for being emotionally inadequate to deal with the stress. *Not* to acknowledge and confront your feelings in the present would be the only regrettable action. Remember: one legitimate use for shoulders is for crying on. Today others may be lending you theirs, but soon, you will be offering yours to someone.

You probably never imagined that you would need a Savior for just such a time as this. He knew it. His provision for you is not merely eternal salvation, it is restoration to wholeness and balance *now*. The area of your hurt is His field of expertise. Jesus reaffirmed to the people of His day the calling He had received from the Lord:

> The Spirit of the Lord God is upon me, because the Lord has anointed me to bring good tidings to the afflicted; he has sent me to bind up the brokenhearted . . . to comfort all who mourn; to grant to those who mourn in Zion—to give them a garland instead of ashes, the oil of gladness instead of mourning, the mantle of praise instead of a faint spirit; that they may be called oaks of righteousness, the planting of the Lord, that he may be glorified. —Isaiah 61:1–3 (RSV)

Jesus' intention is not only to restore you but to make you stronger, more joyful than you ever have been before. He does not deny your mourning and faint spirit, but He acknowledges His adequacy to re-establish you. Have you ever wanted to glorify God? For years I used to wonder how a human being could bless God. Paul gives us a clue when he affirms that Jesus said, "It is more blessed to give than to receive" (Acts 20:35, RSV). If, in our need, we reach out to Him and receive His gift of inner healing, then not only are we restored, but it allows Jesus to be the Giver and thus, receive blessing from our lives!

Even though you may suffer emotionally today, look forward to His healing ministry, making you stronger for the coming tomorrows. No story, no life stays in the abyss of crisis indefinitely; your emergency will be resolved as well.[14] From the low point of your experience with heartbreak, you have gained valuable perspective on the compassion of God and have learned how vital it is to show this tender kindness to others. You will successfully ascend from the valley you never expected to explore. You are survivors.

> And I [Jesus] will pray the Father, and he shall give you another Comforter, that he may abide with you for ever. . . . I will not leave you comfortless: I will come to you. —John 14:16, 18 (KJV)

> I will not leave you as orphans; I will come to you.
> —John 14:18 (NIV)

"Then Jesus entered a house,
and again a crowd gathered,
so that he and his disciples
were not even able to eat.
When his family heard about this,
they went to take charge of him, for they said,
'He is out of his mind.'"

—*Mark 3:20–21 (NIV)*

"Then Jesus' mother and brothers arrived.
Standing outside, they sent someone in to call him. . . .
And they told him,
'Your mother and brothers are outside looking for you.'
'Who are my mother and my brothers?' he asked.
Then he looked at those seated in a circle around him and
said,
'Here are my mother and my brothers!
Whoever does God's will is my brother and sister
and mother.'"

—*Mark 3:31–35 (NIV)*

CHAPTER EIGHT

The Affirming Family

What a privilege to have been a member of Jesus' own family! Imagine that: your son, your older brother, your cousin—Jesus.

Jesus' birth had brought unexpected renown to the family circle and had caused a genuine stir in the otherwise colorless happenings of His small hometown.[1] He had been a delightful child: cheerful, intelligent, inquisitive, helpful. Joseph and Mary found Him easy to manage, never the cause of trouble—well, except once when He stayed in Jerusalem instead of returning with the family to Nazareth! Other than that, His youth had been without incident. He was well-liked by all.

His adulthood, however, had disappointed the family, His widowed mother in particular.[2] She was, no doubt, concerned about Him. He, the eldest son: what kind of example was He setting for the rest of the family? How could she make Him realize how much He had been neglecting her and His responsibilities at home? Others had noticed His nonconformity, too. Although Jesus was a most eligible bachelor, He had shown no interest in any of the nice girls in the neighborhood, nor had He indicated an intention to settle down. At this rate, when could Mary expect to be a grandmother?

The fact was that shortly after His thirtieth birthday He left home! At first everyone thought that mere curiosity had drawn Him to go along with the others to hear His cousin, John the Baptist, preach. The others returned, however; He did not. They brought news that He had been baptized and afterward had felt compelled to head out to the desert. He stayed there for forty days—fasting. More disturbing yet, He then began to attract the oddest assortment of strangers He had met on the streets. No one in the family knew any of them, but they soon *heard* plenty about some of them!

Through a gracious invitation all thirteen of them had recently attended a wedding reception which Mary had helped to hostess.[3] It was a good thing Jesus came, as He averted a terrible kitchen crisis by producing some incredible wine. Indeed, He could be practical when He wanted to be. The whole family had been proud of being related to Him that night.

From what they had been hearing, however, they doubted that Jesus had eaten a good meal since that feast. In fact, the latest news was quite distressing. Jesus' ministry was in such demand that He had been going without eating or sleeping properly. He was headed for burn-out!

His friends and relatives were all in favor of going en masse to bring Him home—at least until He could come to His senses. After talking it over, they decided to send the male members of the family to get Him. His mother and sisters would stay at home to prepare His favorite food and get the room on top of the roof ready for Him. That would keep Him away from people. Everyone had His best interests at heart and would guard His privacy to insure His having a good, long rest. They loved that young man, in spite of His naive idealism.

The rescue party set out and headed to where Jesus was speaking nearby. Upon arrival, they quickly made their purpose and presence known so that they could accomplish their ends and have Him back to Nazareth by late afternoon for the family reunion.

At the designated hour, however, they were still trying to maneuver through the crowds to get close to Him. They were so split up and spread throughout the entire packed-in throng that they could hardly see Jesus, let alone each other! As sunset blanketed the crowd with shadows, they began to congregate once again at the back of the house.

It was worse than they had been told. Plans would have to be changed. There was only one thing to do: return with their mother. Better to have Jesus home and eat leftovers than to feast without Him.

So, Mary and her sons turned out the next time (ten short verses later in Mark's gospel). Certainly no good Jewish son would refuse His mother! But the house was so crowded they could not approach Him.[4] The only way to reach Him was to send a message to Him.[5]

The noise diminished markedly when the crowd saw that He had received a message. He looked straight back, over the throng, at His own. Focusing on those familiar faces He announced, "Who are my mother and my brothers?" Then, His glance left those by the door, and He looked into the eyes of the many people gathered about Him. As His hand swept around indicating them, He explained, "Behold, my mother and my brothers! For whoever does the will of God, that is my brother, and my sister, and my mother."

Jesus apparently did not find an affirming family as He launched into His public ministry (Ps. 69:8; John 7:3–5). Their reaction did not control His life, but it no doubt formed a part of His human grief experience that came from being misunderstood and rejected by men. How we react to the needs of our family members can be a source of great release or anguish to our loved ones.

My husband and I know a childless missionary couple from a family with several members serving in missionary capacities around the world. They expressed to us that they realize more all the time how important to them their family is. They refer to them as the Back-up Team. As family members go to and from their fields of service, they route their trips through each other's countries to spend what time they can together. If storage space is needed at home or emergency items are required on the field, the family comes to the rescue. Although out of sight and far away, they are very much united and aware of each other's concerns.

At times the larger family serves as the Buck-up Team. They may be the first ones, after our Savior, to whom we can express our pain. I witnessed a delightful example of that kind of relationship while attending a baby shower along with more than one hundred people, nearly as many men as women. The reason for such a joyful celebration was the adoption of a baby girl. The adopting couples' relatives came from various states to welcome their new granddaughter or niece. For years they and the church family had prayed for and consoled this couple who struggled through the trauma of not having natural children. This night the young father expressed his thanks to everyone for the scores of baby gifts and then said simply, fighting back tears, "And for our families, who have had to put up with some grouchy times and times of frustration on our part—we're grateful for your support." They had an affirming family.

Of course, being childless does not negate our commitment to our own relatives. Our encouragement may be particularly helpful precisely because we have learned to adjust to a lifelong disappointment. But for us to be affirming family members to those who are, likewise, "out of sync" with family norms, requires a strong partnership between our heart and our head. We, who receive a limited amount of affirmation during our continuous trial, will minister encouragement in our turn to perhaps dozens of relatives who pass through a brief or extended time of personal groping. Contemplating that fact convinces me of my need for resources outside myself to replenish both my desire and my ability to edify my loved ones.

So where do I start? Prayer. I bring my own personal needs to the Lord—questions, heartbreak, and desires for personal affirmation from others. Recognizing my necessity for God to provide for *me* either directly or through people, I can then pray the same blessing for my brother, my sister, my mother. By our being their prayer partners—usually silent ones—we play a vital part in their resolutions and victories which establishes a stronger bond among us. Interceding for one another helps us maintain right attitudes as we move through life together and makes us sensitive as to how we can be of practical service for the other.

Virtually every family must wrestle with a certain amount of intellectual questioning as its members face life's changes. Together we are forced to confront the problems of understanding the why's of such things as cancer, poverty, or death. Childlessness is one of these significant issues.

Historically and almost universally, people have considered marriage and parenthood as expected stages in personal development. Being an adult has been synonymous with taking responsibility for a household, and eventually becoming grandparents, elders, and the wise and experienced of a society. Biblically this was the typical pattern.[6] There have always been exceptions, of course: the widowed, the unmarried, the celibate, and the famous, such as Joan of Arc, Queen Elizabeth I, Henry Thoreau and Mother Theresa. But let's face it: most people have traditionally married and raised a family.

It is difficult to be an exception to the rule, any rule. Being *childless* in a *family* means that having been born into an on-going family structure we are, in our turn, letting the ages-old "bough break and the cradle fall."

Many times the fault lies with the graph of "expected success" which has been unconsciously programmed into our brains. If someone does not "progress" on that scale, then, we reflect, there is something wrong with the person. Instead, we must learn how to reason anew: "There is something wrong with the scale on which I have placed myself and others. We are all individuals, directly responsible to God. Not only must I relinquish control of my own future but that of my loved ones." This conscious decision frees us to relate to each other as we really are; it puts us all on an equal footing.

This relationship of freedom and equality is particularly difficult to establish between parents and grown children who remain childless.[7] All of the expertise gained by our parents through pregnancy, birth, child care, and the raising of teenagers is lost on us, the bachelor son, single daughter, or married, but childless, children. In fact, it may be the last thing which we wish to discuss. Parents often hardly dare speak of these experiences for fear of offending or hurting us. It puts them in a very awkward position, particularly if *all* of their children are childless.

More complicated is the situation of the parent-grandparents who try to be fair with all of their children. Even inheritance arrangements are difficult to make equitably. One young family, for instance, counted the combined years of marriage among their brothers and sisters and found it totaled 47 years. And yet they alone had parented children, two darling girls. Other families may have several children who are married with numerous offspring and one who is childless. Who needs the family monies more? To whom should the heirlooms go?

A more immediate struggle may be for parents to understand the terrible plight of a son or daughter who cannot, in this age of advanced science, manage to produce children under any circumstance. The parents may have struggled throughout their married lives to limit the size of their families, constantly under pressure to avoid having an unwanted baby when family planning information and methodology were not so available. How could they, fertile parents, have produced an infertile child? Is it their fault in some way? Maybe they should have taken more seriously a childhood disease or fever. Now, through their "negligence," their descendants stop through that child. These issues are difficult to admit, let alone discuss.

Such disparities not only isolate our life experiences but tend to destroy family unity, as well. A loving, caring family feels deeply for the member who is "losing out" or suffering. But if relatives with children feel sorry for those of us who are without, we feel uncomfortable with their pity, as if we were in a lower, less fortunate state. Our feelings of equality or acceptance within the family are threatened or actually damaged.

So, what can be done? The whole family must recognize that those who are childless are engaged in a growth process different from their own. The childless are moving into a level of maturity through learning not to base feelings of self-worth and confidence on having a mate and/or children. We are moving into the future with confidence that God will supply all of our needs. That demands a tremendous combination of faith and independence. Others in the family may be able to learn from us about trust and facing fear. We may profit, on the other hand, from talking to childless relatives: a bachelor uncle, a maiden aunt, a widowed grandmother.

Communication is our vital link to each other. It is essential that we talk about our life journeys, aware that ours is a shared venture. None of us can expect to know every human experience personally; but by honestly sharing our differing life walks, we learn vicariously and grow together. This honesty and open relationship necessitates, of course, a conscious investment of ourselves in each other. We need to know when others are hurting so that we can be available to listen, to try to understand, perhaps to cry with them, and to do what we can to make their load lighter. Likewise, we have to share our moments of confusion. We must be committed to comfort one another, regardless of our personal pain.

But what does one say to a loved one who wants desperately to have children? First, let me reassure anyone who is afraid of saying the "wrong thing." Even if you should happen to do so, if the childless person knows that you really care about him or her, no harm has been done. The confidence the person has of your genuine love and concern outweighs any possible mistake. The Scripture explains the pattern for communication as "speaking the truth in love" (Eph. 4:15). Those two ingredients of truth and love apply in this case as well, but note: we must *speak* them.

Voices of our loved ones are perhaps more important to us than we realize. When my husband and I return from a tour of mission duty, I often receive great pleasure sitting back and listening to the sound of our families talking. Just so, hearing a familiar voice in the midst of our trial is a comfort in itself. Those who know our childhood nickname hold a special place in our lives. When someone addresses me as Vicky Faye, my guard is down. That person really knows me; it's someone I can trust. Yes, we want—we need—our family partners to express their personal interest in us.

Some who have ventured to do so, however, have met with apparent rejection to whatever they have tried to say. Frequently a childless person will respond in such a way as to seemingly shut the door on communication: "But *you* don't understand!" If that happens, agree that indeed you have never experienced this particular trial. Express your sincere desire to be a learner.

"You are so right. Would you share your feelings with me? I want, as far as I can, to enter into your experience."

Those who have never suffered this hurt must be prepared to listen to disjointed expressions of feelings. Almost no one who is suffering acutely can logically arrange his or her thoughts about the immediate experience. If you note carefully what is being said, perhaps you can, at least at a later time, help your loved one put those thoughts and feelings in a more definable form.

In the meantime be prepared to hear us ask hard questions, almost demanding ones: "Why is this happening to me?" "How can I go through life like this?" "Why doesn't God give us a baby? Doesn't He know how badly we want one?!" "Why does He let people abort their babies and abuse their kids and we can't even get pregnant?" These examples are calm compared to what you *may* hear.

For obvious reasons, what we do *not* need to hear at such a moment is: "It's not so bad as all that. Other people have it worse." "You'll (get married and) have a family. You'll see." "Try not to think about it. You'll feel better tomorrow." "Why don't you just adopt a baby?" "I knew a couple who had a baby after twenty-five years of marriage." "You're lucky. Our kids cause us nothing but grief."

Listeners must realize that those of us battling our way through childlessness have already spent a lot of time studying out the possible answers to our questions. It is unlikely that there are any simple solutions which we have not already considered. No such "comfort" is likely to satisfy our intellectual questions and heal our hurts.

Sometimes just an understanding statement or question on the part of someone is what we most long to hear. I needed that opportunity one Christmas Eve when I was struck by the reality of a new, second-stage hurt. We were enjoying unwrapping gifts with Jerry's older sister's family and her two grandchildren. To see the little grandson three times pull off every stitch of clothes (and almost the stitches themselves) in order to scramble into his latest gift of pajamas or underwear was hilarious.

Afterward, as we washed dishes, Jerry's sister commented softly, "It must be awfully hard for you sometimes." I didn't have to keep the tears back; I could freely explain how it felt not only to miss out on every joy of having our own children, but grandchildren as well. "Ruth, enjoy your kids and grandkids. I have to live without ever having a child or a grandchild—not even for one day." To have someone I loved invite me to open up kept me from having to twist a tourniquet against a fresh wound. I could bleed a little bit and get the healing process started.

What can others say to us? "Thanks for sharing. Feel free to talk to me anytime you want to. I may not have any answers, but I am glad to listen and count it a privilege to have you include me in your pilgrimage. Besides, it makes me not resent so much having to wash diapers." If my not having children can in any way help others appreciate their own families more, I feel that my experience has had value.

We who are childless, do not expect—nor would we want—the rest of the family to cater only to us and our need. We may frequently find ourselves on the other side of the kitchen table being supportive to a relative whose child is on drugs or whose spouse is an alcoholic. Our response to these loved ones will give them an indication of how we wish to be treated. We may express our conviction that we will not feel sorry *for* them, although we may well feel sorrow *with* them. Who can encourage them more than we can to expect God to bring good out of their situations? A word of testimony as to some unanticipated or alternate blessing that the Lord has given *us* may free them to expect Him to work sovereignly and effectively in response to prayer.

A family's mutual encouragement will not always be spoken. Our attitude can be expressed in thoughtful, creative acts which indicate our feelings. Over the years family members can send cards and letters expressing sentiments of love and appreciation. A mother can send her daughter a plant for Mother's Day. Personal interest may be taken in the childless person's pursuits, hobbies, or life's work.

Sometimes it is what the family *doesn't* do which makes the difference. Care should be taken not to make demands of a loved one who is emotionally vulnerable or physically tired. When a couple is experiencing a crucial stage of adjusting to childlessness, going through a fertility study, or meeting adoption requirements, there will be times when they should not be asked to baby-sit for relatives or host family events. The rest of the family should provide these needs and, in addition, show kindness to the couple under pressure. An invitation to dinner, tickets to a play or a sports event, or an outing planned just for fun can be a godsend. To do or not to do? The sensitive family will first ask themselves the question, and then move in the direction that love points them.

A family is also able to do something else of unique value: carve out a place of importance for one another. My husband and I have experienced this repeatedly in our family. Not having produced playmate cousins for our nephews and nieces, we could easily have faded out of their sight and memory, particularly since we have been outside the United States, returning home only rarely. In our absence, however, the relatives have obviously spoken often and highly of us to their children and in-laws. Because of the bridging which they have done, we feel an almost instant rapport when we are with them, even if we have never previously met! We reap the efforts and genuine love of everyone else; we form an integral part of the family.

Within this natural context of the family, we must all come to grips with the reality of our individual and combined situations. We who are childless can avoid many of the pressures of society in relation to our personal lives, but we cannot escape being part of an expanding family. Here our strongest feelings and greatest inner turbulence may be expressed and eventually, play themselves out. During this process it is difficult to say at times who suffers most: the childless or the greater family. In a real sense, we all do.

My husband is more than a decade older than his little sister. When we married she was a beautiful and very bright eleven-year-old who, along with the rest of the family, formed part of our happy wedding party. Jerry's parents had married when his mother was sixteen and they had produced four wonderful children. His older sister, married at seventeen, had a family of seven. Understandably, our first child was eagerly awaited.

My husband's parents enthusiastically encouraged us by setting up a piggy bank into which they dropped their spare coins, building up a fund for their next grandchild: ours. Time went by and the coins increased, but our family didn't. Meanwhile, Jerry's little sister married at sixteen. Two years later she and her husband announced a proud event: they were going to be parents!

Of course we were glad for them. But living nearby, I saw this exquisite young woman blossoming ever more expectantly before me month by month. I can honestly say that it wasn't jealousy that I felt for them, but rather, an utter and lonely sadness for myself. It drove me to press Jerry into considering adoption immediately. I so much did not want to be left out.

Perhaps you have already predicted that the moment arrived when Jerry's parents in Alaska contacted us. "What we want to know is, should we break the piggy bank and give them the money? Or should we count it, setting it aside for you, and give them an equal amount?"

Nonchalantly we replied that certainly they should smash the pig and give the money to Charla and Rob. It was thoughtful of them to even ask us and let us make the choice. (They would never do anything to hurt us.)

But it did hurt. Who cared about a piggy bank? Even less, the money? That meant nothing, of course. Symbolically, however, it meant everything. It represented our dream, our baby. Suddenly, we were being passed by. Our place was being taken by little sister. My prayer life became reduced in those days to, "O God, God, don't let me cry in front of her. Don't let me spoil their joy."

The day came when my husband and I went to the airport to pick up his mother who was arriving from Alaska for the baby's birth. The talk all the way to our home was about family and friends in Alaska, and then, the expected arrival of the new baby. I did quite well. I had been praying my simple prayer for days in preparation so as to be valiant in the presence of Jerry's mother. Talk turned to us and I successfully masked my gut feelings with surface conversation: "We're pursuing adoption, now. We went in the other day for our first interview." She assured us that they would love a little adopted grandchild. She meant it.

Reaching the house Jerry carried her luggage inside. Excitedly, his mother began to tell us that a few days before she left, our mutual friends in Alaska had given Charla a baby shower in her absence and one small trunk was completely full of baby gifts! She removed all of the lovely presents and told us who had given which. Then, she opened an over-sized suitcase to show us what she had brought personally.

She laid back the lid, and inside was the most magnificent collection of handmade baby items that anyone could imagine: a baby blanket with animals hand-painted with textile acrylics, sweaters, booties, bonnets, little outfits, sleepwear, a hand-crocheted baby blanket, some items in pink, others in blue (what would not be used for this baby could be saved for the next). . . . I had never knitted or crocheted anything in my life. To see all that handwork was overwhelming. She did not observe my tears because it was quite a process to get everything folded up and put back into the suitcase.

In a few days a real baby would be wearing all of those lovely things, but it would not be ours. It was essential that I experience God's grace in order to be gracious in that hour. I would need to receive my little niece or nephew as a loving aunt. Mentally, at least, I could comprehend that.

The day came when I would do it. The call arrived: Charla was at the hospital. I drove the thirty miles alone to a comfortably old, small-town hospital. Three of us were there: her husband, her mother, and I. Suddenly Charla did a surprising thing. She expressed to the hospital staff that she wanted *all three* of us with her. In the midst of what was a new and difficult experience, that loving young girl showed an amazing maturity. Instead of relegating me to the waiting room, she included me in her hours of labor.

There was no way that I could express to her what that meant. I, who would never be able to experience the birth process personally, was being allowed the vicarious opportunity to know of it firsthand through her. If the situation had been reversed, I am sure I would have lacked the open-heartedness to have invited my sister-in-law to be present during the last stages of labor. We really were family.

The hospital personnel let us remain with her until she was taken to the delivery room. We walked the hall together until at last we heard a cry! Before long, we were able to peer from the hall doors through to the inner double doors where the surgical-gowned doctor was holding our fresh new baby who had yet to be bathed. She was all damp and matted-looking, but she was perfect.

Soon after Charla was wheeled back into her room we were allowed to enter. Her husband and mother lovingly congratulated her with quiet, happy praise. I bent over her, too. "Charla, she's beautiful. She's just beautiful."

Groggily, Charla replied, "That's nice."

"That's nice." That's nice?! Was that her only response? Why, if that had been our child I would have been shouting for joy! I would have been telling everyone what a miracle God had done: a baby. A real, live, perfect baby! I'd have been ecstatic. Or so I thought, not reckoning with the anesthetic.

After a final view through the nursery window, I headed toward the car. By now it was dark and rainy. I could talk aloud to God; no one would ever hear me with the cars spraying Oregon rain over each other on the freeway. But I was wrong about doing the talking. After only a few minutes of thanksgiving for such a wonderful experience and the blessing of that lovely baby, I stopped talking and began listening.

For the first time God began to talk to my spirit about my own childlessness. How long I had waited for Him to tell me something, to reveal to me part of the mystery as to why I was put in a position of beggar, not receiver. None of the drivers in the fast lanes sloshing by could have heard His part of the conversation. It was inaudible, but in a deeply calm place within my own heart He whispered, and I greedily gathered in the meaning of His words.

"Vicky, you have known for a long time that joy does not depend on *things*."

"Yes, Lord." No struggle at that point.

"Tonight I am showing you that it does not depend on *people*, either."

He had spoken to me on two issues at once. I had received the Lord as my Savior on the night of my first date with my future husband, but a doubt had lingered as to whether I could continue living a victorious life in Christ if he were taken from me.

"It doesn't, Lord?"

"If you were to have a dozen babies, you would not be any more joyful than you are right now. If everyone were taken from you and you had only Me, you could still be joyful. I am the only source of joy."

Jesus—speaking to me about joy. What a strange way to begin my healing. The very thing I felt I had been missing out on, and it was within me!

The verse! What was the verse from Psalm 4 that He had given me years before?

> You have filled my heart with greater joy
> > than when their grain and new wine abound.
> I will lie down and sleep in peace,
> > for you alone, O Lord,
> > make me dwell in safety.
>
> Psalm 4:7-8 (NIV)

At last I was learning about rest in God . . . with joy.

In some real, yet mysterious way, family affirmation frees the childless for deeper elements of emotional and spiritual healing. The relationship of each family member with the childless has a direct bearing on—and may be a key factor in—alleviating the pain of what otherwise could be a permanent psychological injury.

After the initial acceptance on everyone's part, other hurdles have to be faced. Sometimes being childless means the end of the family name as is so in both sides of our own families. In my husband's family, since his brother is not married, the surname of the family tree is fast meeting its fate. Having all enjoyed our name we wish that someone else could, as well. No one wants *Love* to die, but so it may. We are finally able to see some humor in the pun—even if at times it is mixed with a twinge of regret.

Parents of those of us without children suffer their own private losses as well. While their friends experience an unending series of events—weddings, new babies, growing grandchildren and great-grandchildren—the plastic photo pockets of our parents' wallets remain empty. People are interested in seeing pictures of the newest arrival; no one cares very much about seeing one's fifty-year-old son. Parents begin very really to enter into some of the sense of loss which their children experience. This can lead to a deep bond of identification and understanding. Our personal feelings become inter-personal; there is a new level of unity and equality between non-grandparents and their non-parent children.

One mother told me that for a few years she continued to prod her son, "John, when are you going to have children? I'm waiting to be a grandmother."

Finally one day he replied, "Mother, just stop talking about it."

She realized, of course, that he was right. With the passing of time there has come a welcomed relaxation in their relationship to the extent that she recently felt comfortable making the following introduction, "This is my son, John, and his wife, Joyce, and (indicating the cat), my grandchild, Fluffy."

When the laugh replaces the cry, you know there's been progress!

The entire pilgrimage will take a lifetime. Throughout that walk we all experience countless changes. Given the normal course of events, first our grandparents will die, and then our own parents. The final chapter of our lives will end as Jesus', leaving no earthly heritage behind. But, as He did, we can write a beautiful story with our life. Considering our gifts, under God's direction, we can construct our plot. We don't wait for the happenstance inkblots of life to land on our pages; our story will have meaning. It will influence the lives around us who see us as an open book with Jesus' likeness printed on it.[8]

We can make indelible impressions on the sons, daughters and grandchildren of other family members. We will find ourselves praying continually for them, inviting them to accompany us on a trip, opening up our home to them, slipping them the cash they need for extras while they are in school, being available when they need us.

At one o'clock a.m. our phone rang. It was long distance; one of Jerry's newest relatives was calling us. "You know I wouldn't have called you unless it were a matter of life or death," she said, almost breathless. We were glad that she had the confidence to know that we would want her to wake us up instead of waiting until the next day.

"IT'S A MATTER OF LIFE!" She had made a significant step in her spiritual walk and wanted to share it with us on the spot.

We need more such "matters of life" happening daily. Just because we are not leaving a future generation does not mean that we do not have a stake in the regeneration of the present. What we do for others is just as lasting as if we were doing it for our own children. Jesus has already told us what import our actions have: "I tell you the truth, whatever you did for one of the least of these brothers of mine, you did for me" (Matt. 25:40b, NIV).

Further, we aren't limited to spending ourselves on the young. We can help bring life to, or make life worth living for, people half or twice our age. Nothing prevents us from finding "family"—people who need a relationship with us. Let's create new traditions or carry on the old and include these new loved ones. Hundreds of people can to some extent be nurtured by us. We can be an affirming family today to someone who needs one as Jesus did yesterday. And while doing so we shouldn't be surprised if we hear Him whisper to our own heart, "Here are my mother and my brothers! Whoever does God's will is my brother and sister and mother."

Ah, if only we really knew what would please Him that much. Wouldn't we rush to do it?

> Sing, O barren woman, you who never bore a child; burst into song, shout for joy, you who were never in labor. . . . Enlarge the place of your tent, stretch your tent curtains wide, do not hold back; lengthen your cords, strengthen your stakes. —Isaiah 54:1a, 2 (NIV)

What a privilege to have been a member of Jesus' own family! Imagine that: your son, your older brother, your cousin—Jesus. . . .

"A wife of noble character who can find?
She is worth far more than rubies. . . .
She gets up while it is still dark;
She provides food for her family. . . .
When it snows, she has no fear for her household;
for all of them are clothed in scarlet. . . .
Her children arise and call her blessed,
her husband also, and he praises her:
'Many women do noble things,
but you surpass them all.' "

—*Proverbs 31:10, 15a, 21, 28, 29 (NIV)*

SECTION THREE:
POINTERS AND PROBLEM-SOLVING

CHAPTER NINE

Happy Mother's Day!

A fresh spring evening of my husband's first year in the pastorate settled in. What exciting, challenging, difficult months these had been—yet we considered ourselves to be two of the happiest, most fulfilled people alive. The awesomeness of ministering to our small congregation continued to invigorate us.

That night the church board was meeting in our apartment above the educational unit. Serving refreshments and refilling coffee cups, I was semi-present as financial matters and other items of business were discussed. One of the decisions to be made was selecting an appropriate person to organize a children's program and Mother's Day Tea following the morning worship hour.

From the living room drifted the suggestion, "Why don't we ask Vicky? After all, she's not a mother."

Stab! Pain thrust its way through my heart.

Of course I was willing to plan and conduct a Mother's Day event. Who could be more worthy of being honored than our mothers? What greater participation with God on an earthly level than the creation and preparation of a human being? My own mom had been the most sacrificial, giving mother anyone ever had.

Then, what was my problem? I knew that the board members appreciated me and would never intentionally crush me. But powerful feelings hammered away at my heart all the same. I felt as if I had suffered the blow of burying my father one day and someone expecting me to conduct a Father's Day service the next.

Clearly, there was no "reason" for me to decline the nomination.

In the weeks before the program I battled with my private "Cinderella Thought Syndrome": "If I were a mother, I would be one of those honored on Mother's Day. Since I'm not, I do all the work and they get all the benefit." And worst of all, "It is going to be like this for the rest of my life!"

Of course that was pure, rather, impure self-pity. And it didn't rule my life. I left it time and again in the hands of my Savior and enjoyed teaching my little group of children their songs.

Late on Mother's Day Eve I entered the wood-creaking silence of the looming sanctuary to begin my volunteer janitor service. Since I taught school during the week and did my housework on Saturday, I almost never launched into the church clean-up detail until this hour. Jerry was upstairs making final preparations for the next day; he would be preaching his first Mother's Day sermon.

With the sanctuary and Sunday School rooms in order, I entered the fellowship hall, scene of the following day's event. The refreshment table was already in place. "Tomorrow the little children will be singing in this room." I spread out the lace tablecloth. "Everyone will be here." I was working on arranging the napkins, "And I will be the hostess for the Mother's Day Tea . . . because I'm not a mother." The napkin-folding stopped; I realized I couldn't do it.

The wooden floor felt hard under my knees as I sought the nearest chair to support my elbows. "Lord, I can't do it, can I?" How strange to become impotent in such a simple matter. I could think of no big challenge which had ever overwhelmed me. But this? "How am I going to make it through?"

I realized that simply because the program was my responsibility wasn't enough incentive to bear up under the torture of going through with it. Then, as a helper to my dear husband, I would do it for him, encouraging him in his ministry! That was a good thought—but it wouldn't work. I couldn't do it, not even for Jerry . . . much less for the people who would be attending.

"Lord, You know I cannot do this." A jumble of Bible verses flooded my mind; they all seemed to indicate that I could. Well, they were "wrong." The only one who was going to be able to put on a Mother's Day Tea to the honor and glory of God was Jesus himself. If He wanted to host that event, then I would help *Him*.

"Okay, Lord, You will have to give me the strength to carry out each detail." I pushed myself up from the chair seat. The yellow napkins lay scattered where I had left them. "You'll have to fold this napkin through me . . . and this next one."

That's the way the whole process went. We put out the spoons, the punch bowl, the cups. Then came the mints and nuts. The sugar bowl posed the biggest challenge. The church cupboards collected moisture and the sugar had to be pried out of the bowl and spoon. We washed and dried them thoroughly and brought new sugar down from the apartment. With everything finally in order, I could turn off the lights by myself.

The next day the women of the church brought the refreshments, and the children sang their well-rehearsed songs. All of the mothers enjoyed the tea, and some of them stayed to help wash and dry cups. I was secretly relieved when the last one felt free to head home and celebrate her day with family and friends.

It was easier for Jesus and me to do the rest of the clean-up together; I could cry in front of Him. What a mixture of sorrow and appreciation He received that day during the final crumb sweep: "Lord, thank You for being with me last night. Thank You that I could hold back the tears until right now. Thank You that we could lead those children together and that I didn't have to do it alone."

Does God have rewards waiting for those who clean spoons and replace lumpy sugar in damp churches? We aren't able to measure the present against the future. But if only for a moment in time He gives grace to get us through an emotional difficulty, isn't that in itself an expression of His love which has an eternal dimension?

My husband gets restless—not emotional—on holidays. On other days he is delighted to be at home working on some project. But on holidays he is in and out of the house. The store from which he wanted to buy a part is closed; the mail doesn't arrive; the paper came yesterday. Once he stated plainly, "I really don't like holidays."

If we had children, we would go on a picnic or to a lake or an amusement park or a swimming pool. In fact, there are all kinds of places one can go with children which are not appropriate for adults: the children's zoo, for instance. Not that we don't "borrow" someone else's children occasionally, but on a holiday everyone wants to be with his or her own family.

Being invited to celebrate with someone else's family may be fun, but it can also reinforce the painful truth that other people have families and we were invited because we don't.

Of all the year's special days, Christmas is the most difficult for many who are without children. Some friends whose families live at a distance told us:

> At Christmas I think about "next year." Next year I'll be decorating and these little things I'll be putting up will be for our child. That's what I said last year. Now another year has gone. Maybe next year. . . .

Maybe it will be "next year," but maybe it will be never. That is one reason why holidays can be so devastating: they mark off the years. Other days are just days that go by; holidays are years. The blue Danish Christmas plates tell us so: Christmas 1983.

Childless people are particularly vulnerable to emotional lows during sentimental times. And have you noticed how many holidays or special days emphasize love or marriage or babies—even if, seemingly, unrelated to the occasion? New Year's Day, for instance, has practically become "Honor-the-Baby-Day." The newspaper headlines feature the first New Year's baby born in the state and in the nation. There are often consolation articles, too, about the infants born minutes after midnight, disqualifying their parents from an extra income tax exemption.

Even anniversaries may not be without a slight sadness. "We've been married 15 years, now. Just think, we could be parents of a boy about the age of that one," and there stands a boy, someone else's dream become reality.

To complicate the matter, new holidays are added to the calendar. Now there is even a Grandparent's Day!

That there are such holidays doesn't distress us, but rather the "set-up" which precedes and surrounds them. Much of it is pure commercialism, of course, and can be disregarded, but some of it affects us directly. Let's consider the experiences of a non-parent during the Mother's Day season. Much the same could be reported for Father's Day, as well.

About a month before, the advertisements come out and cards go on sale. I personally like to shop for our mothers at this time as it gives me time to think of them at leisure and send gifts and cards so to arrive well in advance of the day. The longer I wait, the more difficult it becomes to focus on our own mothers because I have to deal with *me*.

As the day approaches, there are Mother-Daughter banquets (this year was quite a victory for me: I spoke at two of them!), Mother's Day magazine articles, TV specials, children's programs, gifts, and plans for the day. Some of us can distance ourselves from such bombardment more than others, but almost everyone who works with children is involved with Mother's Day.

At this time of year we who are childless discover where we are in our healing process. Expecting a grieving non-parent to celebrate Mother's Day, as my husband observed, "is like asking a man who has been out of work to celebrate Labor Day." The private pain would be particularly intense if he were never again to find a job, but were to be expected each year to join his friends and family in rejoicing over their being employed.

Mother's Day places those in sorrow in a particularly stressful situation. Husbands and wives may feel the strain from early morning. What does a husband do or say on this occasion? He can't ignore the day; his wife is only too keenly aware of it.

My husband has made it a point to be thoughtful upon first awaking. After a good hug and kiss, he usually says something like, "I really love you. I'm so glad I married you; I'm the luckiest man in the whole world. I want you to have a really nice day today, and I just want to enjoy being with you."

The next difficult moment is confronting our church family. Churches are usually festive this day and people often arrive with guests or out-of-town relatives. Mothers and mothers-to-be appear especially radiant on this, their day, and many churches enhance their joy by pinning a corsage on each attending mom.

Even such a simple and meaningful gesture can be awkward. I have known the official pinner, ready with a flower, to suddenly pull it back and say, "Oh, you're not a mother, are you?"

For just such a reaction, I try to keep some stock replies on hand, "That's right. We decided to skip the parent stage and become grandparents instead. They have a lot more fun."

It seems hard to think that some people could be so insensitive, but I have been told of a guest at a mother-daughter banquet who was handed a potted plant until someone learned that she was single, and then it was quickly snatched away!

Bless the generous hearts of those congregations who give each woman a flower. Some churches have a custom of pinning a carnation on everyone: men, women and young people alike, with red representing a living mother and white for one deceased. If we are aware that it may be painful for some persons not to receive a flower or a plant, we can take steps to change that. Speaking ahead of time to the persons in charge may be all the action necessary. Volunteering to pin or distribute the flowers may take the personal pressure off. Perhaps we can help contribute the funds so that everyone can be a recipient. If not, let's buy ourselves a beautiful plant ahead of time!

Being one of the few women in a congregation without a Mother's Day corsage is bearable, particularly if one is wearing artificial flowers or an ornament. But participating in the morning worship service may be more difficult, depending on our stage of inner healing. "Faith of Our Mothers" often begins the congregational singing with "Happy the Home," describing mother, father and children, closely following. A special number, perhaps "God, Give us Homes," is presented and, finally a Scripture reading, such as Proverbs 31:10–31, "prepares" us for the Mother's Day sermon . . . if we are still in the pew to hear it.

Obviously, we who have been trying for years, decades even, to fulfill our dream of parenthood may not fare very well on Mother's Day. So, what are we going to do about it? There aren't many Bible references or how-to-books to help us survive Mother's Day.

Perhaps the closest we can come biblically to someone in our situation is Anna.

> There was a prophetess, Anna, the daughter of Phanuel, of the tribe of Asher. She was very old; she had lived with her husband seven years after her marriage, and then was a widow until she was eighty-four. She never left the temple but worshiped night and day, fasting and praying. Coming up to them [Mary and Joseph] at that very moment, she gave thanks to God and spoke about the child to all who were looking forward to the redemption of Israel.   —Luke 2:36–38 (NIV)

Anna was a woman who had lost out, whose earthly dreams were dashed when her husband of seven years died. She may have been only in her early twenties, with sorrow instead of full life ahead for her. How much a jolt the initial loss of her beloved was, we do not know. It must have made a considerable impact, perhaps on the whole community, because the event was remembered and dates were attached to it.

But God's plans for her life didn't stop when her own did. She was to be an intercessor. It would have been difficult for her to pray for others had she not known great need herself. How encouraging to find that after more than fifty years alone she was a whole and healthy woman! She had a vibrant relationship with God and a prophetic ministry to the congregation of her time. With ease she initiated social relationships, approaching Mary and Joesph directly. She recognized and appreciated this special baby, and she was able to communicate her joy to others. What more could anyone ask from an eighty-four-year-old woman?

But shortly after the death of her husband, would she have been prepared to have identified the Messiah? . . . spoken of His ministry to others? . . . and performed her gracious presentation of this little babe to the world He was about to enter?

So with us: the end of our life and ministry cannot be equated with our present losses. Like Anna, we, too, can make steps toward fulfilling our purposes in God. She went to the house of God for worship and praise. Can't we do likewise? And she began to serve others, a real help in alleviating sorrow. Although we may have fresh and deep needs, we ourselves are somehow edified through doing something for someone else.

I have since realized that if I expect to have victory over my "foe," whether it be Mother's Day, Thanksgiving, or Christmas Eve, I must attack the enemy as a general would. First, I have to evaluate my weaknesses and see where my defeats are likely to come. Then I can take a hard look at my strengths and capacity. If I know that attending morning worship service is presently not good strategy, I must decide on an alternate plan. Taking the offensive, I can volunteer where I am sure to succeed. That may be working with children's church or being in the cry room. Sometimes my husband closes up the ranks and joins me.

You and I can be decisive. Taking the initiative puts us at a strong vantage point emotionally. We don't have to stand woebegone on the battlefield drawing all the fire. In fact, we mustn't let holidays "happen" to us because they happen too hard. Let's forget about survival techniques and learn how to advance!

How we do that for the holidays may differ, but the key is advance planning of something pleasant for that day. Being with our own parents or relatives would probably be our first choice for celebration. If that isn't possible, we may think of other moms, dads, couples, or singles to have in—perhaps friends from a retirement center, or divorced neighbors.

One year Jerry said, "I know someone who will be alone this Mother's Day." To my curious response, he told me he was thinking of Laura, a Latin American woman who lived in a two-room store-front building. That was it: we would invite Laura!

She was as happy to be with us as we were to have her. Before the afternoon was over she shared with us her multiplied heartache. One son, addicted to dope, had not returned the night before. She had not seen her second son for days and feared something had happened to him. In addition, she had been very ill and would have to enter the hospital that week for surgery. My small sorrow shrank considerably in comparison just thinking what kind of Mother's Day she would have experienced alone that year!

A number of ladies in an urban community have tackled the holiday problem jointly. They take turns hostessing their single friends, male and female, for special occasions. When they celebrate Mother's Day or Easter they make quite a day of it.

One inventive couple make it a practice on Mother's Day to invite other childless couples over for dinner after church. It is one of their yearly family events, and they do it in grand and unforgettable style.

Where we live in this world and what we enjoy doing will be determining factors in how we observe holidays. Gladys was for years a missionary in Africa. During her furloughs she packed fifty-gallon drums with items she would need during the next four years. She always tucked away an especially generous supply of pencils, handkerchiefs, pens, and other small items. They were destined to be presents which the missionary children, her pupils, would eventually give to their parents for Christmas, Mother's Day, or Father's Day.

One day in Zaire she heard a knock at the door. There stood several of "her" kids who shouted, "Happy Gladys Day!" and presented her with little packages and a cake. She didn't understand what was happening until one of the children explained, "We asked Mother, 'When is Gladys Day? She's always giving us gifts for Mother's Day and Father's Day, but we never give her anything!' " Hearing that, the mother declared that very day 'Gladys Day' and they searched through *their* missionary barrels to find some appropriate gifts for her and even managed to make a cake out of the ingredients they had on hand. Gladys still has her invaluable mementos.

Such love service may create celebrations which end up being more meaningful and satisfying to us than traditional forms of passing the holidays. Furthermore, some of us will experience our greatest pleasure by giving to others instead of receiving. Helping to prepare or serve a community Thanksgiving dinner for people who would otherwise be alone or spending New Year's Day at a rest home or a children's hospital may be the most fulfilling way to invest our holiday—one we'll look forward to throughout the year. I recall a mature businessman, very much loved and respected in the community, who rang the Salvation Army Christmas bell every cold December in Alaska. It wasn't a chore for him, but a delight.

If we desire a heart-enriching or life-changing holiday experience, we may come to the place of recognizing that being without family has served for our good that we may concentrate on loving those around us.

Missionaries in Ecuador once welcomed back some colleagues returning from a year in the States. They bombarded them with questions: "How was everyone?" "What did you do?" "Did you have a good time?"

Answers were all positive until the final inquiry. Well, yes, they *did* have a good time. Christmas, though, had seemed empty. While surrounded by their family, they had missed being with their Ecuadorian friends, singing Spanish carols, and spending Christmas Eve with their staff for an annual smörgasbord! Now *that* was really Christmas.

Personally, one of our most intimate special days is not a holiday at all. It began one May when my husband suddenly announced that *we* were going to begin a new tradition. (Since he shows almost no sentimentality, not even for Christmas, this was quite a surprise!) I had nothing to say about it; he had decided. "We're going to celebrate Wife's Day. And do you know when it falls?" I must confess, I had no idea. "The Saturday before Mother's Day! We'll do something special together on that day." And so we have. We go shopping and he buys me something I help select. Then, we have lunch or dinner together, perhaps pick out a potted plant, and later attend some event in the community. It is amazing how this satisfying break softens the impact of the following day.

Is such activity selfish? No, it is personally affirming. When we have a genuine need—including psychological or emotional—Christ desires to provide for us in that area (Phil. 4:19; Eph. 3:20–21). His work is to bring us to a place of self-acceptance and balance. He is no more pleased than we when we sit around sorrowful; He wants to work with us as we come through our personal trials (Rom. 8:28). Often He will use someone close to us in the Body to be His emissary for our good.

Those who have been blessed with a strong sense of inner security and self-esteem will seldom need reassurance, even in nostalgic moments. My husband is one such person. At a Father's Day banquet when all of the other men have stood to their feet to be recognized as fathers, he has remained seated, wholeheartedly clapping in their honor—and he is unaware of the special grace that he demonstrates.

But many are the situations when others are edified while the childless may feel uncomfortable, if not almost condemned. A public reading of Proverbs 31:10–31 which speaks of the virtuous woman, for instance, can undermine our confidence. What if a woman has no husband or no children? Doesn't this passage hold up such an ideal as the ultimate for womanhood? And what of the bachelor who hasn't found the woman who would complete his life in the ways spoken of in this chapter? We might never find the courage to confess that such portions of God's Word disturb us, but they *do*.

Those who walk in obedience to Christ are meant to receive His Word with gladness. He has already stripped away our real condemnation and He intends to eliminate false condemnation. So, what we must learn is to be heartened by truth, not downcast because we cannot personally identify with every good testimony which someone else lives to God's glory.

Could Paul have given witness to having been blessed by such a good wife and family as herein mentioned? Could Mary, the mother of Jesus, probably the most inwardly beautiful of all women, have laid claim to each of these verses? Did she ever consider a field and buy it? Supply merchants with linen garments and sashes? Dress in fine linen and purple? Clothe all of her family in scarlet? Arise early to provide food for her servant girls? I doubt it. In the first place, she wasn't wealthy. Secondly, she wasn't called of God to do those acts. Ah! But was she a virtuous woman, one who feared the Lord, and one whose works speak her praise?

I am not certain that any one person ever accomplished all of the concrete examples in this passage. But together in the family of faith we have. Our value is clearly not dependent on our station in life or the performance of specific tasks but on our heart attitude toward God and our faithful obedience to Him. The value He places on each of us, His children, is "far above rubies."

Commemorative days were meant to lighten our life, not drag us down. If they hang over our necks, then somehow they have become a law to us, a burden. That's the very yoke Christ came to break. Let's examine our lives and see if we have come into a liberating experience of grace in this area. We may be surprised at the joy He has waiting for us.

One of the best days of my life was a Mother's Day! Can you imagine *me* saying that? It's true. It happened the year I was a "mother." My husband and I spent the weekend in the country caring for the adopted children of friends. While the Wellers served as youth retreat counselors, we stayed behind and reveled in being a family. On Mother's Day we turned up at church with three children! It was great fun for all us us, even if it was just temporary.

Although our "family" was only borrowed, that experience has caused me to reflect on real families. No family remains static. One by one, youngsters leave babyhood and childhood to enter adulthood, and then, sooner or later, they leave. Period. Someday even the Wellers will be a couple again and their children will be grown. Real or substitute parents have to bind their children tightly to their hearts while holding them loosely in their arms, because children never really "belong" to any of us.

Everyone may face down the road what the childless have already surmounted: aloneness. And what will happen to the new "familyless"—when they are faced with an empty nest, the sudden loss of a mate, or their children celebrating with their mates' families? We need to be sensitive to the changing families around us and provide by example, and perhaps invitation, some new alternatives for them.

If you are stuck for ideas of what you can do to make holidays times you look forward to, share you dilemma with others who may be conscious of the same need. Maybe several of you will face the challenge together. You may be amazed at the number of people who suffer Christmas, Valentine's Day, or even Easter blues! There are many shades of blue. Take steps to change yours from icy, night-sky indigo to warm, cloudless-day pastel. God will be honored by your creatively finding a way to say from the depths of your heart *each* day:

> This is the day which the Lord hath made;
> we will rejoice
> and be glad in it.
> —Psalm 118:24 (KJV)

*"Now a bishop must be above reproach,
the husband of one wife. . . .
He must manage his own household well,
keeping his children submissive and respectful in every way;
for if a man does not know how to manage his own household,
how can he care for God's church?*

*"Let deacons be the husband of one wife,
and let them manage their children
and their households well. . . ."*

—*2 Timothy 3:2a, 4, 5, 12 (RSV)*

CHAPTER TEN

The Church and the Childless

Our church family, our Christian friends—how much of life we share. Together we *are* one in Christ.[1] On the screen of God's love, the church, the life of each one is projected as we move through our individual stories and, in combination, present a composite picture of Jesus, Redeemer of lives, Lord.

Those who are single or married and childless have a particular appreciation for this corporate, global, eternal unity in Christ. The childless person may experience the closeness of family-type relationships in the home church as nowhere else. Personal influence which can never touch one's own children can be felt by generations of believers through the years.

But along with the many undeniably positive aspects of having an extended Christian family are certain accompanying realities:

—Christians form an on-going relationship which we may neither break nor withdraw from at will.

—In any given church Body it is possible that sensitivity to each other's deepest needs does not generally exist.

—Further, perhaps *no one*, including the pastor, can identify personally with the particular trials which some members experience.

—We have a love obligation to others whether or not our own needs are thoroughly met; Christlikeness is reflected in servanthood (Matt. 20:28).

—Each one's private pilgrimage with Christ authenticates the work of the Holy Spirit and amplifies the ministry potential of the local church.

My husband and I were first jolted into fuller awareness of the nature of the Body of Christ when we attended a new and exceptionally warm church. The people, sincere believers, were effective in reaching out to the community; the church had a devotional spirit and a good program. And yet, there was something missing. What could be wrong with such a church? At last someone observed: "We don't have any members over forty!" Had any of us been of retirement age we wouldn't have been so blind. (Time, by the way, has since corrected the church's lack.)

So it is that our individual differences, even if we feel isolated or lonely because of them, actually contribute to wholeness and balance in the Body. The church and wider community profit from the spectrum of grace displayed through the varied lives of the members of the church. Others can feel comfortable and be comforted because of our individual walk of faith (2 Cor. 1:3–6).

But how does this unique blending of countless individuals come about? Focusing on the interrelation of families and the family-less within the church, let's search for some clues to unifying these two specific groups. And who knows? In the process we may strike upon some underlying truths which contribute to love-bonding in general.

One key factor seems to be the church's attitude toward brotherhood. If community, inter-personal relationships, and caring are important to the Body, almost any vehicle of church programming can be effective in achieving and expressing unity.

Some churches, however, are notably successful in embracing new contacts and promoting mutual ministry among their parishioners. For example, one such church has placed everyone in the congregation in nurture groups composed of families with children, singles, older persons, childless couples, and teens whose parents aren't church attenders. Twice a month each group meets: once as adults only for a planned evening suitable to their interests, and again as a "family" with activities for all. They have serious as well as hilarious times together and everyone benefits from the inclusive character of the group. Those without families can form close attachments to the children, and young people develop significant relationships with mature Christians. As members of the group face such changes as marriage, an empty nest, or widowhood, the group remains a constant in their lives.

The size of the church often determines what is available specifically for the childfree. Larger bodies have the staff and resources to provide full-blown ministries to singles, young marrieds, or the elderly. Indeed, these homogeneous groups may become more meaningful to the attenders than the general church! Smaller churches may find it impractical or impossible to organize programs and activities which benefit the childless. Their factor of strength is that each member becomes a vital part of the church as a whole.

Regardless of the number on its rolls, if a church has a strictly family-centered philosophy, those without a mate or children may be allowed to disappear (or feel that they have) from the fellowship. Childless people will be uncertain as to where they "belong":

> I tend to hang around with the younger crowd (high school) because in some ways they match my status more. It's easier to teach Sunday School than to figure out which class I fit into.

> When I came to the church I now attend, there were three adult Sunday School classes: one for the older adults, one for men, and one for mothers and others. I never go to Sunday School.

By undergoing slight adjustments such a congregation can make a whole segment of society feel more at home in the church setting. Even small churches can successfully cut across age-sex-and-status barriers. Christian Education in some churches has become decompartmentalized by offering a variety of adult classes with periodically changing topics, Bible studies, materials and even locations. Other churches have experimented with such new approaches as multi-generational methods or team-teaching using leaders with distinctive gifts and personalities who appeal to class participants from varied backgrounds.

As a local church we desire to minister effectively to all the persons in the congregation and reach out to people in the community. But are we making it easy for individuals who don't fit molds to feel at home with us? One dedicated Christian single explains:

> The church's attitude seems to be to ignore the non-parent. It's only with a great deal of initiative on my part that I feel part of the body . . . with, of course, the help of the Spirit.

Another shares her predicament:

> I'm probably expected to do *more* than the parent, although there is *less* for my own personal enrichment in the church program.

Are the childless among us receiving spiritual refreshment, or are they confined to service?

Further, can we be more effective, even while operating within our given programs? Some churches, for example, have potluck dinners which few of the childless attend. Investigating, one finds that whole tables and empty seats are reserved for family members, singles end up sitting by themselves, and often only the pastor or a few others invite the family-less to join them. In contrast, other churches find that Wednesday's family supper is the highlight of the week for those who otherwise eat alone. Obviously, success doesn't depend on the spaghetti sauce!

If our programs are adequate, perhaps it is our perception of each other which is faulty. Frequently the childless hold idealized conceptions of family life. Likewise, church families may lack sensitivity toward the childless. The mother of three preschoolers may view the single working woman as having plenty of hours for doing church work, not realizing that she has a very responsible position with heavy professional obligations and spends almost no time at home. The career person, on the other hand, may not understand why the homemaker cannot accomplish more since she has only her family to care for.

Once we are sensitized to our differences, we may then tend to overlook needs and desires we hold in common. A single friend of ours in her middle years discovered that families may underestimate the importance many childless people attach to having a home, for instance. As she was excitedly telling some of the ladies at her church about a set of china she had purchased the previous day, one of the listeners remarked: "China? What do you need china for? You're not even married."

Perhaps the intent of such a comment is clarification, not cruelty, but the single has difficulty interpreting it positively. Imperceptibly, through just such small exchanges, the church can lose credibility with its non-families.

Childless individuals find themselves particularly vulnerable in a church setting because of its uniquely intimate and, at the same time, public nature. Couples experiencing an infertility problem or considering adoption often struggle with presenting their private need for prayer. Broaching the subject openly exposes a very personal matter to public domain. Even if the couple chooses to say nothing, they may experience psychological discomfort. One such friend, married to an older widower, began to feel very awkward on Sundays after she noticed that the women of the church automatically glanced at her waistline before looking at her face when she walked in.

The familiar question of why you have no children will always come up. Should the question be posed in a purely social setting, the couple could feel free to say, "We really prefer not to discuss it." But in the family of Christ that reply seems inappropriate. Neither does a purposely shocking answer, such as, "Because I'm sterile!" true as it may be, seem a loving way to respond.

The "Why?" should be asked only if there is already a genuine caring relationship between the two parties. But to the inevitable casual inquiries, I personally feel most comfortable giving a sincere, but non-technical, response and attempting to move to a new topic:

It has been the greatest sorrow of my life not to be able to have children. But for that reason, I can really appreciate the children of others. Do you have a family?

Sad to say, even Christian people can be thoughtless, if not crude. A friend of mine, during a period of great frustration while undergoing a fertility study, poured out her feelings to a lady in her church: "We've just been beating our heads against a wall. . . ." To which came the response: "That's not the way you do it, you know." My friend added one more frustration to her list.

More often the unfitting remarks take the form of pity, ignorance, or false hope. "Just relax. Take a cruise." "Quit work; stay home." "Adopt a baby, and then you'll have one." "I know a couple who had a baby after twenty-five years of marriage. Remember Sarah." This kind of comment is particularly unappreciated by the wife who has had a hysterectomy.

Some people are careless in tossing out an "I understand." Others reduce the couple's problem to seeming insignificance. "Be thankful it's not something serious like cancer." It *is* serious. And do you really understand? If not, be honest: "I really want to understand your hurt."

The biblical principle for interacting one with another in the Body of Christ is to prefer the other in love.[2] Our goal should be to respond to each person as Christ himself would. Let's allow what we know of Him to be our guide in our conversations with and relationships to others, in this case, the childless.

The church is potentially the most affirming body in the world. Are we letting our caring show? A Christian woman came up to me once and said simply, but warmly:

> You have really come a long way in a healing process. When your husband spoke publicly of your situation, I knew you must have come to a deep level of inner healing not to break down. I'm a widow. It took me about two years to talk about it.

Often nonverbal statements of love are what most encourage those who are hurting. Friends who are just "there" may be the childless person's best support. One young woman spoke of her experience with others in the Body this way:

> I realized I had to not be afraid of shedding tears. Letting others know of our hurt won't make us cry more than we already have.
>
> Some friends just let me blab away for twenty minutes on the phone. That's all they did.
>
> Others were closer and could interact more. They could talk back to us.

What a relief to the childless to know that the church understands when one of its members is not able to join in the fun of a shower or a father-and-son outing. Likewise, to have a sensitive pastor who has compassion for someone in his congregation who cannot bear to attend baptismal or infant dedication services. A pastoral prayer which includes "those who are suffering at this holiday season" quietly opens the door of availability to the hurting listener. It is to this church and pastor that such a person or a couple will feel free to turn during times of decision-making or crisis. Thus, instead of *forcing* the pace of inner healing, the caring pastor and congregation *promote* it.

Through the years, our various church families have been thoughtful in a number of ways. One person called to tell me about a radio program on adoption being aired. Others have handed me an address for a support group or a publication that I hadn't known about. A church librarian has sent me articles and books which could be helpful. Somebody else has ordered us a tape about a topic related to childlessness. An adoptive mother has touched me on the arm on Mother's Day and said, "I have you on my heart today. I remember how Mother's Day is." One friend called me on the phone because she recalled a sermon her deceased father had once preached and related the encouragement of the theme and Scripture to me. Many have prayed.

Women who have been trying for years to have a baby have told me of pregnant friends who have been kind enough to call and say, "I wanted to share the news with you first. I knew you might want some advance time to handle it."

Not only those who have no children, but those who have lost children or cannot have more will also experience special times of pain. The issues for them may be particularly complex:

> I have a little girl, but I can't have any more children. She keeps asking me for a brother or a sister. I don't know how to tell her (she's not yet three), and she won't let the issue rest.
> My friends are all having their second babies now. I feel so depressed. I can't get into it like I did when I was pregnant, too. I don't want to knit a little baby sweater for them or anything.

These people are not unspiritual; they are in the midst of a great trial. Not that the church need tiptoe around them! Others simply need to recognize that in this area, at this moment, the person who is suffering is the "weaker brother"[3] who needs loving support, not an uncaring or judgmental attitude.

On a spiritual and emotional level, Jesus himself experienced the agony of childlessness—even while accompanied by His disciples. On one occasion overwhelming sorrow poured from His heart as He looked over His beloved city and realized that they didn't belong to Him:

> O Jerusalem, Jerusalem . . . how often I have longed to gather your children together, as a hen gathers her chicks under her wings, but you were not willing.   —Matthew 23:37 (NIV)

Of course, Jesus' affliction has dimensions unknowable to other human beings. His longing for the *re*-birth of the people He loved, knowing what *eternal* life for them would mean, is not comparable to our own experience of childlessness. But even though we only imperfectly understand *His* loss, from the depth of His suffering He can certainly understand *ours*.

Why did He raise Jairus' daughter and the widow's son?[4] In the account of the widow, the Bible tells us:

> When the Lord saw her, his heart went out to her and he said, "Don't cry." Then he went up and touched the coffin, and those carrying it stood still. He said, "Young man, I say to you, get up!"—Luke 7:13–14 (NIV)

He was moved to compassion because the parent's loss was so grave. He cares just as much for those suffering through childlessness today, and one of the principal ways He shows us His loving concern is through His Body.

The church can take many specific actions to alleviate this particular sorrow if only it is aware of what helps. One thing families can do is to "share" their children with their childless friends. My husband and I, for instance, have very little fun going alone to a swimming pool. But when we can borrow a couple of little children to play with in the water, we all have a great time. The same could be said of going to Disneyland, a fair, or the zoo. Friends who loan us their children once in a while do us a genuine favor.

Just so, taking children to a retirement center or to visit those who never have the pleasure of being with youngsters serves to delight and encourage these childless persons. Simple hospitality—inviting others in who aren't often in a family setting—may not be difficult to do but may meet real needs.

One of the most humbling and yet reassuring actions which Christian parents have ever done for us has been to will us their children. Through the years, either formally or by verbal agreement, we have assumed responsibility for ten children should something happen to their parents. For families who lack relatives who could rear children in the event of the parents' death, childless persons are ideal candidates to consider. It's a mutual service, one of the many which we can perform in the Body of Christ.

In another vein, older singles or couples are often the choicest persons to minister to younger ones who are facing the various stages and struggles of matelessness and/or childlessness. They *do* understand and have years of experience and perspective from which to help soulmates learn to thrive in their barren circumstances. One of the kindest acts members of the congregation can do is to put such persons in contact with each other so that they can communicate, pray for one another, and share God's specific comfort.

An often-overlooked resource for church families is the objectivity of the childless person. Being free from the daily cares of parenting places an individual in a uniquely impartial position for observing parent-child interaction and relationships. Sometimes the best insights for problem-solving come from one who is outside, and yet the childless person is aware that to volunteer such information may not be well received. Parents who seek counsel from a wise and trusted non-parent greatly honor him or her and may well receive thorough consideration of the issue and personal encouragement as from no other source.

An almost equally delicate matter is that of conversations involving pregnancy, babies, children, and problem teenagers when childless people are present. Since non-parents have no child-bearing or -rearing stories, the tendency is to unconsciously leave them out of the tete-a-tete. A childless person's only contributions may be to ask questions or affirm the parents as they talk on about their children—their problems and their futures.

The childless person doesn't want to be left out of family-centered talk any more than the single person never wants to communicate with others about marriage. What the childless individual longs for is to be able to participate positively in the conversation.

Leads like, "My son will be fifteen next week. You work with the youth group, what kinds of things are they doing at parties nowadays?" or "Have you noticed if Stacey is joining in during Sunday School? Since the baby has come she has been really insecure at home," are naturals. Such thoughtful spontaneity brings us into a mutual, comfortable exchange

Thus, informally the relationship of families and childless persons within the church offers many opportunities for reciprocal love. But what about our formal interaction? How does our community of faith respond to passages such as that at the beginning of the chapter:

> . . . a bishop . . . must manage his own household well, keeping his children submissive and respectful in every way; for if a man does not know how to manage his own household, how can he care for God's church?   —1 Timothy 3:2a, 4–5 (RSV)

Do we tend to generalize that the Body of Christ is entirely family-oriented with male domination? Does the Scripture exclude all those who aren't family men from taking a responsible role in the church? Surely not. Our consideration must include other pertinent scriptural and God-given models for our faith such as: Christ, the bachelor; the prophetess Anna; the church-homeowner, Lydia; Paul's co-workers,

Priscilla and Aquila; the deaconesses, and the fact that in the Body we are to submit to one another out of our reverence for Christ.[5]

We are many members in this church universal. Those with households can minister to those without. And those who have none to manage can love and serve those who do. Come to think of it, how could we have read the last Scripture if it hadn't been for this love principle in action in the life of one voluntarily childless individual: Paul, the Apostle?

"You know what has happened throughout Judea,
beginning in Galilee after the baptism that John preached—
how God anointed Jesus of Nazareth with the Holy Spirit
and power,
and how he went around doing good
and healing all who were under the power of the devil,
because God was with him."

—*Acts 10:37–38 (NIV)*

CHAPTER ELEVEN

Pointers for Pastors and Other Professionals

You in the service professions are carrying on in a great tradition. Jesus himself was one of your colleagues. His titles included: Great Physician, Counselor, and Good Shepherd. And didn't He dedicate himself to those pursuits which by human standards were most difficult, but most necessary? No wonder at times your case load seems staggering and your hours pitifully insufficient! Working conditions for the professional have seldom been commensurate with the value of the results.

But a valid question is: Who helps you, the people-helpers?

Considering the limited information on childlessness in texts and journals, amazingly, the Bible may still be the most enlightening book on this subject. Another basic resource which Jesus had at hand is likewise available to you—those of us who are childless: your patients, clients, and parishioners. We must be willing to help you tool-up because it's your skill, in turn, which will aid us during our process of healing.

This chapter, written from a counselee's point of view, does not detail medical or social service procedures, but gives practical suggestions to facilitate your helping us face and manage life without children. Because only part of our search will involve your professional help and this specialized information, we invite you to read the entire book and explore the rest of our childless life with us as well.

I. *Increasing the Comfort Level*

The race is on these days to produce "friendly computers." But why? Obviously the professional computer programmer is not disturbed by a sophisticated machine. But the layman, experimenting with one for the first time, may be.

And so it is with those of us who seek your help. Examining tables, case studies, shelves of reference books, and diplomas are part of your everyday environment, but they are cold to us. Our *first* need, therefore, is assurance. Seeing your relaxed face, particularly when it's smiling, helps us tolerate the unfriendly props.

Those of us who come to discuss our infertility, adoption dreams, or sense of childlessness will be sharing on the most personal level imaginable. Usually we arrive in a super-sensitized state. It's not a root canal we are talking about, but a terrible sense of loss.

We are prone to suffer "room-arrangement anxiety" in such moments. Almost every time I have been in a doctor's or pastor's office, I have found myself automatically moving my chair so that I can have more direct contact with the person I came to see. When you use a table or a desk, place it so that we can communicate freely in spite of it. If it's a big desk, pull the chairs up close and invite us to rest our elbows on it. Or perhaps we can just sit in chairs in a more natural manner.

We come expectantly because you can provide something that we need. But underneath we often harbor fear: "What if he tells me that we can't have children?" "Will she approve our application for adoption?" "What if there is no spiritual answer to my problem?"

You are in a position to allay that unspoken terror. If you are personally appreciative of our problem and supportive of us, then we begin to feel that even if we don't get our heart's desire, our doctor, counselor, or pastor cares deeply for us and wants our best.

Coming to you may be a last resort. Perhaps the previous professional let us down. We may turn to the social worker, counselor, or pastor because the undertaker closed the coffin on our stillborn child as we stood there alone, or our doctor diagnosed our physical case as hopeless but failed to assist us in meaningfully processing that information and evaluating our alternatives. We may feel desolate.

II. *Confronting the Issues*

The encouraging factor, however, is that we see you as a bridge from our bleak present to a future which we can face confidently. We expect that you will deal directly *with* us, not just information *about* us. Even our words may be superficial and you will be forced to understand below what we vocalize to the level of what we are really expressing.

If it's vital that both partners be present to resolve a life issue, we depend on you to recognize that fact and insist that we come as a couple. "We just never once considered that we wouldn't have children," cannot be explored fully if "we" are still not confronting it. With both of us present it is time to get down to work, "Well, let's consider it. . . ."

Coming into unity in this hard matter may be one of the most profound learning ventures we will ever undertake. The wife of a childless couple expressed their discovery this way:

> Our experience has taught us that it's okay to keep asking God for something we really want. We've learned the importance of praying TOGETHER for something. It's taught us patience.

Our counselor or pastor may need to initiate this process, forcing us to expose our gravest present concern. "What would you say causes you the most anxiety about your situation? What's your biggest fear?"[1]

Once we can declare our fear, we can look at it more objectively. Even so, that which we dread may be absolutely repugnant to us. "I don't see how I can go through life without having a child of my own."

"What if your worst fear came true, what do you think you would do? How would you handle it?" Considering such an eventuality does three things:

1. Removes the issue from its intense personal nature to a less threatening position of supposition.
2. Forces the childless to make a few tentative projections or decisions.
3. Relieves some anxiety feelings by confronting and attacking the recognized foe directly.

If we have obviously been agonizing over our situation, the professional may shed light on our intense feelings by informing us of the various stages of grief: denial, rage and anger, bargaining, depression, and acceptance.[2]

You may then ask us, "Where would you say you are in that grief process?" Usually we will be able to recognize what we have passed through, where we are, and then, how far we have yet to go. Understanding the course of mourning helps to authenticate our grief experience and gives us a reasonable goal to reach.

Some of us will never pass through such a defined process, or if we do, it will be delayed. Our immediate problems will be of an entirely different sort. We may be experiencing interpersonal conflict as husband and wife, blaming each other instead of seeing the combined nature of our problem. Or, we may be suffering from stress due to a prolonged infertility study. Perhaps we will be struggling with matters of guilt. Issues such as these must be recognized and dealt with as in any counseling situation.

Sometimes your job will be to help us accept our limitations when we would prefer to be "normal." A young woman, who had a hysterectomy before she met the man she would later wed, thought she had accepted her sterility at the time of the operation. After two years of marriage, she suddenly found herself working her problem through at a different level:

> I have trouble understanding why so many limitations have been put on me. I feel that God has given me a loving heart and I wonder in what ways I am supposed to use it.

We don't want to face the fact that our bodies don't function the way other people's do or that for some reason no one ever found us attractive, or vice versa, and we never married. Talking these issues through until we can accept ourselves as we are, created by God as unique individuals, or brought together as a couple with a very special blend of personalities and gifts, is your contribution toward our resolution.

We may be wrestling with a philosophical question which has religious overtones. Each year in the biological sciences moral lines get a little fuzzier. Partners may be facing such decisions as: What about *in vitro* fertilization ("test tube babies")? Should we consider donor sperm? Or, we may wonder about the use of a surrogate mother. (See Gen. 16–17, the story of Abraham, Sarah, Hagar, Ishmael, and Isaac.)

Sometimes we will be questioning how much money we can conscientiously spend on a percentage chance that pregnancy will result. At other times we will have to consider major or minor surgery. Should I put myself in a life-endangering position for possible resultant fertility? How about a second such procedure? A third? An experimental technique?

Ultimately, the couple must arrive at each decision based on sound evidence and biblical principles which satisfy them. Whether the professional would have reached the same conclusion is immaterial. It is your job to help us understand our choices, not make them for us.

At times you will find yourself working with persons haunted by a past choice. A sense of loss—even years later—may overwhelm those who have aborted their unborn child. They may experience a terrible awareness of conviction and guilt. Their healing will come by working through that guilt until they have the assurance of forgiveness, and grief until they have an inner rest that their innocent baby is safe in the presence of Jesus (Ps. 139:13–18; Jer. 1:5; Matt. 18:1–4, 10; Luke 1:5–7).

A further ministry will be to help those of us who are suffering acutely. We may just have received an unfavorable prognosis for fertility, lost a baby through miscarriage, or sustained a blow such as a rejection for adoption. If we are in emotional shock, words may be largely meaningless to us. Touching, listening, accepting our tears, assuring us that you care, sharing a cup of tea, repeating some simple reassurance from Scripture, staying by our side, or arranging for someone to be with us, and later, calling us frequently may be your most appropriate responses.

Helping us receive a verdict and assimilate its meaning is one of the most difficult, and yet needful, services you can do for us. Perhaps a judge rules that our children will be placed with another family. An adoption agency decides we cannot receive a child because one of us has a heart condition. Or an examiner determines that our child has died of Infant Death Syndrome. Even a vague diagnosis such as "unexplained infertility" aids us in our acceptance process. We need to know what it is we are confronting.

If you are to break such news to us, tell us gently, caringly. Explain to us in simple vocabulary because our immediate inner panic may screen out technical terminology which we would normally comprehend. Treat us as you would your own loved one. Afterward we will think many times about the moments in which we received our devastating news; it helps us when we can recall the meaningful relationship we had with the messenger or the one who stood by during those moments. We may need to turn to you later for clarification, expecting you to remember details that our numbness blocked our receiving.

Whatever our specific trauma, when we can react rationally, encourage us to live in the present and to open our hearts to Jesus *now*. Can we live through this very moment without a mate? Can we survive another hour without holding a baby in our arms? Will we be brokenhearted this afternoon if the door doesn't fly open with children coming home from school? Has Jesus given His grace in the past? Is He providing a way through for us now? And can't we trust Him to continue doing the same in the future? When we realize that we can answer yes to these basic questions about Christ's adequacy to keep us in the midst of our trial, then we have assurance of available victory for the rest of life (1 Cor. 10:13).

Sometimes hope-killing information has long ago been delivered to us in a cruelly blunt fashion when we had no one near to help soften its impact. Although we may have survived the initial blow, we may yet have unrecognized hurt or unresolved feelings about it. One such woman suffered the indignity of being termed an "habitual spontaneous aborter." She wept time and again over this designation until her husband, in a stroke of genius, grabbed the paper with the diagnosis, ripped it up, and said, "That just means you're *special!*"

You, the professional, have the privilege and responsibility of helping us come to know and adapt to our brand of specialness. If you should find yourself unable to do so because our need lies beyond your sphere of expertise, assist us in finding the person who can help.

III. *Exploring the Possibilities*

As we move through and beyond our time of despair, we may continue to be deluged with inner questions. Before we can consider the future, we have to try to make sense out of the past and present.

Invariably, we wonder "Why? Why me? Why us?" To jog us out of a rut, you may have to help us ask some positive *why's*:

1. Why not? If God has chosen or allowed a different pattern than the norm for me and my family, why not be in agreement with it?
2. Why would God, perhaps even miraculously, prevent us from going through the door others walk through with ease?
3. Why would I (or we) be particularly successful living a life which doesn't include having my (our) own children?

Point out to us that we may not know the answer to that *why* for years, until we can look back and see God's hand at work in all of life. One interesting observation I have made in interviewing older childless people is that invariably they have been able to point out reasons for their state which satisfy them this side of eternity.

—"Over the years we have taken in a nephew and other relatives."
—"We teach the young people at our church and it involves a lot of time. They are like our children."
—"We have cared for all four aging parents."
—"We have been able to pour all of our heart and energy into the work God has given us to do."
—"If we had had our own children, we never would have adopted. God meant for us to raise this child (these children)."

Our answers differ, but our God is a master at bringing beauty out of what appears to each of us as only a pile of ashes.

The time may come, though, when you will have to challenge us to get up from our ash heap so that God can proceed with His divine sculpture. Through the years Christians have tried to do that by encouraging us with the Scriptures. But they've used the wrong passages! They have selected those pertaining to Abraham and Sarah, Isaac and Rebekah, Jacob and Rachel, Ruth, Zacharias and Elizabeth—all of whom became parents. Not only that, but to them were born special children destined to the lineage of, or preparation for, the Messiah! Clearly, God's leading in their lives does not preclude His taking a different track in our own.

Childless people have been plagued with, "If you just have faith like Sarah. . . ." By that reasoning not only do we have a physical problem, but we have a spiritual one as well!

Point us to Jesus himself. Hold up Paul's example and teachings. Lead us to passages such as Hebrews 11, but don't stop with verse 11:

> By faith Sarah herself received power to conceive, even when she was past the age, since she considered him faithful who had promised.

Go on to tell us about the others who had faith in spite of not receiving a visible reward for it:

> . . . Some were tortured, refusing to accept release, that they might rise again to a better life. Others suffered mocking and scourging, and even chains and imprisonment. They were stoned, they were sawn in two, they were killed with the sword; they went about in skins of sheep and goats, destitute, afflicted, ill-treated—of whom the world was not worthy—wandering over deserts and mountains, and in dens and caves of the earth. And all these, though well attested by their faith, did not receive what was promised, since God had foreseen something better for us, that apart from us they should not be made perfect.
>
> —Hebrews 11:35b–40 (RSV)

There is nothing at all wrong with our faith. Why, we may never before have recognized how great a confidence we have shown in the Savior! Faith is expressed in more than one way, and ours trusts God alone for himself alone.

Once we know we have been obedient in our situation, we are open to making the next move of faith. That is to look at the strength of our unique position, evaluate our gifts and potential realistically, and begin to make some decisions.

You can help by feeding us questions:

—What would you most like to do with your freedom?

—Do you (to a woman) want to pursue a home-centered ministry or a career?

—Would you like to launch into additional education?

—Are you living where you would like eventually to be?

—Do you see yourselves as a team in any way, in business or in ministry?

—Have you considered opening your home to foster children? . . . troubled teens?

—Do you wish to investigate adoption?

—Do you feel that the Lord has been pointing out to you an option which you wish to look into?

You may find investing time in us one of the most personally rewarding endeavors of your professionl career because our successful steps in faith will be traceable, in large part, to you.

IV. *Reaching Conclusions*

A little boy came to his father with a riddle: "There were three frogs sitting on a log: a bullfrog, a tree frog, and a leap frog. The leap frog decided to jump into the water. How many frogs were left on the log?" His father answered, "Two." "No," the little boy gleefully replied, "there were THREE! The leap frog only *decided* to jump; he didn't really do it!"

Not only must we decide how we are going to express our family life and ministry potential, we must take steps to actually do so. Eventually we must learn to live within our means—what it means to be us. Our concept of family will broaden, breaking out of its previous stereotype. We will accept the fact that as single persons we can be a family unit, that as husband and wife we can have a multitude of "changing children" by becoming a foster family, or that by being a resident counselor for a dormitory or children's home, we can be a parental substitute for hundreds of young people.

You can assist us in making our personal "leap" by loaning us reading materials or getting us in touch with a peer support group such as Resolve (for infertility and pre-adoption help), The Compassionate Friends (for parents mourning the death of a child), Candlelighters Foundation (for the parents of children with cancer), and many more. You may be able to suggest some volunteer ministries or paid positions which need personnel and for which we are well suited.

You can refer us to some successful singles, childless couples, or adoptive families so that we can find out from firsthand experience how other people have managed a comparable life. If no such person is available, perhaps you can suggest an individual to whom we can write. We may long to pour out our hearts to someone who understands us exactly. I have received many letters through the years, often from strangers, a number of whom were referred to me by a minister or pastor's wife. A reply written by someone who cares can be a source of encouragement time and again to the reader. Life-changing decisions can be made as a result of receiving such an answer in the mail.

Sometimes we simply need a facilitator. In the event that we should wish to pursue adoption, you can help us in your specialty field, whether it be to locate addresses of adoption agencies or homes for unwed mothers sponsored by your denomination, submit a recommendation, or prepare a medical opinion. Physicians in some states can arrange for private adoptions. Contacts can be made with overseas adoption programs if the prospective parents wish to take that action. Be our advocate; that is a service which we cannot perform for ourselves.

Pre-adoption counseling is often underestimated because the myth prevails that adoption will "cure" a sense of childlessness or loss due to, let us say, infertility. Adopting does not negate our feelings for the child who "never was" or for a child who died. Nor does it mean that we are no longer infertile. We must reconcile these issues separately. Entering into adoption before doing so is a serious mistake. Even if our unresolved feelings are not evident at the time of adoption, we will have to acknowledge them later when our life is complicated by being a parent.

An adopting mother revealed the perspective she and her husband gained through their formal pre-adoption sessions:

> It was another whole process of soul searching and questioning. We were so fortunate to have a Christian caseworker—one who asked many tough questions, and probably some that will come up again and again through our lifetime.

Some of us will not be ready to handle such microscopic scrutiny successfully if we do not have some advance preparation. Lacking this preliminary groundwork, my husband and I found visiting our state adoption agency a very unsettling experience.

We went to inquire as to what would be required of us if we were to make an application for adoption. I expected a place having to do with babies and children to be "warmer." Instead it was a drab-colored, straight-walled government building. Only the sign by the door and the pamphlets on a counter distinguished it from any other state office.

The social worker, a young woman, and quite pleasant, was bent over the secretary's desk as we walked in. She offered to spend time with us even though we didn't have an appointment. After a brief and impersonal introduction, she explained to us the regulations of a state-agency adoption. She was realistic about the minimal numbers of placeable children and the abundance of ready homes. Once we were processed, our name would be placed on a list for one year, during which time we might receive a child for which we were qualified. At the end of that time, if no child had been placed in our home, our name would be withdrawn from the elegibility list. We could then wait a calendar year and file a new application.

I hadn't anticipated such tremendous competition for adoptable children nor the emotional upheaval an applicant could suffer waiting to receive one. I wasn't sure that I could bear the suspense of not knowing if I were to be a parent imminently—or never!

The social worker then began to ask us a few leading questions. "If you were to adopt, what would you say to your preschooler about his beginnings? Would you tell him he was adopted?" "How would you deal with this issue with an older child?" "What would you share with a teenager?"

I wasn't prepared to confront those inquiries. We had just walked through the door to pick up an application form. I gave a superficial answer to the first question, not knowing that more were coming. My husband fielded the second and third questions. Those were the kinds of questions we had expected to be able to ask *her*! Not only did I not know how to answer, but I was fighting back tears. By fastening my eyes upon Jerry, I hoped that the caseworker wouldn't notice.

She was calm; this was routine for her. But it was an all-important moment for us. I felt my level of stress and my emotions rise. But why? I worked professionally with social workers and families on a daily basis, so why should I suddenly feel so intimidated? She was there to help us. Or was she? She didn't seem to be offering us any positive hope, any sure solution. What if she didn't like us? That was it: I felt threatened. If we were ever to be approved as adoptive parents, she would have to recommend us. She had the power to deny us parenthood—and she didn't even know us!

That wasn't fair. What right did the state have to decide if we would make good parents? How would we ever convince them? Right now I was not making a very good impression. That would probably count against us. What if they rejected us?!

They did. Not in the office, but on the way home, before we proceeded further. Reading the application form out loud in the car, we realized that we didn't qualify. We had to submit medical proof that we could not have natural children. For years doctors had been referring us from one specialist to another; we were still in that medical process and they continued to hold out hope for us. We even had a little hope left for ourselves. How could we end all that and have it stated in writing that we would never have a child of our own? That would almost be presumptuous.

In addition, there were strict financial requirements. The prospective father had to have been employed by the same company for a number of years. His income, not counting the wife's salary, had to cover all of the family's budgeted expenses with a percentage above that as a financial cushion. My husband was just getting started in his own business. It would take years before he would be in that kind of position! We could not even *apply* until then, let alone begin the case study and finally, the wait.

Where was a line on the application asking about our faith in God, that He would provide for a family of three as well as for two? The awful realization struck us that families with financial means could be approved, but loving couples without such material resources wouldn't qualify. We hurt for all the couples that we represented.

Costs for having our own child would have been minimal because of good insurance coverage. Adopting a child privately, however, would cost thousands of dollars for prenatal care and birth expenses plus lawyer's fees and court costs. Perhaps more at issue: families entering into private adoptions in our state had no guarantees because the courts had set a precedent of upholding the right of a birth mother to reclaim her child. We felt we needed the benefits of an agency.

Our anguish increased through the succeeding weeks as we contacted every adoption agency in our area. Salvation Army's White Shield division did not have babies available. Boys' and Girls' Aid Society had such a long waiting list that they were not accepting other applicants. International adoption was not feasible because it would complicate our missionary candidacy. And so the search continued fruitlessly.

After some years we were forced into reaching a double conclusion: we could not have natural children and we could not adopt.

The pastor or counselor ministering to such a person at a post-closed-door stage may find the counselee in despair. What we need now is an infusion of common-sense realism that, although our rejections or disappointments have been personally experienced, they are objective in nature. The wife of a family refused by numerous agencies because of the husband's health, came to the following conclusions:

> We finally learned that there is no one to blame. It isn't the fault of an adoption agency or an unwed mother who keeps her child. We can talk about it and not feel ashamed. We don't have to explain it to anyone.
>
> Because the adoption agency says "No," doesn't mean you're a freak. It's just not for you. It took us a long time to reach the point where we could say, "We weren't meant to have children."

So, what were we meant to do? The four final chapters of this book suggest management options available to the childfree. You may wish to refer to the specific ideas contained there as you help us expand our horizons. Your objective insight into our interests and abilities will help us get a realistic perspective on our alternatives.

You and we may go through a lot together, perhaps forming a lifelong bond. But even a short, meaningful relationship may make a radical difference to us. We will welcome it if once in a while you check back, casually asking how it's going or suggesting we get together for coffee. When we close the door to your office, we want to leave assured that you are willing to turn the knob on the other side if we knock again in the future.

V. *Preventing the Problem*

As a professional you have a unique edge in attacking the growing problem of childlessness in our society. In some ways you can contribute to limiting or preventing its occurrence, at least in specific cases.

The physician has many opportunities to do so. Premarital examinations, for example, provide an excellent occasion to note any detectable physical obstructions to later conception. Some women are predisposed to an early curtailment of menses; males may evidence testicular varicocele. Being frank about such findings can alert a couple to potential difficulties even before marriage and contribute to their taking steps to prevent the later heartache of irreversible infertility.

From our perspective, we would want you to make available services and trained personnel for our high-risk pregnancies and neonatal intensive care facilities for our premature infants, to keep abreast of advances in the field of infertility, and to refuse to perform abortions for non-life-threatening reasons.

Other professionals exert influence in complementary areas. The pastor through teaching, preaching, and administering the church program is responsible for establishing a firm biblical basis for the people in his congregation. Among other benefits, this strength will contribute to preventing childlessness due to such avoidable causes as separation, divorce, and abortion.

Furthermore, the pastor or counselor has unparalleled possibilities to help parishioners or persons seeking Christian counseling. Premarital sessions can introduce the family-in-formation to the fact that about one out of six couples of childbearing age will be involuntarily childless.[3] Especially if the couple is older, if one of them is infirm, or if they are planning to delay child-rearing indefinitely, such realities should be explored while discussing family planning.

If there is good reason for a couple to examine the issue further, you can pose realistic questions which are better faced before marriage than afterward. Some issues should be discussed with each partner alone, others with the couple together. "What if you should find you cannot have children? What do you think you would do?" "If you were to discover that your mate is infertile, would you still be satisfied that you married this person?" "Are you convinced of God's having brought you together as a couple whether or not your marriage results in your being parents?"

Another of the pastor's privileges is infant baptism or dedication. While discussing other matters—both spiritual and practical—encourage the family to provide for the child in a legal will. They can then specify to whom they wish to entrust their child(ren) in the event of their death. Some couples may come to the conclusion that there is no family member who could assume that responsibility. The pastor may then suggest that as they consider possible legal guardians, they entertain the possibility of designating a childless couple or a family who has lost a child.

You will also undoubtedly be counseling the unwed mother or the married woman who doesn't want to carry the child she is expecting. Beyond ministering to the person herself, you are responsible for presenting honestly the options which exist for her unborn baby. The world abounds with information and resources for bringing death to the infant; those facts will not be hard for her to come by. But you are in a position to present an alternative: life for her child and, according to the case, joy for a Christian family.[4]

The person before you may feel: trapped, desperate, angry, betrayed, violated, abandoned, unprepared, victimized, afraid, alone. She may be very young or in the middle of a flourishing career or educational program. Seldom will she be physically incapable of bearing the child. Pregnancy is usually most injurious to her sense of pride and self-esteem, her reputation, her job, her educational opportunities, her family relationships, or her hope for a happy future.

Your challenge is to help her focus on two truths:
—the redemptive power of Christ
—and the good life possible for her child.

She will need to be affirmed in making life choices based on an objective standard, the Word of God, and in so doing she will recognize whether her thoughts and feelings proceed from self-interest or Christ-centeredness. Further, she will need to be satisfied that a pro-birth decision will result in a life worth living for her child. Because of today's adoption crunch, you can assure her that there is no such thing as an "unwanted baby" and that her child can be placed in a loving Christian home should she wish to make that choice.[5]

Through active listening and effective questioning you can help her face her situation honestly and clearly: What personal gain does she want to receive from her experience? Does she wish to learn principles of problem-solving which will be applicable throughout life or is she interested in seeking an immediate escape? What constitutes "good" and how does one determine the highest good in any particular situation? What is the most redemptive way God could move in her life and her baby's life? How does Christ interpret "love"? How did He express that kind of love for us? What does she think Jesus would do if He were in her place?

You may be called upon to ferret out information vital to her immediate future. What financial and social assistance is available to her? Are there individuals or facilities she can turn to for practical help? What provision does the denomination or a Christian adoption agency make for persons wishing to avail themselves of prenatal and/

or adoption services? What, if any, are the obligations imposed by such a group? Find out what assurances a birth mother is given as to the family in which her baby is placed. Discover what resources are at the disposal of a single parent. What, for an already-overburdened mother? Think, talk, and act together until the person is ready to proceed independently.

VI. *Evaluating the Effort*

As a professional person, you serve others. As a Christian professional you are committed to representing and following Christ while engaged in your profession. Ideally, you will be free to interact with those you serve on a spiritual, as well as a physical, psychological or practical, plane.

The leading of the Holy Spirit and your adept handling of the Word of God are essential if you are to be a catalyst, allowing His hope to grow in the hearts of individuals. The style you use will be unique. Depending on your career and personality, you may at times use medical procedures, questions, well-chosen illustrations or humor, fitting testimonies, appropriate literature, or prayer. The end result for the believing client or parishioner should be that even while engaged in personal struggle, Christ's character is increasingly formed within and expressed without.

Each person you touch will be a composite of multi-levels of spiritual growth. Some will be, overall, more mature than you are! You may end up receiving more through them than they ever will from you. Their exercise of faith and experience of joy in the midst of regrettable circumstances will give you incentive to hold out a similar victory to others.

Remember, however, that even though Christ ministered to the whole person, He did not always see the life changes He desired. Just so, you will not witness all of the positive results you know to be possible. But He will effect changes—eternal ones at that—through using the skills and gifts He has entrusted to you.

Think of the hours that Jesus spent working with imperfect people—teaching, preaching, healing, and counseling. Those exchanges through which life passed from His laid-down life into an area of human need were *ministry*. His whole purpose in being physically present was fulfilled in those divine-human transactions. He explained to His twelve "interns":

> . . . the Son of Man did not come to be served, but to serve, and to give his life as a ransom for many.   —Matthew 20:28 (NIV)

You who follow the Christ in the essence of His lifework know what a personal investment you make as you pour time and energy into people. But nothing else is more satisfying. Yours is not merely a job, it is a calling. As Christ himself found that His meat in life was to do that which He was sent to do,[6] so you are edified in the very act of meeting our needs. We thank God for His provision for us: you.

We have different gifts,
according to the grace given us.
If a man's gift is prophesying,
let him use it in proportion to his faith.
If it is serving, let him serve;
if it is teaching, let him teach;
if it is encouraging, let him encourage;
if it is contributing to the needs of others,
let him give generously;
if it is leadership, let him govern diligently;
if it is showing mercy, let him do it cheerfully.

—Romans 12:6–8 (NIV)

"... ye have received the Spirit of adoption,
whereby we cry, Abba, Father.
The Spirit itself beareth witness with our spirit,
that we are the children of God:
And if children, then heirs:
heirs of God, and joint-heirs with Christ. ..."

—Romans 8:15b–17 (KJV)

SECTION FOUR:

POSSIBILITIES

CHAPTER TWELVE

The Option of Adoption

She wrapped the blanket snugly around the wriggly body, still slightly damp from his bath. His brown eyes could focus on her now. Those eyes looked so like his father's—wise, and yet somehow, vulnerable. His broad forehead, covered with sparse, dark baby hair, would soon be more exposed as the fine fuzz dried.

Having him was one of the most important events which had ever happened to her. How accustomed she had grown to her son in these brief three months. She could hardly remember what life had been like before she had first held him. But this time as she held him so tightly, instead of gladness, she felt an aching deadness. So different from her first eager clinging to him was this, perhaps the last, embrace she would give her son.

She breathed into his miniature ear words he would never understand, "My grief is deep, son, but my love is deeper." Tears slid between her cheek and his. "I never knew there could be such sorrow in doing what's best for you, sweetheart. You are so young to leave your mother. But from now on, you are in the hands of my God, and yours, my baby."

With that, she placed him in a handmade basket and fastened the lid down noiselessly over her baby, Moses.[1]

A close-up of this one biblical baby helps us see adoption as a family unit formed through *loving surrender* on the one hand and, if we were to follow Moses into Pharaoh's court, *prepared willingness* on the other.

My husband and I became acutely aware of this partnership when we were invited to speak to a youth group. Over a powdered-sugar doughnut we began to get acquainted with the young people, including a newcomer from Colombia, a girl who was obviously pregnant. She had been invited by the most enthusiastic blond sixteen-year-old in the group. Afterward she confided, "I have just recently come to know the Lord. But my baby is going to be born in January and he is going to have Christian parents. I've been praying about the family who will be adopting him."

Adoption is a faith-demanding step for all the parties involved, often the most profound experience of joy and grief which they will ever know. Birth parents bring a child to life, only to turn that new baby over to strangers. The child who is *theirs*, physically, is not theirs to keep. Adopting parents know the joy of receiving their long-awaited child. But they may suffer final death pangs over the demise of their own personal genetic future and the disappointment that characteristics of their adopted child are unlike those their natural children might have had. Adoption will never cure their infertility, nor will it erase the loss of natural children. The child who is theirs to keep is not *theirs*.

Adoption as a calling is as God-given as that of natural parenting or celibacy. As is true in other areas of our Christian walk, being led *to* or *not to* adopt is a matter which the Spirit of God can initiate and confirm. If we are to adopt, it is because the Lord has created a child or children whom He has gifted us to parent.

Such a conviction probably will not come to us during the immediate emotional upheaval of failing to conceive or of losing a child. As one new adoptive mother reflects, "You can't get psychologically 'up' about getting pregnant and adopting a child at the same time."

So how do we get "up" about alternatives?

In finding our life's new direction, we must reach a point of seeing that children are not a "solution" to our "problem." Otherwise we follow the same shortcut reasoning that impressed some of us watching a film on infertility. After presenting interviews with childless people and showing a series of medical procedures, the final scenes showed these various couples with their babies. We were left with the distinct impression that only those who manage to get a child can be happy.

The truth is, we must be content *before* we adopt. This inner relaxation comes after we have reevaluated who we are and, more particularly, who we were meant to be in Christ. One friend described it this way:

> My reasons for wanting a child now seem to have changed. The reason is not necessarily because I want to fulfill my own desires and inner needs, but because I am really, really burdened for homeless or parentless children. I feel that we have so much that we could give. I know that we could never be perfect parents, but with the Lord's help, I think we could do a pretty good job.

Getting a child has ceased to be an end in itself. This family sees adopting as part of fulfilling Christ's purposes for them.

As clearly stated in Scripture, God's express will *is* to provide for the orphaned:

> But you, O God . . . are the helper of the fatherless.
>
> —Psalm 10:14 (NIV)

> Religion that God our Father accepts as pure and faultless is this: to look after orphans and widows in their distress and to keep oneself from being polluted by the world.   —James 1:27 (NIV)

But because God is the great advocate for the orphan does not mean that each of His childless children should adopt!

Our responsibility before Him is to receive His specific guidance for our lives. On our part we will make the possibility of adoption a matter of prayer, seek spiritual counsel, study the Scriptures which speak to this issue (a concordance can help us locate passages on the fatherless, adoption, the family), read articles and books on the topic, and speak to persons who have adopted. Such a lifelong commitment mustn't be based on the encouragement of well-wishers or our own perceived emotional needs. The Lord is the Head of each of our families and our only dependable Guide. A friend, even though thrilled with her new baby, has had the courage to tell us: "I would rather be in God's will and not have gotten this baby than be out of His will and have the baby."

I have personally spent days in prayer and fasting to prepare my own heart and to be in harmony with my husband while considering certain children whom we might have adopted privately. We have discovered that just as important as knowing whether to pursue adoption is that of receiving peace about *not* adopting. Those of us who reach this latter conclusion, however, can expect to be misunderstood and, at times, criticized. "I can't believe God wouldn't have you be parents" coming from the mouth of someone we love is a strong goad. To avoid being unduly influenced we need a deep assurance that, whether or not we can offer this person a logical rebuttal, our family size is perfectly all right the way it is.

Someone who was probably never encouraged to adopt a baby was a virtually unknown carpenter, Joseph! Precisely because he never intended to be an adoptive parent, he serves as an ideal for many of us. Although Joseph had been chosen to receive as his own child the very Son of God, he himself was unaware that he was especially suited to such a task. God had to reveal to him his unique calling. The consistency of his responses, however, leaves no doubt as to his being the perfect candidate. Let's shadow him, and in so doing see if our profile matches his to a significant degree.

Perusing the passages of Matthew 1:18—2:23 and Luke 2 we discover numerous character-revealing details about Joseph. We first encounter him encapsulated in the most anguishing heartache of his entire life: his fiancée is pregnant and he is not the father of the baby. Since the Word of God informs us that he was a "just" or "righteous" man, we can well imagine his agony of soul. Yet instead of reacting brashly, he was considering the matter at length before attempting to reach a decision. Amazingly, he was weighing the effects of alternate decisions to determine which would be kindest toward Mary!

When the will of God was revealed to him, he unhesitatingly responded in faith. He welcomed his God-given responsibilities and carried them out precisely and sacrificially. He was a man whom the Lord could trust to be disciplined, diligent, and obedient, even to making an international move, with its accompanying cross-cultural adjustments, in the interest of the Christ Child. Joseph's treatment of Mary undoubtedly patterned Christ's own high regard for women which has subsequently influenced social reform throughout the world. What a model of fatherhood! Although Jesus may have been poor, He certainly was not underprivileged; if He lacked material possessions, He did not lack the personal investment of His parents.

Our interest is further challenged upon noting that Joseph gained not only spiritual rewards, but earthly blessings as well. In addition to his adopted son, he had at least six natural children (Matt. 13:55–57; Mark 3:31–33; John 7:5). He might have seconded the statement of a modern father:

> I never could understand why anyone *wouldn't* be able to take and love another's child as his own.
> Adoption is not a second-class option. We have one [child] of each. Both [choices] are preferrable.

Through such transparent examples, we begin to develop a clearer understanding of what constitutes "family." After all, a husband and wife are not related by blood. But they love one another and become the most intimate family unit. Since the Lord is not limited to giving us children which were formed from our own bodies, He can create our individual family in various ways. The couple mentioned above could have only one child. And so, they began to pray for the child gifted to be the sister of their little boy and vice-versa. The foreign baby they adopted has been just such a child.

If you are serious about exploring adoption, the best general advice I can pass on to you is that which has been given to us. Investigate first the medical possibilities of having your own children. (This is often a prerequisite for adoption proceedings.) Then, dedicate yourselves to pursuing the avenues open to you for receiving an adopted child. If, after a reasonable time of prayer and leg work, your efforts seem not to produce the results you desire, begin to consider other ways to invest your life. The final three chapters of this book should give you more specific direction.

Let us assume, however, that you wish to pursue adoption, but don't know where to start. Talk to your pastor. Your denomination may have facilities for the care of unwed mothers and placement of babies. The Junior League or other service organizations in your area may have a list of adoption agencies which you may contact. Some international agencies are listed at the close of this book. Adoption agencies usually have literature available describing their own services and requirements as well as pamphlets from other organizations. Speak to your personal physician. Many states and countries allow doctors to be instrumental in private placements.

Some infertility support groups recommend spreading the word— even in written form—through friends, neighbors, work associates, former classmates, and your local church. Describe yourselves and the kind of child you are desirous of adopting. Someone you least expect may have contact with an unwed mother who has not chosen to go through an agency, but wishes to place her child with a family known and recommended by people she trusts. Whatever avenue you choose, you will need the confidence that your adoption will be legal and will protect the three parties involved: the birth parents, the child, and you as the adoptive parents. If you do not use the legal services of an agency, talking with people who have adopted can help you make contact with a lawyer well-versed in this area of legal practice.

Now, if we were to live in some African states our plight would be greatly simplified. Aware of the pain which family members who lack children suffer, relatives respond by placing their own children on permanent loan to loved ones to complete their families!

But we shouldn't expect that kind of consideration if we live elsewhere. Family and friends, unaware of how hard it presently is to adopt, may not even take our trial seriously. A pastor and wife with an adopted son discovered both the tight adoption market and this prevailing attitude when they ran into difficulty trying to adopt a daughter. One well-meaning parishioner offered them this comfort: "Why don't you get a puppy?"

The pastor's wife commented afterward, "I considered asking the woman if she would take a dog in place of one of their children, but on second thought I was afraid she might take me up on the offer!"

In spite of such occasional times of "levity," this pre-adoption time begins to settle in as an interminably long period of suspended animation. Oh, by all appearances we are engaged in plenty of activity: contacting agencies and individuals, filling out forms, going through interviews and examinations, engaging in a case study. But the next frame to show up on our life's screen—our baby—refused to drop into view. We are living on hope and dreams . . . with not just a little dread that our dear desire will never become reality.

If we have already endured years of waiting for natural children we may reach a moment of final overwhelming frustration. I recall one night following almost 10 years of medical appointments, adoption disappointments, and waiting for a missionary appointment. Very aware that I had to arise at 5:30 the next morning for work, I sat in a cold car outside a country church. My husband, meanwhile, was talking at length with our pastor. When Jerry finally got into the car, my patience was exhausted. For the first time in my life, I screamed at him.

"You're always making me wait!" I cried.

While I continued my outburst, my husband calmly drove on. When at last there was a pause from my side of the bench seat, he assured me that he was sorry he'd made me wait and would be more aware of my feelings in the future.

Suddenly I realized how wound up I had been over an insignificant event. On so many fronts I had been waiting, waiting, waiting. But instead of recognizing the emotional impact of these combined frustrations, I had been living through each new wait as though it were unrelated to the others.

Faced with my ineptitude at handling this overwhelming burden, I found the Lord to be even more gracious than my husband. He began to show me a way to cope with my fresh experiences of waiting. Knowing that in such moments I found it impossible to pray effectively or concentrate on Scripture—since all I could think about was my desire for an immediate end to the waiting—the Lord set my heart at rest. I didn't have to pray; I didn't have to read. Most importantly, I didn't have to *just* wait. I found that I could choose one characteristic of God and think on that. With this primitive form of meditation, I began to invest my waiting time contemplating the patience of God, His mercy, or His loving care toward the people He created—whatever came to my mind at the moment.

The waits still occurred, but when they did I had something specific to do: think on one of the Lord's attributes. A reprocessing was taking place as the Lord set about to defuse my inner TNT. I began almost to appreciate each new wait: "Well, today I have a chance to think about Jesus' practical concern for people." Amazingly, I found myself anticipating the future: "Next time I have to wait, I am going to meditate on God's ability to make even evil serve Him."

Granted, this long preface to our future may at times still appear to resemble punishment more than essential preparation. But we may take comfort reckoning it to be parallel to what parents go through the final weeks of pregnancy—or better yet, overdue days! Let's keep in mind that our wait, well-invested, contributes toward our success in the coming venture of parenting. As we shed stereotypes and gain new insight, we become ever more suitable candidates for a non-typical family life.

For the waiting couple, therefore, this is a time for specific "work" in many areas simultaneously. A family who could have only one natural child shared the part that prayer played in their pilgrimage toward adoption:

> We prayed that we would love our adopted child every bit as much as our natural one. Our own child was special and our given child would be just as special.

Once our decision to adopt is made, those of us who suffer from infertility still have to confront our physical limitation:

> We can't get away from the fact that it's going to bother us to hear of our friends getting pregnant. We can't have a biological child which would be our first choice.

> Four days after we adopted I found out that a nurse friend was expecting for the third time. I said to myself, "That's okay. We're where we are because we're supposed to be here. We're blessed."

In the midst of handling our old feelings on a new level, we begin to receive some special advantages as adopting parents. One benefit is an extended time of personal and family counseling if we go through an agency. Our feelings of isolation begin to recede. We receive support from persons who are in a position to be objective. They help us evaluate whether we could successfully receive another's child as our own. Our confidence is no longer just subjective; it's based on a series of interviews, research data, and the concurrence of others.

This process, a home study, begins by our making a formal application which includes submitting personal and financial information, educational and employment history, medical records, and recommendations. The social worker assigned to us will conduct a series of interviews following a pattern such as this:

1. Why are you here? What has brought you to this point? (After this husband-wife interview, homework is required of each to write a personal and family history for the following session.)

2. Personal family biographies are explored to see the strengths and weaknesses of each one's background. Christian agencies require

details of one's religious beliefs and experiences as well. (Following this joint interview is an assignment for each partner to write a courtship and marriage history.)

3. The husband-wife relationship is examined together.

4. Each partner is interviewed separately and given the freedom to express personal feelings about one's marriage and perspective on adoption.

5. One or more home visits will be arranged. Practical requirements regarding health and safety must be met. Emotional matters which can best be considered in a home setting will be discussed. "Do you really think you can handle an adopted child?

It may seem grueling, but on the other hand, what natural parents have such an opportunity to get to know themselves, each other, and their united goals? As one newly-adopting mother remarked:

> Agencies are pretty protective and jealous of where their children go. The caseworkers ask heavy questions. They make you think how you will react in fifteen years to a high school student. If they choose to place a child with you, they want to be pretty sure of you.

With good cause adopting parents may feel particular stress at any time during the home study. For some, the narrowing-down process to determine the specific child for one's family is extremely disconcerting. One acquaintance expressed a sense of self-incrimination over being unable to receive "just any child." She was unaware that we were never expected to be able to adopt every child, as if we should be thrown together as a family without regard for unique personhood and parenting grace.

We find ourselves facing multitudinous decisions at this stage:

> Does it matter to me what sex my baby is? Do I really want a child of my own race? How much do I need to know about the natural parents? Can I accept a child with a handicap? If so, how severe? How old a child am I willing to take? Do I really want a newborn, or would a six-month-old satisfy my needs?
>
> Am I willing to take what they give me and leave much of the choice to them? Do I want the best? Should I take the "leftovers"?

One couple, upon stating their various preferences to a social worker, was relieved to hear her understanding response:

> Maybe it's God's way of compensating those of you who can't have your own. You can at least have some choices.

As she got up from her desk and walked to the door, the couple noticed that she had a decided limp. The wife said later:

> My heart ached. How many times had she heard a couple say they wouldn't take a handicapped child?

God wants us to be willing. He'll give us far more than we ever expected.

Thus the qualifying process may be anguishingly painful. We may find it difficult at times not to resent natural parents. They have only to engage in a love act to engender their child. We, meanwhile, must submit to intense introspection, the judgment of others, physical examinations, agency stipulations—even the indignity that others have the right to decide whether we would make suitable parents.[2]

We cannot dwell on our circumstances just now; we must concentrate on our Savior. He it is who restores our equilibrium, affirms our worth, and assures our meaningful future. He sees our present and future family life. If He gives us peace about adopting, we must press on! We are performing many acts of love to receive our child. Let's take any disappointment as only a closed door in our search for the door He is opening for us.

The norm is that sooner or later we will make a waiting list. This in itself is cause for celebration! We now have assurance that we will eventually receive the child for which we have been longing. Since each agency has its own procedure for placement, one cannot generalize as to how long the exact matching process will take. Usually our caseworker will be able to give us a fairly accurate estimate—whether a few months or up to five or six years.

Some agencies work on a "lottery-type" system whereby every approved family has a fairly equal chance of adopting each available child. Since one will not necessarily have to wait to receive a baby, everyone remains fresh to the possibility of imminently becoming a parent. The disadvantage, of course, is that newly-approved candidates may receive a child before those who have been waiting a considerable time. Other agencies have a policy of going strictly in order. Prospective parents know where they are on the list and are moving forward.

Let's listen to the feelings and faith of some of our waiting friends:

We believe very simply that God has His timing as to when we will get a baby through adoption.

Luke 18 keeps giving me courage and persistence in asking God to continue to help us through the time of waiting in our adoption proceedings.

We've been waiting for a baby for one and a half years and are first on the waiting list as of now!

In this time immediately before and after placement, adopting families may be required to attend a number of helpful seminars. Topics such as the physical care of the newborn, child development, sex-related matters, and the adopted child's special needs (learning about one's adoption, developing a unique place in the family, searching for genetic history or biological parents) are presented by qualified professionals. These sessions give families the opportunity to ask specific questions now that parenting has already or is to become a reality.

At some point the agency representative can often suggest to the family a time frame for expecting their baby. Adopting parents of newborns, even without meeting the birth mother, are thus able to identify strongly with her experiences in the final days before "their" special baby is born. This period may be a necessary one for some new parents such as one adopting mother who finally received a call from her agency. She spent a tender moment with her husband that evening as she said, "This is the closest I can ever be to telling you I'm pregnant."

And then it happens. The phone rings; the baby is here. Arrangements are made for seeing the child, for taking the baby home. Conversations are as varied as are the persons involved. One woman was confronted with:

> You mentioned that you would be willing to consider twins. A set has just been born; are you still interested?

She and her husband became the happy parents of those twins, and have since had two additional children of their own.

The moment of viewing the child finally arrives. Some agencies arrange for the new parents to be with the child on one or more occasions before making a final decision:

> They ushered us into a room where he was on a changing table and left us alone. They had wrapped him in a fuzzy flannel blanket. His little face was all red and broken out. As we unwrapped him we found out he had a rash everywhere! He was allergic to the blanket.

> We had a choice of three babies (indigenous children in a culture foreign to that of the family). They moved the cribs of the prettiest two closest to us and kept showing them to us, convinced we would want one of those. We chose the ugliest one. She was so homely she was cute. Besides, if we didn't take her, *who would*?

Adopting parents often experience a great rush of emotion during these moments of greeting their baby for the first time:

> I was so full of thanksgiving the day we went down to see our caseworker. I had this sense that I wanted to thank the birth mother. If someone out there hadn't gotten pregnant and decided to give up the baby, we wouldn't be a family.
> I didn't know how the agency deals with their mothers. But the social worker thought that it would be very appropriate for her [the mother] to hear that her decision was an answer to our prayers.

Then, I thought: "I don't want to say what a wonderful baby she is or it might make the mother change her mind and want her baby back!"

I thought and re-thought. I finally wrote *not* a three-page letter but a three-line note to help her close that chapter of her life:

"My husband and I wish God's leading for you in the future with whatever plans you have. I want you to know that with the help of God, our family and our friends, we will do our best to fill your daughter's life with love.

The Adopting Parents"

And then, at last, the child begins its new life with its receiving family.

Adopting parents have an "unknown bundle" in their care. Genetic health problems or tendencies in the child's background may not be known—nor the color of great-grandfather's hair, nor the special talents and abilities of the child's biological relatives. New parents thus exercise great faith that they are the ideal people to foster the growth and development of this unique child.

Parents' initial reactions are unpredictable. Whenever a new baby inhabits a house, a lot of changing can be expected, the least of which is diapers! One new mom comments:

It's quite a switch from being a strong friendship to being a triangle. Books [advising of difficult adjustments] don't always say unrealistic things!

Neither do social workers. They try to orient each new family to the peculiarities of bonding to an adopted child. One such professional wisely counseled: "Don't be alarmed if at times you feel a strong dislike for her being around; 'If you weren't here. . . .' Don't be hard on yourself if you don't feel an instant love and attachment for her." For many parents the process of bonding is an on-going saga. Even what may begin as an apparently easy relationship of affection can be strained as the child becomes capable of talking back or refusing to do what the parents expect. The issue of parent-child bonding is so critical that books and periodicals dedicated to research in this area are now readily available.[3]

Happily for some parents and children there is an immediate love attachment which time serves to strengthen: "Maybe it's because she was such an attractive baby, but we really did love her immediately. We keep saying it: 'Steph, we love you and are glad you are part of our family.'"

Upon adopting, parents must confront feelings not only about the child, but about themselves and their occupations as well. A father is faced with formerly unknown family responsibilities. What kind of new—perhaps unexpected—needs will his wife have? Does his schedule permit the kind of interaction his expanding family demands?

An adopting mother may have given up a professional career or an enjoyable job to raise her new child. Now that she has no contact with the business world, what will substitute to give her a sense of accomplishment? What goals will challenge her? She may well miss her job and the association with her peers, especially if she had very little lead time to become accustomed to the idea of shutting down a satisfying area of life to launch into her less predictable future as Mother.

I've always worked before. Now I have to find my style as a mom. What am I to major in: a career and mothering, mothering, or mothering and a ministry?

I have to keep myself from being a smothering mother. I have to set priorities. Monday nights we work with young people and the child goes to a baby-sitter. I have to teach her flexibility and confidence in others. A child is not "everything" and needs to know it.

A new perspective is added to a family's social and church relationships. The significance of this little life long ago moved beyond the boundaries of two people and invaded the thoughts of those who cared. An adoption becomes an audio-visual aid, aptly conveying truth to those close at hand. As one new parent describes it:

I have probably had a special conversation with every member in the church. We have shared with different ones at different stages—and everyone at one time or another has ministered to us and may never know it!

When we adopted it was as if the whole church were adopting her, too. Maybe it's better that this adopted baby came after the end of a baby boom in the church so that the other babies wouldn't be underplayed!

It was an opportunity for the whole church to comprehend the concept of adoption. It may have caused some people on the edge of the Christian life to think about adoption. It gave people a chance to take another look at how we all got into the family of God.

And don't we need some firsthand experience with adoption to comprehend the great spiritual parallels God draws to this vital, living relationship? Perhaps one of the main reasons that God allows some of us to go through the agonizing process of personal loss leading up to the receiving of another as our very own is to model himself to the world, to the church. We who adopt are living out a great parable:

. . . ye have received the Spirit of adoption, whereby we cry, Abba, Father. The Spirit itself beareth witness with our spirit, that we are the children of God: and if children, then heirs; heirs of God, and joint-heirs with Christ. . . .   —Romans 8:15b-17 (KJV)

Adoption depicts God's expression of Fatherhood as clearly as it does our experience of spiritual identity and bonding to Him.

The entire process of adoption, from the legal aspects to its significance and duration, is alive with marvelous spiritual symbolism (Eph. 1:2–14). Think about this the next time you find yourself waiting!

Finally, within six months to two years—depending on the laws of your nation or state—the legalities of your child's adoption will be completed. According to the birth records this child was born to you. From this point on all financial responsibilities for the child, including insurance and health care, rest with you, the new family.

Adopting parents may have the right to learn the name of the birth parent(s) at this time if they should so desire. Some new parents find this a difficult decision to make. One couple decided to place the mother's name in a sealed envelope left in trust with the lawyer at court. If the child later asks for the information either parent is prepared to respond: "I don't know myself, but I can tell you where you can find out."

If their daughter wishes to search out her natural family, the parents will uphold her and accompany her through the process, thus affirming their love and enfolding her in their security as she pursues an otherwise lonely and scary undertaking.

During the present period of legal indefinition on the issue, information about one's biological parents remains difficult or impossible to obtain. Courts, agencies, and lawyers are careful not to violate confidences or the legal rights of birth parents to retain their anonymity.

But such knowledge, if obtained, needn't threaten the adoptive parents. Even ancient Moses knew his roots and "looked up" his birth family. Modern adoptive families are usually equally open with their children and let them know early, "As far as I'm concerned, you can talk about anything you'd like to talk about—anything that's important to you."

Understandably, an individual who is adopted has specific issues to settle. Never knowing one's blood relatives and not belonging to the physical family tree of one's adopted family may create a longing within to discover one's biological heritage, particularly if the adopted person is very different from the adopting family. Some cases of hereditary disease or a medical problem (for example, one which requries that a close relative be an organ donor) may even make a search for one's biological family a necessity.

Curiosity as to why natural parents would place one for adoption may surface. Adopting parents can foster positive impressions of the natural parents' real and sacrificial love for their child. The birth mother didn't reject her child. Abortion would have been rejection; birth and placing of her baby in the hands of a loving family when it was beyond her control to provide adequately indicates great personal maturity and sensitivity to the needs of her child.

Sometimes it won't be the adopted child who will need parental consideration, but the natural child or children of a family. A friend, the only physical offspring of her parents, admits having been plagued as a child with the horrible thought: "My parents can't have any more babies. It had to be something I did in my mommy's tummy." But she was never able to communicate that with her mother and thus lived for years with unresolved "guilt." Others will want to know where they stand in their parents' affection if a new baby is adopted. Brothers and sisters are important persons in the adoption affair, and some agencies even prefer to place their adoptable children in homes with other children rather than with childless persons.

Whether they have siblings or not, children who have been told positively of their adoption early on have a great lifetime opportunity to grow in the appreciation of their being "chosen children." Baby books and picture albums with "their story" of how they came into a family who needed and loved them may be favorite pieces of literature from their tenderest years. Experiences which they will have with other adopted children will increase their understanding, too. A minister's wife mentioned that two adopted girls in their congregation have become close friends. When another couple in the church adopted a baby the two of them rushed up to see the newborn and have taken a special interest in her ever since. One of the girls has commented: "That's how it was for my mommy and daddy when they were young."

Such identification with parental feelings facilitates communication at the next stage of growth: adolescence.

All teenagers can be expected to confront the "Who am I?" question. But it can hit adopted teens particularly hard. They may feel justified in charging that their parents don't really understand them. Some will become expert at wielding their particular weaponry against one or both parents: "If you really loved me you would . . ." or "You're harder on me because I'm adopted." The temptation for parents is to become wounded by such attacks and, further, to try to compensate for the child's "loss" or placate one's own feelings of false guilt by giving in.

Obviously, these overreactions give immediate victory to the teenager, increasing his or her prowess in manipulative strategy for the future. At such a time your teen's security will be strengthened by two factors: your own inner security in not retaliating or surrendering because of such verbal attack and your continued consistency in following a wise course of action in the treatment and discipline of your teenager. Juvenile delinquency doesn't thrive in homes where mom and dad, in agreement, clearly demonstrate both love and limits.

We may, of course, anticipate the same general problems with adopted children that would be true of natural children. But with adoption there is a further matter which must be faced: what of the rare case in which bonding never occurs and the adoption doesn't "take"?

I met an acquaintance at a social event one evening and commented on her new white teeth brace. "I have to wear this now as I almost ruined my teeth. I've been under such pressure for the last two years that I've been grinding my teeth down."

To my inquiry as to what had caused her such anguish she shared her recent experience. Unable to have more children after their little boy was born, they decided to adopt an older child. A nine-year-old, from all appearances a sweet girl, was placed with them. It wasn't until after the adoption was finalized that the child's serious emotional disorder surfaced: she was diagnosed as having a split personality.

The parents could never anticipate how she was going to react. Even a simple expectation—for instance that the child go to her room upon misbehaving—could trigger uncontrollable rage and violence. Only later during psychological treatment was the truth uncovered that, as a young child, upon being sent to her room she would be subsequently molested by her father.

Despite the loving efforts of the adopting family, the girl blatantly announced that she planned to destroy them to get back to her foster parents. One day in the presence of the little brother she took a butcher knife and tried to kill the mother. At this point the parents determined that they could not risk their safety and emotional stability for the sake of the child and returned her to the custody of the state.

The adopting mother reflects:

> We still feel we were led to adopt her. The Lord only knows why. In her good times she would tell us how she wanted to go all around the world and tell people about Jesus. I pray for her constantly. Legally she bears our name and we will continue to support her until she's an adult.

Her picture is on the bookcase along with their son's, and the two of them appear in photo albums and the little boy's baby book. The family writes to her. But perhaps their main ministry to the child will be that of intercessory prayer.

As in natural parenting, there are pitfalls and can be heartache on all sides in the adoption venture. That should only point us to the necessity for making our decision with eyes wide open, in sincerity seeking God's will and then, trusting Him with the consequences. We need the full security that we are the ones who should be caretakers of the child(ren) we adopt. Otherwise, we are later open to deep questions and doubts. Adoption is for life—to last however long that may be and to bring full life to the child and the parents.

Beyond the immediacy of this parent-child relationship, however, the greater family, the community, and the child's future must be considered. In a sense everyone in the child's environment will be involved in the adoption process—receiving and incorporating this child into the larger circle of interrelationships.

Presently international adoption is often the easiest—and perhaps the only—door to open for those of us seeking a child. Interracial placement is also a very real possibility for many families as is the receiving of an older or handicapped child. Singles are often able to qualify more readily for certain of these children than for newborns.

In each of these cases, however, our own desire and ability to accommodate such a child is only part of the picture. As prospective parents we must determine how well the child is likely to be absorbed into the family and social setting. If our own relatives or community have strong prejudicial feelings, will a child of another race be accepted and welcomed? If not, is a tight circle of parental love sufficient? Are there medical facilities and educational programs available in our community for children with special needs? Do I as a single adopting parent have the support of persons who can provide role models, care, and family-type experiences for the child I am considering?

Of course, the major factors are personal. What is the state of my health and stamina? Over the years, have I shown an interest in encouraging young children? Have I felt a certain attraction to persons different from myself? Do I enjoy cross-cultural relationships on an adult level? Do I feel fulfilled providing physical care for family members? What are my normal reactions when people, even strangers, shy away from me or criticize me? Do I receive more satisfaction in my relationships with many people on a number of levels, or do I prefer to concentrate my time and energy on one or more specific individuals? Are my mate (or family) and I in agreement over the basic issues of this particular adoption?

Such an evaluation may make it clear that we have both a nonjudgmental character and special capacity to nurture others. If so, we are the very ones who *should* make ourselves available to children who need our kind of parenting.

Not that such a task for anyone is easy. Just ask a single mom who adopted two older children with physical problems. After a year of coping with operations and adjustments, she assures us: "It's not perfect, but it's sure a lot better than being alone!" The children echo her sentiments.

Every family *is* unique in God's economy, and He forms each one with particular care according to His own design and purposes. Those of us who have adopted can look back over the circumstances and admit to the individualized way that the pathway to adoption opened up:

We got ours the easy way. We adopted.

Everyone said that it was impossible. But we have adopted four children.

We were serving with the Peace Corps in a Third World country. When we went in to see about adoption, they thought we were trying to get a cheap maid! We finally convinced them of our sincerity by pointing out that if we had wanted a maid, wouldn't we be trying to get a child instead of a fifteen-month old baby?

Maybe what we needed was to get our feet wet (by adopting a newborn of the same race). Perhaps now we can cope with an international child. Sometimes I smile at myself and wonder just where we're headed.

The same kind of excitement was probably felt by our model adoptive parent, Joseph. Not only did he face taking in an unexpected child, but he entered into the most monumental parenting task of all. His child was conceived by the Holy Spirit. His name would be called "Immanuel," which means "God with us." Who could possibly meet the special needs of this amazing Son of God? How could an ordinary man, not wealthy or highly educated, think to be able to succeed in such a venture?

Simple: he was called to this ministry by the God who created him. He did not presume to be capable, just obedient.

Likewise, all adopted children have a great pattern, too. Perhaps they may never be able to feel a kinship to Joseph as we do, but for their example they can certainly look to his adopted son: JESUS.

*"After this, Paul left Athens and went to Corinth.
There he met a Jew named Aquila, a native of Pontus,
who had recently come from Italy with his wife Priscilla,
because Claudius had ordered all the Jews to leave Rome.
Paul went to see them, and because he was a tentmaker as they
were, he stayed and worked with them.
Every Sabbath he reasoned in the synagogue,
trying to persuade Jews and Greeks.*

*"Paul stayed on in Corinth for some time.
Then he left the brothers and sailed for Syria,
accompanied by Priscilla and Aquila."*

—Acts 18:1–4, 18a (NIV)

CHAPTER THIRTEEN

The Priscilla-Aquila Approach

If ever there was an amazing story of love and labor it was this one. Having arrived in Rome from Pontus, more than one thousand miles to the East, Aquila found himself at the hub of the world. There not only did he practice his trade and religion, but he met his mate. Even their names blended smoothly together: Priscilla and Aquila. Priscilla must have been quite a prize for a tentmaker from Asia Minor. Inscriptions on the walls of the catacombs in her native city indicate that she was an accomplished woman, the daughter of a highly-distinguished family in Rome.[1]

Following this couple through the New Testament, it is remarkable that they are never mentioned apart from each other. So well-matched are they that Priscilla's name appears before her husband's in four out of the six times they are mentioned in Scripture.[2] Truly, they were a pair equally yoked together.

Tents were their stock in trade. When they were forced to leave Rome because of a decree against the Jews by the Emperor Claudius in A.D. 49, it was only natural that they should move east to reestablish their business.[3] To have returned to Pontus would have taken them away from the vigor of East-West trade opportunities and far from the large city environment to which Priscilla was accustomed. They selected Corinth, Greece's major commercial center, an attractive, recently-constructed city which even had cold-water plumbing for the shops in its main market place.[4] Paul evidently arrived in that progressive metropolis about a year later.[5]

Being Jewish tentmakers, they struck up a friendship and made a business arrangement whereby Paul would both live and work with them. One need only imagine the hours they spent in close fellowship to envision the personal one-on-two discipling process which was going

on between Paul and his newfound friends. Each Sabbath the Apostle
made it a practice of publicly reasoning and persuading both Jews and
Greeks in the synagogue, Priscilla and Aquila's place of worship. The
couple observed him closely on a daily basis and in his public ministry
when, on occasion, he was powerfully moved by the Spirit.[6] Quite naturally, Priscilla and Aquila became spiritually the two best-prepared
believers of the Jewish community.

And then it happened: Paul's ministry to the Jews in that city
ended—abruptly. He announced one day to the Jewish congregation,
many of whom had set themselves against him and had blasphemed
the Lord, that he would no longer minister to them. He would dedicate
himself to the Corinthian Gentiles. Proceeding to do so, he left his
Jewish acquaintances that very day and moved in with a Gentile be-
liever, Justus, who lived next door to the synagogue.[7]

There stood Priscilla and Aquila, among their Jewish contempor-
aries. In one instant they had lost their star boarder and their private
religious tutor. In addition, they seem to have inherited his former
parish, being the best-schooled of all in the Christian faith. By then
even some of the rulers in the synagogue believed in Jesus, but it is
unlikely that they would have availed themselves of Paul's teaching
as he worked with the Gentiles. More probably, they turned to Aquila
and Priscilla as their spiritual mentors. Paul, remember, was not a
pastor of a congregation: he was a missionary. His job was to plant
churches—working and praying until people were convinced and converted. Then he would turn that newly-created flock over to a pastor
so that he could repeat the process elsewhere. In this case he unhesitatingly let the staff fall into two pair of able hands.

After a time, Paul at last departed from the city, sailing for Syria.
But he did not leave as he had come: alone. This time he invited
Priscilla and Aquila to accompany him. It must have seemed to them
quite an adventure to set off with the Apostle Paul! Their first stop
was Ephesus. Upon arrival, however, they were treated as brusquely
as before. Paul left them in Ephesus and continued on.[8]

It appears that Paul was delegating authority and that Aquila and
Priscilla were a pastoral team seeking a new parish. The Apostle had
succeeded in training his friends, only to uproot them and transfer
them to a strange city, Ephesus. There they would care for the nucleus
of a small church and continue as development pastors. Aquila and
Priscilla were once again filling the place left by their discipler.

Then, one day, their turn came to repeat the process which they
had experienced originally with Paul. A well-bred Jew, Apollos, arrived in Ephesus from the culturally-advanced city of Alexandria. He
was an eloquent man, gifted to proclaim the Scriptures and instructed

in the way of the Lord through the baptism of John. He spoke boldly the things of God in the synagogue, courageously imparting the spiritual instruction he had received.

Priscilla and Aquila, however, discerned one missing element as the man preached: he did not yet know Jesus. He hadn't heard the full story. Aha! The former discipleship roles were to be reversed: here was one sincere Jew with two apt teachers. They recalled how Paul had worked with them. Instead of confronting him publicly, they drew him aside privately, and on that occasion Scripture mentions Priscilla first as though she may have taken the initiative.[9] Very conceivably they invited him into their home for a time. And in that intimate company, they expounded to him in detail the whole truth about the Savior.

It must have been all delight to them to function as a perfectly meshed team to help this special servant of the Lord discover his particular lacking pieces so that he could finish assembling his spiritual puzzle. Paul's personal relationship with them and the principles of discipleship he had taught them—train, trust God, and turn loose— had paid high dividends.

When Apollos emerged from their careful instruction, he was a dynamo for God. The congregation wrote a letter of recommendation for him so that he could travel to the young Corinthian church to help foster their spiritual growth and refute those of the opposition. By vouching for his credentials Priscilla and Aquila opened the way for a new messenger of the Gospel to be accepted by and begin ministering to their former flock. Not only did they form a pastoral team themselves, but they were able to prepare a pastor in the Way and the way before the pastor.

We next see them through a view from one of Paul's letters written from Ephesus to those believers in Corinth who had by then prospered spiritually under Apollos.[10]

> The churches in the province of Asia send you greetings. Aquila and Priscilla greet you warmly in the Lord, and so does the church that meets in their house.   —1 Corinthians 16:19 (NIV)

They had successfully planted a church in their house. If that were all that we knew of this amazing couple, it would be more than enough to evoke our admiration. But we have more.

Paul writes of them again, not so long afterward, but this time, surprise of surprises, they are no longer in Ephesus! They are now in Rome:

> Greet Priscilla and Aquila my helpers in Christ Jesus: who have for my life laid down their necks: unto whom not only I give thanks, but also all the churches of the Gentiles. Likewise greet the church that is in their house.   —Romans 16:3–5 (KJV)

Paul had never been to Rome to visit the believers or preach the Gospel.[11] This time his former disciples, Priscilla and Aquila, have forged ahead of him. And what's more, they have another church meeting in their home. This is their third congregation!

Imagine: they returned to Rome from which they had formerly been forced to flee. Paul spoke of them as his co-workers, his equals, who cooperated with him in spreading the Good News of Christ. We don't know when or how, but at some time they had both put their lives in jeopardy for Paul. Whatever that service, the testimony of their courageous ministry and willingness to suffer for Christ Jesus and His servants had reached the churches Paul had founded. The Apostle, mentioning Priscilla first, gives the couple the greatest possible praise and commendation. Paul's former pupils had become an example to the teacher himself.

We come to Paul's final written word in which he is giving Timothy his last advice and encouragement. This young preacher must take up the baton from Paul and lead forth the church at Ephesus. Paul is about to be martyred. Times are extreme; Christians are being handed over to evil men and their schemes. All of Paul's companions, with the exception of his personal physician, Luke, have abandoned him.

Paul's final postscript begins: "Greet Prisca and Aquila, and the household of Onesiphorus" (2 Tim. 4:19).

There they are again, approximately twenty years after their first meeting with Paul.[12] This time it is Paul who is in Rome and they have once again relocated in Ephesus! Paul cannot be with young Timothy, but this faithful couple can be. They know how to encourage, how to remain faithful in adversity, and how to help God's work and His workers prosper. They will stand beside Timothy in his ministry and insure that his youth and lack of experience do not hinder his service for Christ.

How appropriate that Aquila's name means *eagle*; even his training had been like that of an eaglet. Closely protected while young, the eaglet at last must soar into the very heavens, seemingly alone, while the wings of its airborne parent remain securely below. Aquila's lifetime flight for God was noble indeed.

Luke, speaking of Priscilla in the Book of Acts, uses the familiar, diminutive form of her name, Priscilla. But Paul in his epistles refers to Aquila's lady as Prisca, choosing the most formal, respectful usage, meaning an elder or older woman.[13] She and her husband have reached their senior years. They have moved through life agreed with each other and with the purposes of God. Probably no couple in the New Testament has had a more fulfilling ministry together in service to others.

Perhaps you noticed that nowhere is it suggested that Aquila and Priscilla had a family of their own. It is doubtful that Paul would have invited them on his missionary journey if they had had children to care for. Of course, their family could already have been grown and independent. Yet it is unlikely in the culture of that day that they would have separated themselves even from grown children.

Perhaps there is a further clue in Paul's final postscript in which he greeted them and "the household of Onesiphorus" (2 Tim. 4:19). Why, if through the years Priscilla and Aquila had had children of their own, would Paul never have greeted their whole household?

The simplest answer is probably the correct one: Priscilla and Aquila were childless. They had only each other and a continually changing "house." But what a house it was, always being filled anew with people. Their gift of hospitality turned visitors into spiritual children.

Tentmakers by trade, no doubt their home was simple. Priscilla, who may have sampled the best of Roman cuisine in her home as a young woman, was very possibly an excellent cook. Conversation at their house was stimulating, knowledgeable, and full of hope for the future. They were thinkers and doers. Neighbors were attracted to this couple whose religion gave them joy in undertaking even difficult or dangerous tasks for others.

Priscilla and Aquila had a beautiful old-shoe quality about them. They were equally at ease with older, mature people like Paul, those in the full of life such as Apollos, and young people like Timothy. Likewise they had the energy and vision to devote themselves whole-heartedly to loving and serving entire churches. This, then, is a biblical example of a childless couple whose lifetime ministry is intricately linked to what could have been their greatest personal devastation. Together they were nurturers, not of their own flesh and blood, but of recent converts and new ministers.

Sit back with me a moment and contemplate that couple. There is something about them personally, their marriage, and their ministry, that fairly shouts: *contemporary!* We do not have a single recorded word of their conversation or teaching, and yet, we know them very intimately because of the life they lived. Does that shared life speak to you, showing its kinship to your own circumstance? Do you feel at home with the lifestyle and interdependent ministry of Aquila and Priscilla?

As you think of your own marriage relationship, would you say that you enjoy being almost constantly together, finding each other's company ever-satisfying? Does agreeing about minor and major areas of life come easily? Do you both feel comfortable listening and ministering to people's spiritual needs? Does it seem more natural to minister together than separately? Do people seek you out more readily as a couple than singly? Can you rejoice when the other gets credit or public recognition? If so, the possibility that this is your kind of ministry could catch hold of your imagination and serve as an insight into who you and your mate really are in the Body of Christ.

When I unemotionally consider the potential which being a couple represents, I realize that the Lord has given us perhaps the strongest of all life positions in which to serve Him. Since we are a family, we thus have the support of each other and a home base from which to reach out to anyone: families, couples, young people, and children. Single men and women often identify more readily with a couple than with friends who are also mother and father to children. In many ways couplehood is very little removed from singleness and the two lifestyles share many common bonds.

Realistically, then, the only obstacle to my taking advantage of what may be the finest opportunity for ministry which exists is: *me*. My attitudes and selfishness alone could stand in the way of experiencing a satisfying life of service to others. Selfishness surfaces in such thoughts: "But I don't want to reach out to other people's kids. I want my own!" "If I get involved with *that* family, Lord, there will never be any end to it." "A weekly commitment of working with this group would mean never having Friday night to myself." "We're free, and so, why tie ourselves down?" Are you as intimately acquainted with those inner protests as I am?

Family freedom: we have it whether we wanted it or not. And now, well, now that we enjoy its benefits we find ourselves not so eager to surrender some of it—perhaps not any of it! Ah, yes, we are waging our second big spiritual battle. First we rejected being childless, but now we protect and embrace our freedom as if it were our dearest treasure.

After all, we are at liberty to live as we wish. There is no thought of having to provide college educations for our children or an inheritance for our posterity. There are no personal commitments to P.T.A., Boy Scouts, the local swim team, Little League, or the church young people. Our life is adult; our schedules need only be communicated one to the other.

At this juncture we can easily become self-directed and, even more dangerous, unconcerned about others. With great intensity we may pursue further education, secular careers, or our businesses. Each of us may separately become so deeply involved in our own life that we scarcely think and react as a couple anymore. Quite literally, *we may spend* our freedom.

Over and against such a pattern, Aquila and Priscilla's approach to life stands out as a color television alongside a black and white set. They led a secular life with its business as usual. But at the same time they lived and shared an abundant community life and engaged in God's business which was most *un*usual. Ministering as a couple seemed to come naturally, but while doing so they were blessed quite supernaturally.

Today's opportunities are even greater. Childless couples are needed everywhere, in every church. They are ideal "on-call" people who can go in an emergency to visit a family, pick someone up, spend time at a hospital or lend their supportive presence at the police station. Their home can be spontaneously available for invited (or unexpected) guests, temporary living quarters for someone in transition, a place where people can go for privacy, or perhaps, to retreat. Theirs can truly be an "open invitation" to others with no concern about conflicts of "family" versus "visitors." All have equal status with them.

If we honestly evaluate the possibilities open to unencumbered couples, we realize that there is almost no end to opportunity. There are relatively few things which we cannot do because we do not have our own children. But there are many things we are *free* to do for the very same reason. Have we ceased viewing our childless state as a curse and begun to open up to its blessings? Further, and almost more revealing, are we hoarding or investing the gift of time which accompanies the childfree life?

The mobility of ministry is a very separate factor. Had Priscilla and Aquila been directed to stay in Corinth where Paul had originally encountered them, they could have remained in the work there indefinitely. We do not have to go somewhere else in order to minister effectively; we may do so wherever we are. If God is leading you to launch out, you will sense it and He will confirm it. He knows how to put a restless uneasiness, accompanied by a vision for service, into the heart of His children. You will then clearly recognize His inner prompting, "You must follow me regardless of what others are doing."[14] If He truly is calling you, at some point others in the Body of Christ will concur.

For years my husband and I lived with two great inner frustrations: not having the family we so desired and not being able to complete the missionary call we had received as teenagers. Neither longing would leave us and yet we were powerless in ourselves to fulfill either. Time passed and more distant became our hopes of parenthood or missionary service. Our medical study and all the careful measures we had taken proved fruitless. Likewise, our mission plans with a beloved denomination were aborted when we mutually came to the realization that our need for Christian freedom was greater than that particular group could afford us.

We spent these years serving a little community church as laymen. As one childless woman recently remarked, succinctly telling our story as well, "Our life has been characterized by two words: *wait* and *hope*." The age limit of thirty-five was drawing steadily nearer. Almost no missionary society will consider new candidates beyond that age because of the adjustment and language difficulties involved. So it is with many adoption agencies who will likewise no longer process applicants. In contrast to any outward evidence that God answers prayer, we had only His inner, personal assurance that He knew exactly who we were and what He was doing. We were forced to lean on His vision and provision.

As if by accident we at last came in contact with a short-term missionary training group, made up largely of young people, with whom we felt an immediate kinship. Although we were in our thirties, they agreed to let us serve full time with them on one condition: that we rid ourselves of all our material possessions except the luggage permitted on international flights. What a step! By then we had a four-bedroom home, several vehicles, and a gasoline station. Even though the timing seemed inappropriate to us, we made the decision one Friday to turn loose of everything and trust God to work out the details. Four days later two thieves broke into the station, robbed it, and burned it down. Thereafter everything else was rapidly sold or parcelled out.

Even at that there was only one reason why they accepted us: *WE DID NOT HAVE CHILDREN.*

Unbeknown to us throughout the whole frustrating experience of heartache, medical studies, and feelings of great spiritual darkness, our God foresaw that what was a closed door naturally was to be our open door spiritually. When we at last understood that, our life finally made sense to us. It was like passing from the basement of our experience to the ground level in the life plan that God had designed. We moved to the second story when, while serving as short-term volunteers in the country of our choice, we met the group with whom we would eventually serve on a career basis.

After returning briefly to the United States for orientation and processing as missionary candidates, when we finally entered our adopted country on career status, Jerry was four months short of being thirty-five years old! And our first year with our new mission board was the last year in which our former denomination had missionary representation in that country. They nationalized all of their churches and sent their missionaries home. Had we been with them, our ministry would have been finished. But with the new group it had just begun. Our Lord had been faithful in every detail to lead us. At last we understood that God works even in the darkness.

Be assured that your deepest night is His greatest opportunity as well. The basic biblical principle for what you should do with your life if you do not experience any special guidance is to continue right where you are, and expect Him to open doors for you there.[15]

If, however, the Lord's plans for you include permanent temporariness, I wish to help alleviate your doubts as to whether you could be satisfied in a life so seemingly unstable. God does not call adventure-seekers to go and do something for Him. He works with people who seek Him and allow Him to do something for and through them. Along with a call to a mobile ministry comes a very special kind of grace which allows us to be content each moment knowing only that we are where God has led us, doing what He has asked us to do.[16]

In different segments of missionary life we have found ourselves living out of a van or truck, in churches, servants' quarters, open fields, mission housing, rented apartments, or nice homes. Every experience has been a good one. We have often commented to each other, even when sleeping out under the stars in a foreign country, "Don't you think we should feel insecure? We don't know where we'll be tomorrow; we don't own anything. Yet I feel really peaceful, don't you?" It was, indeed, a surprise to discover that just being in the center of God's will is *home*.

Evangelists, conference speakers, missionaries and others in traveling ministries find it very complicated meeting the demands of such work and doing justice to their children. Think of all they must provide for each child, especially those living an international life, just to instill within each one a sense of roots and personal security. It is encouraging that in spite of these handicaps many families have done an exceptionally fine job—so much so that a high percentage of their children select the same career as their parents and frequently return to the identical field of service.

Depending upon the kind of ministry and its location, however, some sending organizations discourage or even exclude families with children. It's a great hardship on the family when children must attend boarding school for nine months out of the year while the parents serve in remote areas where communication even in the event of emergency is impossible. The childless couple in the same setting, however, can work with undivided attention, focusing entirely on the tasks at hand. Since many ministries are simply not practicable or appropriate for children, there are, indeed, some doors of lifetime opportunity which are clearly marked: "Singles" or "Couples Only."

What a glad relief came to my own heart to realize that I had been patterning my longing for life after the wrong model. For years everyone tried to encourage us in the same unproductive direction, commenting: "You would be such great parents." "Remember Sarah. Don't ever give up hope." "Why don't you adopt?" There never were any adequate answers.

I now realize that those of us who are childfree do not have to become Abrahams and Sarahs. There are Pauls, Johns, and Annas; Mary-Martha-and-Lazaruses; and there are Priscillas and Aquilas in God's ample and varied pattern book. Find what fits you, even if it is a new creation that has never been seen before, and wear that life and ministry comfortably. Then you will find matrimonial fulfillment and/or self-realization based on what suits you. You are a very specially created child of God who should never be spiritually draped in someone else's hand-me-downs.[17]

The heavenly Father has a way of setting us free within our limitations. Your options and mine may not be as boundless as we have previously thought, but neither are they as narrow as we may have imagined. Hold up before the Light the Aquila-Priscilla approach to life. If it looks as though it just might fit, try it on for size. Perhaps it was tailor-made for you. If so, it will wear well, and you may be sure it will last a lifetime.

Seeing couples ministering in unity with their distinct combinations of spiritual gifts could cause people around the world to echo Paul's personal comment about that original team:

> Not only I but all of the churches of the Gentiles are grateful to them.　　　　　　　　　　　　　　　　—Romans 16:4b (NIV)

"Am I not free? Am I not an apostle?
Have I not seen Jesus our Lord?
Are you not the result of my work in the Lord?
This is my defense to those who sit in judgment on me.
Don't we have the right to food and drink?
Don't we have the right to take a believing wife along with us,
as do the other apostles
and the Lord's brothers
and Cephas?"

—1 Corinthians 9:1, 3–5 (NIV)

CHAPTER FOURTEEN

Me . . . a Minister?

Let's face it, the Apostle Paul's missionary life would have eliminated him as a candidate for the Ideal First-Century Father.[1] As an apostle he excelled; as a family man he would have tallied up his fourth shipwreck. Being the pattern for an apostle to the Gentiles, Paul deserves our admiration for recognizing the advisability of choosing the single life. Clearly, he had a right to marry and take his family with him on his missionary journeys. He undoubtedly made a wiser selection: Dr. Luke.

None of us will ever receive a duplicate of Paul's call—or Luke's, for that matter! But we are as much an individual as either of them, with circumstances and abilities just as distinct. We may find ourselves surrounded, as Paul, by peers who come complete with family. But *we* are not *they*. Members in Christ's body serve complementary, not identical, functions. The only ideal we as individuals or a couple have is that which Christ gives us: His example of being obedient in His circumstances.

Even before the birth of Christ, though, countless childless people lived lives of faith without ever understanding why they were being singled—or "coupled"—out. For instance, what more ideal people to parent a sizable family could there have been than Zechariah and Elizabeth? The Scripture declares that they were righteous, upright people in the sight of God, continually pleasing Him. And yet, their childbearing years passed by without their ever having the thrill of becoming life-givers.[2]

How frequently they must have requested just such a blessing—so much so that it evidently became *the* prayer of their lives. When the angel Gabriel appeared to Zechariah he said, "*Your* prayer is heard, and *your* wife Elizabeth will bear *you* a son, and *you* shall call his name John" (Luke 1:13b, RSV, italics mine).

Elizabeth's reaction shows how personally significant this answer was: "Thus the Lord has done to *me* in the days when he looked on *me*, to take away *my* reproach among men" (Luke 1:25, RSV, italics mine). God indeed responded to their specific petition. He gave them a special mission in their old age: the rearing of John the Baptist.

But what about each of the rest of God's childless followers—the thousands of other *me's*? Only one John the Baptist was necessary. Your answer and mine is not going to be identical to Zechariah's and Elizabeth's. But does this mean that the Lord does not hear our prayer? Has the Lord done nothing for *us* in response to our faith?

Perhaps we've fixed our attention in the wrong direction. What are we *really* seeking? Is it God's eternal plan? Or, our own paternal-maternal one? If we are unhappy in our child-free life, could it be partly because we haven't discovered—or even desired to discover— what we have been set free to be and to do?

Maybe we are waiting to be let in on the surprise! Perhaps its even difficult to believe that God could have a unique ministry for us apart from parenting. Lacking Sherlock Holmes' insight to make an almost immediate deduction of what our contribution can be, we may need to plod along like a Dr. Watson and note the obvious. Teamed up with the world's greatest Sleuth, we will undoubtedly track down the truth about ourselves.

Our first clues appear as we take the glass of self-scrutiny and focus on what lies buried, inherent within us. What interests us? In what do we excel? My own evaluation would reveal that I feel most content and fulfilled while engaged in:

—listening
—creative caring
—teaching (certain methods, materials, and persons)
—writing
—encouraging
—public speaking.

Make your own list. Now is the time to be honest, not humble.[3]

You might ferret out your nonstrengths, as well. I would have to name:

—business and sales aptitude
—mechanical ability
—physical or medical care-giving
—bookkeeping
—youth work.

The more such information we can trace down the less baffling will be our personal puzzle of who we are and what we should be doing.

Our most challenging detective work may be to discover the supernormal gifts and ministries placed within us by our Creator. Many ministries open up to people almost automatically because their natural and supernatural abilities are virtually inseparable. For instance, someone with an exceptional mechanical and electronic bent may come alive while working with the sound-system or cassette-tape ministry of a local church. A gregarious person may constantly be making new contacts who are drawn not only to the individual, but to the Person whom he or she represents. Others have musical talent which the Lord uses to wake up people's spirits to that which is more real than words or sounds.

Every one of us has received something from our heavenly Father to benefit others and glorify Him.[4] You and I are probably already aware of some of God's spiritual investments in our lives which allow us to make eternal contributions to others. By receiving direct teaching, attending a spiritual gifts seminar, or finding titles on this topic at our local Christian bookstore or church library, we may more precisely identify and see a practical application for our God-given graces. Our pastor or perceptive friends may also unravel deciding clues by observing what may escape our own notice or affirming what we feel could be our specific gifts and their application in our unique setting.

However, when all the evidence is finally in, every eye turns to us. We turn out to be the deciding factor in solving our mystery! Only by actually using our spiritual gifts—teaching, administration, evangelism, or helps, to mention just a few—will we at last track down our elusive ministry.

But why should we bother? What benefit is it to us to divert our love gifts to others when we, ourselves, stand to gain nothing? After all, our dream of pouring ourselves into our own flesh and blood has died.

For that very reason we are the ones who can most appreciate life and what it means. A housewife who lost her thirteen-year-old son in a horseback-riding accident discloses the powerful potential of a transformed tragedy:

> Always before when young people came to the house, I would greet them and then go about my business: washing dishes, cooking, cleaning up the kitchen.
> Now, when a teenager comes to our door, I drop what I'm doing to spend time with him. I realize just how valuable every young person is.
> Since Martín died, the teenagers seem to want to come to our house and be with us. Our home has practically become a teen center.

Their personal sorrow has had such a profound effect on their lives that the husband has recently been appointed by his church board as the deacon in charge of visitation. He gives every weekday afternoon to his ministry.

We, the childless, are specially prepared people.

Our task is only too evident. Perhaps that's the problem: it seems almost overwhelming to us. A pastor's wife shares with us her perspective:

> Maybe it's just a rationalization, but with billions of people—more than ever before in history—there is more need for childless people.
>
> We are free to serve.
>
> Can't we see that that's part of God's plan for reaching the bulging population worldwide? We're more necessary than ever before!

Are we not members of the Body, the bride of Christ? Did it ever flicker through our minds that perhaps we were meant to be among those who form the womb of the church? We don't have to be adept at producing physical children to participate in bringing to birth new babes in Christ. Perhaps we are the bosom of the church patiently nurturing those who are too weak and inexperienced to fend for themselves. Our task may be to wean the dependent, gently forcing them to seek that which is solid, to become ever more mature.

These ministries—beyond bringing us satisfaction—result in changing lives, strengthening the church, and producing everlasting rewards.

The Bible presents an unmistakable pattern of positive action in the face of childlessness. When David heard that his child by Bathsheba had died, Scripture tells us:

> Then David arose from the earth, and washed, and anointed himself, and changed his clothes; and he went into the house of the Lord, and worshiped. —2 Samuel 12:20a (RSV)

Ancient Job suffered loss upon loss: oxen, donkeys, sheep, camels, servants, and children—all in one day! What was his response?

> Then Job arose, and rent his robe, and shaved his head, and fell upon the ground, and worshiped. —Job 1:20 (RSV)

What does the childless Apostle Paul recommend to us?

> I appeal to you therefore, brethren, by the mercies of God, to present your bodies as a living sacrifice, holy and acceptable to God, which is your spiritual worship. —Romans 12:1 (RSV)

We also may lay aside our earthly hope, not wrapped in despair, but in worship. In the midst of our personal loss, we can worship God with action just as courageous as that of our biblical predecessors. By fully consenting to our childlessness, we make an irrefutable statement of our unswerving commitment to a sovereign Lord.

I once explained to a well-known writer my burden to comfort and challenge you who are childless. He responded realistically, "Vicky, you have found something in life which is all right for you. Being a missionary is very fulfilling. But what about the other people—perhaps from a small town—who don't have such a call or possibilities? What are you going to offer them?"

For a long time this question buffeted me, time after time eroding my confidence. How could I, after all, dare to confront you if I didn't have a specific solution for you? At last I arrived at the obvious answer: I cannot offer you anything. That's not my job.

I can only recommend to you the same Holy Spirit who has guided and is continuing to point the way for my husband and me. No one else can or should tell you what to do.

His destiny for us is himself. He can use whatever material life presents to build His goodness into us. Paul assures us: "We know that in everything God works for good with those who love him, who are called according to his purpose" (Rom. 8:28, RSV). God is *in* our circumstances, working *with* us to bring good out of them. Since His disposition is clear, the question is: are *we* working with *Him?*

Postponing a decision to do so allows the matter of our childlessness to lie suspended in our hearts like a great bomb of sorrow or anger threatening to fall and burst devastatingly. Our pro-faith choice, however, gives Him access to the detonator—our will—thus allowing Him to dismantle the obstacle to our happiness. At last comes the relief of no longer being at the mercy of our out-of-control foe. The shell of the threat may exist, but it is without its former explosive power.

The inner relaxation which follows is expressed by a childless friend:

> There are times when you wonder, and you feel bad. And then, later you see people who have kids and they too have *problems*—and you get on with other things!

And so we begin the adventure of getting on with the alternate blessings and opportunities in this life.

However, since we don't know what Christ would do or have *us* do in our circumstances, our initial attempts to act in faith may be less than successful.

I recall a time during my infertility treatment when I was taking hormones which induced a detestable nausea. One weekend I made and frosted a chocolate cake for a Sunday dessert—only to be faced Monday with the uneaten half! For several hours I struggled with even the thought of that cake; having it in the house was finally more than my stomach could tolerate. But how could I conscientiously throw out a cake? And our closest neighbors weren't home. I finally packed the cake into the car and headed for Burnside Street, where many of the homeless of our city wandered the sidewalks.

Stopping the car, I eagerly approached a shabby man who was sauntering aimlessly toward a corner. "Sir, I made this cake and we were unable to finish it. Would you like to have it?" A surprised look crossed his face as he replied in the affirmative and took the plastic-wrapped chocolate hunk. That was all—nary an opportunity to talk to him about the motivation of love behind my action. But I was satisfied to note a new sense of direction to his movements. He hurried his pace, walked straight across the street, and marched into the nearest bar to share his good fortune with his cronies!

Obviously rescue work was not my forte.

Where many of us *do* shine, though, is in our chosen career. The Ralph Naders among us find that our job involvement remains intrinsically interesting and virtually all-consuming throughout life. Some of us will purpose not to have children so as to give ourselves wholly to our work, knowing that we could never do justice to both.

A couple told me of a seventy-five-year-old obstetrician in Mexico City. Upon discovering as a young woman that she could never have children, she decided to specialize in the birth of other people's babies. Through the decades she has delivered several generations of families. Yet when our friends requested her services for their final child, she lit up. She still remembered the names and even the birth dates of their two little girls! Her work has never lost its fascination.

We know an always immaculately dressed bachelor. He is a great Christian gentleman who speaks several languages and is an expert in international law. In the past he has held responsible positions around the world, but some years ago he committed the rest of his career to volunteer service with an international Christian group. Instead of having a home of his own, he lives with a team.

He coordinates all of the organization's bookkeeping worldwide. When banking or legal problems occur in any particular country, he arrives to straighten out the difficulty. In emergencies, his is the calm presence sought. I recall the time shortly before Christmas one year when several young members of the group were killed and another seriously injured in an accident in a Communist country. He was sent to the scene to oversee the transfer of the medical patient to the West, identify the other bodies, and arrange for their international transport. His were the letters sent to loved ones expressing esteem for these young people and giving comfort. It was he who mailed the personal effects of the deceased and handled the necessary legal and insurance details. His service is as beautiful as his character.

We can probably all think of persons like these. Could it be that you are such a one? No rule states that self-actualized individuals have to raise children. I remember my high school Sunday School teacher in Alaska, an unmarried science instructor who taught in a school for native students, telling us with conviction, "If you seek happiness, you will never find it. If you seek service, you will find happiness."

But maybe we don't have a burning passion to pursue a career. What can our place of service be?

For many of us volunteering will be the key. Ever-increasing opportunities for volunteer services are announced via radio and television. Depending on our skills, interests, and time available we can find a glove-perfect fit for the investment we wish to make of ourselves.

So that our minds will be stimulated as we consider other potential channels for self-giving, let's examine *one* possibility present in most communities: a retirement home. Many residents have a variety of needs which can never be met solely by paid staff:

Physical care: haircuts, permanents, shaves, and nail trimming.

Practical help: letter-writing and reading, banking, mending, purchasing, calling, handling legal matters, and celebrating birthdays.

Transportation services: church, home, restaurants, funerals, community events, doctors, dentists, and optometrists.

Physical activity: various games, materials such as tools, wood, yarn, cloth, construction paper, glue, or collectable items, or a boutique in which to sell articles handmade by the residents.

Religious needs: fellowship, a listening ear, prayer, contact with a pastor, communion, and services on Sundays, Christmas, and other religious holidays.

We can all find ways to encourage our fellow human beings. Our place of volunteer service may be a hospital, preschool, park program, scout troop, Little League, community choir or with our next door neighbor. If we can give time in such a way to others, let's do it with gusto. Many aspiring volunteers must wait until they retire, hoping then to have time and health to help out. Thank God that our kindness can become catching *now*.

Very likely we may render our most satisfying service through an avenue of the church. After all, how did Jesus spend His time? The Scripture tells us He went about doing good. Jesus was actively engaged in His Father's business: advancing the kingdom of God.[5] Since much of what He began is left for us to carry on, we are assured of encountering temporary or long-term needs in the church tailor-made to suit our gifts.

Hospitality, always a mark of the mature Christian, is a natural area of service for many childfree people.[6] Inviting home Sunday morning visitors, young people, a Sunday School class, new couples, singles, and neighbors can be an expression of caring on behalf of the church—

as well as being just plain fun! Those of us without family responsibilities can often most easily entertain visiting speakers or groups, missionaries, or individuals who need some tender loving care.

Most pastors are searching for people gifted to head up needed committees or programs, do shut-in or hospital visitation, or foster growth in new believers. Those of us who enjoy talking on the telephone may be delegated the responsibility for a prayer chain or the passing on of urgent information to others in our congregation. Church libraries and offices often depend on volunteers, as do many behind-the-scenes operations, such as finalizing plans and arrangements for weddings and receptions. Sometimes an official host and hostess are needed to coordinate the social activities of the church.

We may even find our niche in a team ministry such as puppeteering, music, drama, evangelism, seminars or camping programs, or a Christian community.

But I'm not suggesting that we "throw ourselves into" church or community work to sublimate for not having children! That would almost certainly be a mistake. First, if we didn't recognize what we were doing, our unconscious substitution could prove unhealthy, if not self-deceptive. Second, even if we were purposely trying to fill up our lonely hours, we would never be able to use them all up. At some time we would have to face our sad or angry selves, as disenchanted with our lives as ever.

Equally true is that the kinds of satisfaction we receive—even from serving others in ways we really enjoy—will never be the exact equivalent to the fulfillment a parent receives from successfully rearing a family. But thinking from the opposite point of view, the rewards for a parent's intense personal investment in a few children will never be the same as the joy we receive from having spent significant moments with perhaps hundreds of people.

A single lady shared with us her thrill of having received 76 cards and the same amount of dollars for her seventy-sixth birthday! It wasn't even a milestone year for her; people simply loved her for all she had done for them throughout her lifetime. Who's to say that a parent receives any more pleasure from the cards and presents received from his or her own children?

We may *assume* that we would experience our greatest challenge and sense of accomplishment by being parents. But what if that simply isn't so? Actually, our greatest challenge in life, despite our status, is finding and doing the will of God.

What begins as raw trust in our loving Savior can result in my—and your—having a ministry. In response to our conforming to His choice, He begins to affirm us in that decision, steadily preparing us and directing our operation in the Spirit to that area of service in which we are personally comfortable and can be most effective.

A single friend, Marge, tells us how this process unfolded in her life after reading this verse:

> My people have committed two sins: They have forsaken me, the spring of living water, and have dug their own cisterns, broken cisterns that cannot hold water. —Jeremiah 2:13 (NIV)

She had previously expected her abundance to appear in the form of a marriage-shaped cistern which she had carved out. When God failed to fill up that desire for a husband and children, she became desperate. She went into a terrible state of depression, panting for pleasures to start bubbling up. They never did. She felt justified, therefore, in accusing God of unfairness, railing at Him for His oversight of her.

Then she was discovered by this verse. She yielded her cracked cistern to His final breaking process. When she turned from the ruins there waiting for her was a beautiful new source of blessing! Having learned Spanish during her childhood, she was the ideal person to serve a Spanish-speaking church of bruised people in her city. She now plays the piano, leads a Sunday School class, and helps meet the needs of dozens of individuals in this brand new congregation.

God's provision for us may take any number of forms. Perhaps we'll have a ministry working with people who have been "messing up." On occasions Jerry and I have served as a bridge for individuals undergoing extreme marriage tension, young people who have experienced a collapse of communication with their parents, or someone debating over having an abortion.

Such individuals often require a place where they can temporarily escape external friction and work out internal problems. Even slight noises can trigger headaches, flashbacks to ugly scenes in their lives, or anxiety because of their present, highly sensitized state. Many need to experience a tranquil home setting with healthy interaction going on, a place where they are accepted just as they are. For the first time, or the first time in years, these sufferers will experience peace in the home.

Often such persons have an exorbitant need to talk and be listened to. They are bursting to express their anger and frustration, their great sorrow, their despair. And all the while they are holding to the wisp of hope that life can be different for them, answers found, relationships restored.

But that takes time. And it may take *our* time.

Whatever form of ministry we may be considering, we need to distinguish between being willing to serve and being gifted for a given ministry. God's plan isn't to put us where our service becomes unbearable. He carefully prepares both us and our work, so that His cause will advance. Listen to Him tell us about His way:

> Lord, you establish peace for us; all that we have accomplished you have done for us.   —Isaiah 26:12 (NIV)

> For we are God's workmanship, created in Christ Jesus to do good works, which God prepared in advance for us to do.
> —Ephesians 2:10 (NIV)

Not to worry: the good we are to do has been prearranged by Jesus.

He knows which of us can *only* be challenged by working with the desperately needy. We're the ones who will find our faith adventure in skidrow missions, prisons, homes for the homeless, crisis centers, organizations for battered women or children, telephone hotlines, all-night prayer or counseling services, or rape, drug and alcohol trauma facilities. Some of these settings require both full-time personnel and people who are free from a fixed schedule or family responsibilities so that they can remain with an individual until an initial shock subsides or immediate needs are met. Certainly live-in counselors or staff members would not want to expose their own children to such emotionally-charged environments.

Some of us may be led to adopt, not a baby, but *somebody*. For decades in Chicago, a man and his wife, Lil, invested time in the children of their neighborhood. She conducted Bible clubs, taught Sunday School, and helped a large number of young people, including Sandy, find the Lord. When Lil was left a widow due to an electrical accident, Sandy began to board with her. Through the years as the older woman became more infirm, Sandy has assumed more of the work load for the two of them and has served cheerfully as her almost constant companion.

Instead of a lifetime to devote to such loving action, some of us will experience periods of childfree living, perhaps a number of years being single or of having an empty nest. This time segment presents interesting opportunities as well.

A certain widow in a Midwest state devotes herself to providing a home for one unwed pregnant teenager after another. She provides her "girls" with a pleasant place to live, introduces them to an accepting church and a good physician, and supplies needed transportation. As each girl makes decisions about her future and her baby's, this kindly lady lends her understanding support. Finally, she cares for the new mother (and baby) shortly after birth.

Indeed, there is unlimited "No Child Trespassing" territory in this world, and some of it belongs to us, the childfree.

Perhaps there never will be kids on our block claiming our house as their *property* or bragging on us as the greatest mom or dad ever. Not that we haven't just as much "right" to such a family as anyone else. Paul acknowledged these inalienable rights:

> Don't we have the right to food and drink? Don't we have the right to take a believing wife along with us as do the other apostles and the Lord's brothers and Cephas? —1 Corinthians 9:4, 5 (NIV)

But we, as did Paul, also have the freedom to deny our rights and to consciously choose the life and ministry given us:

> But we did not use this right. On the contrary, we put up with anything rather than hinder the gospel of Christ. . . . I have not used any of these rights. —1 Corinthians 9:12b, 15a (NIV)

In selecting God's way, we replace the bitterness of deprivation with the joy of choice.

You may be asking yourself as you stand on the brink of such a decision, "But does it really pay?"

Only ten years have passed since I finally took my eyes off having a baby and focused them on having a ministry. That's not a lifetime, just my final prime time for fertility . . . physically. But in this one decade I've had the pleasure of learning a new language, discipling twelve women, helping train more than one hundred Sunday School and Vacation Bible School teachers, preparing several church musicians, teaching a number of women's Bible studies, and helping many brand new people come in contact with Jesus.

There is no way to describe the inner exaltation of walking into a church and hearing one of my students play the organ for a congregation of three hundred people or seeing one of the women I trained with her own group of young women sharing the basics of a life of faith—more effectively than I ever could!

But the highlight has been seeing the birth—not of a physical baby— but of a brand new church! We are now helping to bring to life a second infant congregation. And who knows? Perhaps my prime time *spiritually* yet lies ahead.

Your service and mine for Christ will indeed produce fruit—results as real as the those of the Apostle Paul's ministry. Of course, the individuals he spawned spiritually neither took on his physical traits nor grew up in his house. But they ended up in his Father's family: Lydia, Luke, Priscilla, Aquila, Apollos, Timothy, Epaphras, jailers, prisoners, Aristarchus, Onesimus, Justus, Tychicus, Nympha, Titus . . . Martin Luther . . . and maybe even us!

"People were bringing little children to Jesus
to have him touch them,
but the disciples rebuked them.
When Jesus saw this, he was indignant.
He said to them, 'Let the little children come to me,
and do not hinder them,
for the kingdom of God belongs to such as these.
I tell you the truth,
anyone who will not receive the kingdom of God like a little child
will never enter it.'
And he took the children in his arms,
put his hands on them
and blessed them."

—Mark 10:13–16 (NIV)

CHAPTER FIFTEEN

A Child-Blessing Ministry

Why did the disciples try to keep the kids away from Jesus? What was it about the attitude of the Twelve which made Jesus indignant? Was He pinning them down with His eyes when He appealed to everyone present not to hinder, but to help, the little ones come to Him?

These are delicious questions to chew on. But more delectable yet is a tender *why:* Why did Jesus welcome the little ones into His arms, touch them, and bless each one individually?

And what was He doing when He blessed them? Consecrating them? Requesting of His Father the bestowal of divine favor? Pleading protection from evil for them? Maybe He took the action appropriate for each particular child.

There may have been many reasons Jesus loved being in the presence of children. Perhaps they reminded Him of home. From having spent eternity past with the Father, He had come to bring His kingdom to this earth. And who among us were more like the members of His celestial reign? Why, those little ones, of course! Their innocence, joy, delight, and trust were very much like that expressed by heavenly beings in the presence of God.

Compared to Jesus' workaday world of doubt, mistrust, treachery, jealousy, satanic manifestations, misunderstanding, false motives, and broken lives, the world of children was an instant refreshment.

But perhaps there was another reason. Paul attributes to Jesus the statement that it is more blessed to give than to receive (Acts 20:35). As He gave of himself to those children, they accepted His every gesture of love and spiritual care. By receiving everything He had for them, they blessed Jesus!

Have we ever considered that Jesus would want us to get some of the same blessings out of life that He did?

Granted, none of us wanted to miss out on humanity's most creative event—desperately we didn't. We wanted to experience all of life. Those of us who came from a happy home wished to repeat that process. If we came from broken homes we thrilled to the possibility of terminating that ugly chain and forming the first link in a new one which would affect future generations positively.

Some of us, therefore, find it difficult to be near children. While around them we battle sorrow, jealousy, covetousness, or just plain anger. During such stress, in a confusion of emotions, we may confront our mates as did Rachel in her desperation, "Give me children or I'll die!"[1] In these stages, we may not be able to hold a baby without squeezing that child and crying out in our hearts, "I want you *so* much."

Who knows? Maybe Jesus had a hard time giving back some of the little children, too. Perhaps that's one reason His disciples didn't want toddlers around: He lavished attention on them. The Scriptures make a point of the double-touch experience He had with them: "And he took the children in his arms, put his hands on them and blessed them."

Couldn't He simply have blessed all the children from a distance? Why didn't He have all the mothers form a line at the front so that He could pass by quickly or pronounce a group benediction?

Do we see it? He loved those little kids. He really cared about each one. He didn't shortchange the children even when surrounded by adults with problems, handicapped persons waiting for their healing, and heads of families who were sacrificing a day's work to hear Him teach. God incarnate, with only three years on earth to minister, thought it a good investment of himself to spend time with the children.

The direct challenge to those of us who are childless, faced with others' children, is to follow Jesus' example. We must allow what we would gladly have showered on our own offspring to land on the children in our particular world. Kids and the kingdom just naturally belong to each other; we can be links in their coming together.

In some areas of life we have a built-in "excuse" when we fail to pattern ourselves after Jesus. After all, He never was—let's say—a housewife, a bus driver, or a high school principal. But as we observe Him, in addition to whatever else we see Him doing, we've got to admit and admire His ministry with children. He perfectly models the attitude and meaningful interaction with the little ones of others which we, the present-day childblessers, can emulate. Making ourselves available to children presents us with the opportunity to grow ever more into His stature.

One mark of maturity is being able to appreciate other people's children. A teacher friend insists that those without a family of their own are, of all persons, the *most* genuinely interested in children. Although that point could well be debated, we know that children form very special relationships with those outside the immediate family. One mom of two preschoolers comments:

> Have you ever watched singles with children? They give them *so* much. They give them something different from what I as a mother can.

The childfree occupy a position *parallel* to parents: we're not "the same as" but "complementary to" them. Although we provide less direct nurturing than a child's principal care-givers, our contribution can prove nearly as vital to a child's sense of well-being.

Child-rearing might be compared to a nest of birds on a branch. The parent birds are essential as they provide food and warmth. But where would they all be without the support and security of the tree? Trees hold up many nests and come into direct contact with multiplied little ones. Obviously, both the parents and the branch are essential.

Prayer is perhaps the most necessary and influential contribution we can make to children's lives. We may have to start simply with what my friend Olivia calls "pretty prayers." She suggests that when we see someone who is or has what we want—in this case a happy parent, a pregnant mother, a little baby, a handsome child, an enjoyable teenager—the most effective way to combat covetousness is to purposely pray for the best blessings we can imagine for that person. If the temptation returns again and again, we continue to respond, almost automatically, with prayers of blessing for him or her.

Intercessory prayer, our personal faith stretch on behalf of children, goes much further. Often we outside the family unit are able to see a child in his or her uniqueness more objectively than those close by. We may offer "pure prayers" for that individual because our motivation is in no way personal.

Ofelia is the most picturesque example of an intercessor for children that I know. An abandoned Latin American wife left with three little girls, she certainly isn't childless! However, precisely because of her heavy load, her prayer life challenges those of us free from such a weight.

For years a successful Sunday School teacher, Ofelia once had in her class two brothers: Pablo and Guillermo. Pablo, an angel of a boy, helpful and eager to learn, was thought of by many to be headed for the ministry. But Guillermo—the opposite—was sure to become a juvenile delinquent! He disrupted every class, kept other children from benefitting from the sessions, and was the cause of Ofelia's returning home almost every Sunday weeping. She couldn't keep the burden to herself; she asked the pastor and others in the church to join with her in prayer for that boy.

Years went by. Pablo did become a pastor. Meanwhile, Ofelia's own middle child, Ivonne, rebelled. She ridiculed her family's faith and stubbornly refused to have anything to do with Christ. One day she was invited to an evangelistic campaign. Probably she went only because she knew the revivalist . . . Guillermo! (Converted as a young man he has subsequently demonstrated such a remarkable evangelistic gift that he was chosen to be Billy Graham's interpreter during a capital city crusade.) Ivonne came to know the Lord that night and has since received a missionary call and married a Christian in the nation she serves.

Who knows how many young Guillermos, Ivonnes—or Pablos, for that matter—have come to a living faith in Christ in part because someone cared enough to pray? Prayer is a mystery, the invisible side of visible results.

—We offer the Father our faith, love and time on behalf of children,
—He passes the benefit on to the little ones,
—and He ends up with the glory.

Oh, we needn't worry; He'll give us our reward as well. The awesome thrill is that we enter into a partnership with God in which He, the senior partner, gets the credit and the whole company of little ones prospers.

The Unborn

There are no "littler ones" than the unborn. They call up our deepest protective instincts. As childless Christians our most painful cut may come in the form of having personal contact with someone who, locked into an unwanted pregnancy, opts for abortion. We may feel both righteous and personal indignation. From our point of view, the woman in question is not only performing the supremely sinful act of snuffing out human life, but is slamming the door in our own face by denying her baby the privilege of being adopted into a caring, loving family.

My first such encounter came at a very inopportune moment. Shortly after returning from a demanding day at work, I was greeted by our ringing phone. Wearily I picked up the receiver and recognized the voice of a dear friend. She was obviously shaken.

Knowing how I felt about a relationship she had been having with a certain man, she now bluntly dumped on me the news that she was pregnant.

I tried to be very matter-of-fact and replied that our actions do bring consequences and that pregnancy is a very real possibility when we engage in sexual relations.

My comments did not sound matter-of-fact to her! They appeared judgmental and very unloving. In a moment she became lividly, abusively angry with me and all other Christians because of my remarks.

If only I had simply listened to her and showed compassion instead of offering a platitude. She might then have thrown down her defenses and received some much needed love and personal affirmation. My insensitivity cost me the privilege of helping her during her process of decision-making. The most I was permitted to do was to lend her my presence and prayers.

In the weeks which followed I accompanied her on various occasions and invited her to our home in order to be with her during her utter loneliness. When she entered the hospital for a hysterectomy, I visited her before and after school, at lunch break, and in the evening. Nauseated from the smell of anesthetics, I sat beside her, aware of what a long process lay ahead for her to become established in Christ.

Through His wooing she eventually made a lifelong commitment to Him. But my lack of empathy, rising from my own state of hurt and disgust, almost shut her out of a relationship with a loving Savior.

Engraved into my consciousness is the understanding that we must keep ourselves from injuring others even if occasionally it means forcing ourselves to listen and keep silent. We are prejudiced because of our own suffering. But hurting persons are oblivious to our needs because their own pain is so intense. Recognizing this, we are the stronger and have a love obligation to prefer them, rather than judge or heap guilt upon them.[2]

They will be able to discern our attitude. If they determine that we accept them, just as they are with their conflicting emotions and unspeakable confusion, then the time will come when it will be natural for us to share what Jesus says to them:

> Whoever receives one such child in my name receives me.
> —Matthew 18:5 (RSV)

> For I was hungry and you gave me food, I was thirsty and you gave me drink, I was a stranger and you welcomed me, I was naked and you clothed me. . . . And the King will answer them, "Truly I say to you, as you did it to one of the least of these my brethren, you did it unto me."
> —Matthew 25:35—36a, 40 (RSV)

Who needs nourishment, the clothing of human flesh, and the welcome of a loving heart more than the least of mankind, the unborn?

How thoroughly sweet the tones I heard coming from the lips of a single woman who sat across the aisle from me in a plane. She told me about her exciting singles group. Showing me a brochure that listed their services to people in the community, she pointed to the title: "Unplanned Pregnancies." "I'm going to start volunteering in that area when I finish my trip. I'm a little bit scared, but I see so much potential for good in being able to relate to women who are trying to decide what to do about their unwanted babies. I think the Lord can really use me to save a lot of children."

Undoubtedly He will. Can He use us as freely?

The Little Ones

We know a pastor who, as he presents a baby to the Lord, plants a kiss on the child's forehead. It's only a little kiss, but it sounds *big* through the sound system!

Just so, our influence on children, although seemingly insignificant, may be magnified well beyond anyone's expectations.

Sometimes we are made pleasantly aware of this power as was a single friend to whom a mother commented, referring to a specific word of counsel: "I'm so glad that you said that to the kids. When I say it, it goes right over them. Because you said it, they listened."

What we do may be even more significant than what we say. Consider the now retired couple in Minnesota who for decades have spent every Sunday morning in the nursery, freeing parents to have a worship experience. Their twin service to parents and babies is a clear statement of love.

Some time ago an aged lady in a retirement home wrote to me. She told me how through the years she had taught Sunday School, always having just a little group of children. The last year she was able to teach there were only six in her class, but she poured herself into those youngsters. From that group one boy went into the ministry, one of the girls married a pastor, another became a missionary in the Far East, and two of the other children grew up and stayed in the community, frequently stopping by to visit her. As she reviews her life, part of her well-deserved sense of integrity comes from the results of her love labor for kids.

We perhaps all know of individuals who temporarily stand in the gap for children. Some families take in foster children, others care for the handicapped, a few serve the newborn until placement for adoption, still others are Big Brother or Sister to needy youngsters.

These ministries require the ability to invest heavily and then, transfer the trust. Not everyone is gifted to do so.

Twice we have had youngsters with us on an extended basis. For me each experience was an emotional disaster. I became too involved personally to set the boys free for their next step in life. In the case of the first boy who had a slight brain impairment, we had prayed diligently that he would be placed in a Christian home. The county social worker surprised us by finding a family for him in short order—Christians who lived on a ranch with several sons, one of whom was successfully coping with brain damage! The placement was perfect—but it occurred the week of Bobby's birthday. We had already made plans to celebrate his special day and had purchased his present. The social worker, a firm-spoken man, denied us the opportunity to carry through with the promises. "Remember, Mrs. Love, he belongs with a new family now. Did you ever stop to think that *they* will want to celebrate his birthday *their* way?"

Reluctantly, the caseworker allowed us to drive out to the ranch ahead of the date with our gift. Bobby, surrounded by horses and other animals, a barn, corrals, and a woods, had made a magnificent adjustment. His special "brother" explained, "I tell Bobby he can do everything just like I can 'cause I've got brain damage, too."

Bobby did splendidly; I didn't.

But I learned that not everyone can hug and release equally well. For some, temporary care-giving brings fulfillment. But we mustn't feel inadequate if we discover ourselves to be long-term lovers exclusively. Heading in the direction of what for us is a heightened sense of life will open the way for our most positive relationships with children.

In our mobile and changing society, children often have a special need for "aunts" and "uncles." Many of us can recall significant relationships with relatives or volunteer "family" as we grew up. I had an uncle who made me child-sized doll furniture, a sled, and even a clothespin gun! My aunt took time to color pictures with me, pick out tunes on a toy piano, and read me the Sunday comics. What an assurance to know that if anything were to happen to my parents, I would live with my aunt and uncle who loved me. We, in our turn, may have occasion to develop just such a security bond with some very special children.

Youngsters suffering anguish because of their parents' marriage problems, separation, or divorce are ideal candidates for steady third-party relationships. Those among us who have suffered a similar childhood trauma and have made a successful re-entry into life may be the best prepared and most positive models such a child can have. Often our personal childhood wound is ultimately healed as we reach into our unenviable past in order to form an identity bond with today's hurting children. The opportunity to assist a little soulmate may well justify our own painful pilgrimage. Potential evil will not only have been thwarted, it will have produced good results: our being enabled to minister effectively to bruised children.

Clearly, our contribution to kids is an individual, creative matter. Some of us will thoroughly enjoy scooping up young friends or relatives and taking them on outings or travel ventures. Instead of passing our vacations in solitude we have someone with whom we can later reflect, "Hey, remember when?" And they *will* remember. In fact, such moments together may constitute some of the highlights of their life.

We once took three girls on a camp-out vacation in Latin America. The littlest one brought a blue negligee which she delighted in wearing while she twirled around in the sun, and stretched out on the grass. Another, a blond teenager, attracted nearly the entire American water polo team to our trailer site. Those were exciting days. My husband and I never could have created such a pleasant stir!

Practical love for children may end up being more rewarding for *us* than it ever is for the "adopted" kids in our lives. A single friend in her mid-fifties levels with us:

> Some of my funnest Christmasses were those when I went shopping for nieces and nephews. I always bought clothes. I had money and I could do it.

She enjoyed buying, wrapping, and giving. Parents appreciated the help. And the children? They delighted in all the new things that their auntie chose for them.

This is precisely what Jesus says to us:

> Give, and it will be given to you;
>   A good measure,
>   pressed down,
>   shaken together,
>   and running over,
>   will be poured into your lap.
> For with the measure you use, it will be measured to you.
> —Luke 6:38 (NIV)

Not that we give to receive, but in giving we receive.

Blessing the Big Ones

If you've ever heard a fishing tale of the big one that got away, you're aware that probably the big one wasn't so big after all. We encounter the same phenomenon in the world of children. Some of the little ones look—and act—big from a distance.

But they're still growing.

You and I may be instrumental in taking away hindrances or directly helping some of these big little ones move in close to Christ.

The most obvious way to do so is by involving ourselves in their lives. In one Oregon community Betty and her husband, both employed full time, dedicate every Friday night to the young people in their church. No one can remember how many years they have been doing so, but everyone knows that nothing infringes on the quality time which this couple reserves exclusively for each succeeding generation of teenagers.

Jenny, a secretary, living in a small southern town, reflects on the fulfillment that working with youth has brought to her marriage:

> I am so busy working with teenage girls, and my husband with the boys, that it's almost like family. It doesn't end in the Sunday School.

It *is* work and it *doesn't* end—but it's "almost like family."

We may actually become family to some teenager(s). Living with any teenager is temporary because these years are short and action-filled even in normal home life. Thus, our participation in the life and development of a teen may come in condensed form. Key persons in my own unfolding were big-hearted missionaries in Alaska who, when they had an empty nest, opened their attic room to a continuing assortment of unlikely inhabitants. The Upper Room was crammed one particular summer with an Eskimo girl, a fair-haired teenager from New York, a young woman with Caribbean heritage, and myself. Our lives were as packed with learning as our closet was with clothes. For the Lattas to have taken us on, I realize now, they had to be the most adventurous couple I've ever known!

Myrtle, a single, has spent her adult years as a cook in a Canadian Bible college. But her real specialty isn't overseeing twenty-one meals weekly for the young people: it's having them into her home on an informal basis and being available to them in their moments of decision, doubt, and joy.

During the years before they had their own child, Bob and Kathi took in troubled teenage girls, providing a home for those who were unwelcome in their own homes. Although the immediate results were not always successful, they are glad that they didn't spend their time simply waiting to bear a child, but were able to bear up other people's daughters at a critical time in life.

Maybe we are not quite as courageous as these, but perhaps we find that there is space in our life the size of one or two teenagers. Several people have told me of their satisfaction of taking in a niece or nephew during university years. Others have drawn up alongside one floundering young person and seen him or her through rocky times when the individual's own parents were unable to do so.

Perhaps our help will be financial. A missionary wife sat across my table and wept as she told me:

> God is so good. We just didn't know how we were going to be able to send Bettina to the Christian college she wanted to attend. Her grades were excellent and she received a scholarship, but it was nowhere near enough. We didn't know where we were going to be able to scrape up the money.
>
> Then out of the blue this Christian couple in California offered to pay whatever was lacking. They have a beautiful home and they're both working, and since they have no children of their own, they wanted to pay for the college education of a missionary kid. And Vicky, it's thousands of dollars!

They are making a gift of themselves, although it comes in the form of a six-inch piece of paper.

Many such life-gifts are being given every day:
—adults talking to teenagers in person or by phone.
—businessmen or women giving young people their first job opportunity.
—lay persons visiting a crippled teenager, sharing encouraging books or dedicating time weekly to his or her Christian growth.
—adults befriending a confirmand for two years.
—individuals crocheting afghans or offering tennis classes to auction off in order to send young people to a Christian conference.
—someone going weekly to the county jail to teach young prisoners basic learning skills.
—concerned lay people directing youth choirs and Bible quizzes.
—church members writing to young people in the military.

You and I can be such givers.

Unfortunately, many of us who sincerely care about young people and extend ourselves in their behalf will suffer grave disappointments and even losses owing to our relationship with them. Many teens are manipulators. They can deceive, take advantage of us or others, and even involve us in legal entanglements. Some will never repent of such actions against us.

Jesus knew this. He will bless us in spite of their not doing so:

> Blessed are you when people insult you, persecute you and falsely say all kinds of evil against you because of me. Rejoice and be glad, because great is your reward in heaven. . . .
>
> —Matthew 5:11–12a (NIV)

Our motivation, after all, is not personal. When Jesus invested himself in children, it wasn't because their sticky fingers or runny noses were any help to Him. He genuinely cared about them and knew what the Father desired for each one. When He included Judas in His close circle, He knew what was in store for Him. But He gave the young man a chance anyway. His love was not conditional upon His gain or the desired reaction on the part of those He served.

Sometimes we have to follow Him . . . to the cross . . . for others.

Not everyone for whom Christ laid down His life has responded in kindness. But some have! We needn't ask Him, "Has it been worth your risk and investment?" We know how He'd answer. He considers each of us worth His best.[3]

We may find the visible results of our own minimal sacrifice to be not only unexpected, but actually astounding!

Isaí, the teenage son of a national pastor, lived with us for a year and a half, including one Mother's Day. According to the custom in our country, the mothers in our congregation were all awakened in the wee hours that morning to a serenade by the young people who drove from house to house throughout the night. I was able to sleep as normal since, because as you know, I wasn't a . . .

A heavy day was in store for me: the day I found out about grief. And it included a momentous afternoon, because it was then that I determined to write this book.

Isaí came home in the early evening, and thoughtfully made no reference to my tears. He played some numbers on the guitar while I set the table for the next morning. After he had retired, I made my final round downstairs and on the table found a little typing-paper heart trimmed with pinking shears, with a note written in Spanish:

VIKY

ALTHOUGH I AM NOT YOUR SON, I CAN SAY
THAT YOU ARE MY MOTHER.

AND
I CAN'T GIVE YOU ANYTHING BECAUSE
I HAVEN'T ANY RESOURCES
BUT WITH THESE WORDS
I SAY

HAPPY DAY, MAMA!

ISAÍ

"Lord! I expected to be the mother of a little baby who cried and looked like me. Instead, I've become a mother to a rural teenage boy of another culture who speaks a different language and will never be able to pronounce my name! I am overwhelmed by such an honor."

And so it happens. By loving the little ones, the middle-sized ones, the big ones, we discover the truth of the Scriptures:

> Be glad, O barren woman, who bears no children; break forth and cry aloud, you who have no labor pains; because more are the children of the desolate woman than of her who has a husband.
>
> —Galatians 4:27b (NIV)

> He gives the barren woman a home, making her the joyous mother of children. Praise the Lord! —Psalm 113:9 (RSV)

Since the option of family planning does not rest with us, but with Him, then we await the children that He gives us. There will be those who see in us something admirable which makes them want to be our children. Or, better yet, become *His* children.

I would tell you as my husband once said to me:

> The reason why He has allowed you to have this maternal (paternal) instinct is so that your ministry would continue to be a real sacrifice with a real reward.

Your sacrifice is real, as you well know. What you may be just discovering is how real your reward is and shall be.

In this life many of us face one tightly closed door: that which leads to natural parenthood. We have a choice. We can continue to try to beat it down, or we can look around and find the way which is wide open for us in God. I can't tell you which door that will be for you. I can only encourage you to place yourself squarely within the following words as my husband and I have. Be assured that the Spirit of God, as He did for those in the church of Philadelphia (Brotherly Love), and is doing for Jerry and Vicky Love, will show you the way which has been cleared for you:

> These are the words of him who is holy and true, who holds the key of David. What he opens, no one can shut; and what he shuts, no one can open. I know your deeds. See, I have placed before you an open door that no one can shut. I know that you have little strength, yet you have kept my word and have not denied my name.
>
> —Revelation 3:7b—8 (NIV)

Let us choose to go through the unshutable door. And in doing so, we will each find that childless is not less: it's *blessed.*

Notes

Chapter One

1. Barbara Eck Menning, "The Infertile Couple," *Child Welfare* 54 (June 1975, p. 454; and Barbara Eck Menning, *Infertility: A Guide for the Childless Couple* (Englewood Cliffs, New Jersey: Prentice-Hall, Inc., 1977), p. 4.

2. Adrienne D. Kraft and others at St. Mary's Services, Chicago, Illinois, "The Psychological Dimensions of Infertility," *American Journal of Orthopsychiatry* 50 (October 1980), p. 620.

3. See Sherwin A. Kaufman, *New Hope for the Childless Couple* (New York: Simon & Schuster, 1970), p. 94, and Gina B. Kolata, "The Psychology of Infertility," *Science* 202 (October 13, 1978), p. 200.

4. American Fertility Society as quoted by Pamela Abrahamson, Matt Clark, Sandra Gary, Daniel Shapiro, Deborah Witherspoon, and Marsha Zabarsky, "Infertility: New Cures, New Hope," *Newsweek* (December 6, 1982), p. 102.

5. Gina B. Kolata, "Infertility; Promising New Treatments," 202 *Science* (October 13, 1978), p. 200; and "Infertility: New Cures, New Hope," *Newsweek*, p. 102.

6. Adrienne D. Kraft, pp. 624–5.

7. John 14:9; 5:19; 10:10; 15:11; Isaiah 53:2.

Chapter Two

1. Passages on creation: Genesis 1 and 2:1–15; passages on the formation of the family of Abraham: Genesis 11:29–30; 12:1–7; 13:14–16; 15; 16; 17; 18:1–19; 20; 21:1–21.

2. Genesis 17:17; 18:11–15; 21:6–7.

3. Genesis 15:1–3.

4. Genesis 16:1–3.

5. Genesis 12:1–5; 13:5–11.

6. Genesis 13:2.

7. Genesis 15:4–6.

8. Genesis 16:15–16; 17:5–8, 18–21.

9. Genesis 21:1–5.

10. Psalm 100:3.

11. Barbara Eck Menning, *Infertility: A Guide for the Childless Couple* (Englewood Cliffs, New Jersey: Prentice-Hall, Inc., 1977), pp. 12–15, 32–34.

12. J. Stephen Bell (of the Royal Edinburgh Hospital, Andrew Duncan Clinic, Scotland), "Psychological Problems Among Patients Attending an Infertility Clinic," *Journal of Psychosomatic Research* 25 (1981), pp. 1–3.

13. G.B. Kolata, "The Psychology of Infertility," *Science* 202 (October 13, 1978), p. 202.

14. Diane Renne, "There's Always Adoption: The Infertility Problem," *Child Welfare* 56 (July 1977), p. 466.

15. Psalm 139:1–18.

16. 1 Peter 5:7.

Chapter Three

1. Ephesians 1:3–4.

2. 2 Corinthians 10:3–6.

3. 1 Timothy 6:12.

4. Ephesians 6:11–20.

5. Ephesians 5:21–33; Matthew 19:3–9.

6. Adrienne D. Kraft and others at St. Mary's Services, Chicago, Illinois, "The Psychological Dimensions of Infertility," *American Journal of Orthopsychiatry* 50 (October 1980), p. 626.

7. Jeremiah 1:4–5; Isaiah 44:28–45; Ezra 1:1–3; 7–11; Isaiah 40:3; Malachi 3:1; Luke 1:5–80; Mark 2:1–8.

8. Romans 8:19–23; Hebrews 10:14; Ephesians 4:11–13; 1 Corinthians 13:8–12; Revelation 21:5–6.

9. Elisabeth Kübler-Ross, *Death: The Final Stage of Growth* (Englewood Cliffs, New Jersey: Prentice Hall, 1975), pp. 10, 97–100.

10. Barbara Eck Menning, *Infertility: A Guide for the Childless Couple* (Englewood Cliffs, New Jersey: Prentice Hall, 1977), pp. 116–117.

11. *The Covenant Hymnal* (Chicago: Covenant Press, 1973), hymns 389 and 482.

Chapter Four

1. Galatians 2:20.

2. Merrill F. Unger, ed., *Unger's Bible Dictionary* (Chicago, Illi-

nois: Moody Bible Institute of Chicago, 1966), p. 956.

3. See Barbara Eck Menning, "The Infertile Couple: A Plea for Advocacy," *Child Welfare* 54 (June 1975), p. 456; Adrienne D. Kraft and others at St. Mary's Services, Chicago, Illinois, "The Psychological Dimensions of Infertility," *Amercian Journal of Orthopsychiatry,* 50 (October 1980), pp. 624–25; M. D. Mazor, "Barren Couples," *Psychology Today* 12 (May 1979), p. 108; and Diane Renne, "There's Always Adoption," *Child Welfare* 56 (July 1977), pp. 466–469.

4. Renne, "There's Always Adoption," pp. 466–469.

5. Renne, p. 466.

6. Luke 2:41–52.

7. John 19:25–27.

Chapter Five

1. Isaiah 53:2; Isaiah 52:14.

2. Psalm 22:6; Isaiah 53:8; John 10:17–18.

3. Matthew 23:37; Luke 13:34.

4. "The Westminster Assembly's Shorter Catechism as included by John Whitecross," *The Shorter Catechism Illustrated from Christian Biography and History* (London: The Banner of Truth Trust, 1968), p. 7.

5. Daniel 1:1–2:48.

6. Merrill F. Unger, *Unger's Bible Dictionary* (Chicago: Moody Press, 1966), p. 115.

7. Daniel 6:15–24.

8. Henry H. Halley, *Halley's Bible Handbook* (Grand Rapids, Michigan: Zondervan Publishing House, 1956), p. 340 and Daniel 2:48; 5:10–30; 6:1, 25–28; and 10:1.

9. Donald Goergen, *The Sexual Celibate* (Garden City, New York: Image Books, a Division of Doubleday & Company, 1979), pp. 33–48, 173–209.

Chapter Six

1. Ephesians 5:21–32.

2. J. Stephen Bell, "Psychological Problems Among Patients Attending an Infertility Clinic," *Journal of Psychosomatic Research* 25 (1981), 1–3.

3. "Bergman's Talent Endured," *The Times-Picayune/The States—Item* (August 30, 1982), I:4.

4. Matthew 5:23, 24; Mark 11:25, 26.

5. John 8:44.

6. Proverbs 31:12; Ephesians 5:25.

7. M.D. Mazor, "Barren Couples," *Psychology Today* 12 (May 1979), p. 103.

8. Genesis 2:18 (KJV).

9. Judith A. Stigger, *Coping With Infertility* (Minneapolis: Augsburg, 1983), pp. 79–88.

Chapter Seven

1. 1 Samuel 3:1; 7:3–15.
2. 1 Samuel 1:11, 16, 18, 21–28; 2:1–11.
3. Isaac—Genesis 12:1–3; 15:1–6; 17:1–19; 18:1–19; 21:1–7.
   Joseph—Genesis 30:1–2, (3–21), 22–24.
   Samson—Judges 13, particularly verses: 1–2, 24–25.
   John the Baptist—Luke 1:5–25, 39–45, 57–80.
4. Genesis 12:3.
5. Isaiah 54:4.
6. Deuteronomy 23:1.
7. Isaiah 47:9; Leviticus 20:20–21.
8. Galatians 3:13–14.
9. Galatians 3:26–28; Revelation 1:6.
10. 1 Samuel 2:1–11.
11. Barbara Eck Menning, *Infertility: A Guide for the Childless Couple* (Englewood Cliffs, New Jersey: Prentice Hall, Inc., 1977), pp. 102–3.
12. Barbara Eck Menning, *Infertility: A Guide for the Childless Couple,* pp. 118–124.
13. For those interested in investigating in more detail Jesus' practical ministry to others, the following texts are suggested: Matthew 4:18–22; 5:1–2; 8:3, 15; 9:18–25; 14:15–21; 17:6–8; Mark 6:31–32, 45, 50–53; Luke 22:39–40; John 4:1–42; 9:1–6; 11:1–44; 17:6–25; 21:1–13.
14. Menning, *Infertility: A Guide to Childless Couples,* pp. 95–103.

Chapter Eight

1. Mark 3:20.
2. Mark 3:31–35; John 19:25–27.
3. John 2:1–11.
4. Luke 8:19–21.
5. Mark 3:31.
6. 1 Timothy 3:1–5, 12.
7. M.D. Mazor, "Barren Couples," pp. 10–112.
8. 2 Corinthians 3:2.

Chapter Ten

1. Romans 12:5, 12–13; Ephesians 4:4–5.

2. Romans 12:10.

3. Romans 14:10–13, 19.

4. Luke 8:41–42, 49–56; 7:11–17.

5. Anna—Luke 2:36; Lydia—Acts 16:13–15, 40; Priscilla and Aquila—Romans 16:3; Deaconesses—1 Timothy 3:11, note: NIV; Mutual submission—Ephesians 5:21.

Chapter Eleven

1. Sherwin A. Kaufman, M.D., *New Hope for the Childless Couple* (New York: Simon and Schuster, 1970), p. 109.

2. Elizabeth Kübler-Ross, *Death: The Final Stage of Growth* (New Jersey: Prentice-Hall, 1975), p. 10.

3. M.D. Mazor, "Barren Couples," *Psychology Today* 12 (May 1979), p. 101; John J. Strangel, M.D., *Fertility and Conception* (New York: Distributed by Grosset and Dunlap for Paddington Press, LTD, 1979), p. 181.

4. Melody Green, *The Questions Most People Ask About Abortion* (Lindale, Texas: Pretty Good Printing, 1983), n.p.

5. Melody Green, *Children: Things We Throw Away?* (Lindale, Texas: Pretty Good Printing, 1983), n.p.

6. John 4:34.

Chapter Twelve

1. Exodus 1–2:10.

2. Patricia Eichelberger Thompson, "Stress in the Adoption Process: A Personal Account," *Social Work* 23 (May 1978), p. 248.

3. Lois R. Melina, "Bonding: It's a Never-ending Experience," *Adopted Child,* 1982. (Free copy: Newsletter published 12 times each year by Lois R. Melina, P.O. Box 9362, Moscow, Idaho 83843.)

T. Berry Brazelton, *On Becoming a Family: The Growth of Attachment* (New York: Delacorte Press, 1981).

Chapter Thirteen

1. Henry H. Halley, *Halley's Bible Handbook* (Grand Rapids, Michigan: Zondervan Publishing House, 1965), p. 576.

2. Acts 18:2 (Aquila); Acts 18:18 (Priscilla); Acts 18:26 (Priscilla); Romans 16:3 (Priscilla); 1 Corinthians 16:19 (Aquila); 2 Timothy 4:19 (Priscilla).

3. Acts 18:2 and Merrill F. Unger, *Unger's Bible Dictionary* (Chicago: Moody Press, 1966), p. 210.

4. Ibid., pp. 220–221.

5. Ibid., p. 221.

6. Acts 18:5–6.

7. Acts 18:6–7.
8. Acts 18:19–21.
9. Acts 18:24–28.
10. 1 Corinthians 1:12–14; 3:4–11.
11. Romans 1:8–15.
12. Unger, *Unger's Bible Dictionary*, pp. 221, 1101.
13. Ibid., p. 889.
14. John 10:1–14; 21:22 (NIV).
15. 1 Corinthians 7:7–24.
16. Philippians 4:11.
17. 1 Samuel 17:38–40.

Chapter Fourteen

1. 2 Corinthians 11:21a–33.
2. Luke 1:5–7.
3. Romans 12:3; 1 Corinthians 12:7.
4. Romans 12:3–8; 1 Corinthians 12:4–31.
5. Acts 10:38; Matthew 4:23; 9:35; 24:14; 16:16–19; Luke 2:49; 4:42–43.
6. Romans 12:13; 1 Timothy 3:2; Titus 1:8; 1 Peter 4:9.

Chapter Fifteen

1. Genesis 30:1 (NIV).
2. Romans 12:10; 14:10–13.
3. Revelation 22:13–14, 17.

Selected Bibliography

Abrahamson, Pamela; Clark, Matt; Gary, Sandra; Witherspoon, Deborah; and Zabarsky, Marsha. "Infertility: New Cures, New Hope." *Newsweek* (December 6, 1982), p. 102.

Behnke, Lynn C.; Snodgrass, Leslie; and Malcom, Janet, eds. *Stepping Stones: To Offer Hope, Encouragement and Support to Infertile Couples*. Witchita, Kansas: Stepping Stones Ministry, P.O. Box 11141. Four-page bulletin published every other month.

Bell, J. Stephen, "Psychological Problems Among Patients Attending an Infertility Clinic." *Journal of Psychosomatic Research* 25 (1981), pp. 1–3.

Brazelton, Berry T. *On Becoming a Family: The Growth of Attachment*. New York: Delacorte Press, 1981.

Goergen, Donald. *The Sexual Celibate*. Garden City, New York: Image Books, a Division of Doubleday & Company, 1979.

Green, Melody. *The Questions Most People Ask About Abortion*. Lindale, Texas: Pretty Good Printing, 1983.

Green, Melody. *Children: Things We Throw Away?* Lindale, Texas: Pretty Good Printing, 1983.

Halverson, Kaye with Hess, Karen M. *The Wedded Unmother*. Minneapolis: Augsburg, 1980.

Kaufman, Sherwin A. *New Hope for the Childless Couple*. New York: Simon & Schuster, 1980.

Kolata, Gina B., "Infertility; Promising New Treatments," *Science* 202 (October 13, 1978), p. 20.

Kolata, Gina B. "The Psychology of Infertility." *Science* 202 (October 13, 1978), p. 202.

Kraft, Adrienne D. and others at St. Mary's Services, Chicago, Illinois. "The Psychological Dimensions of Infertility," *American Journal of Orthopsychiatry,* 50 (October 1980), p. 624.

Kübler–Ross, Elisabeth. *Death: The Final Stage of Growth.* Englewood Cliffs, New Jersey: Prentice Hall, 1975.

Mazor, M.D. "Barren Couples," *Psychology Today* 12 (May 1979), p. 101.

Melina, Lois R. "Bonding: It's a Never-ending Experience." *Adopted Child* 1982. (Free copy: Newsletter published 12 times each year by Lois R. Melina, P.O. Box 9362, Moscow, Idaho 83843.)

Menning, Barbara Eck. *Infertility: A Guide for the Childless Couple.* Englewood Cliffs, New Jersey: Prentice Hall, Inc., 1977.

Menning, Barbara Eck. "The Infertile Couple: A Plea for Advocacy," *Child Welfare* 54 (June 1975), p. 454.

Renne, Diane. "There's Always Adoption," *Child Welfare* 56 (July 1977), p. 466.

Stigger, Judith A. *Coping With Infertility.* Minneapolis: Augsburg Publishing House, 1983.

Thompson, Patricia Eichelberger. "Stress in the Adoption Process: A Personal Account." *Social Work* 23 (May 1978), p. 248.

Unger, Merrill F. *Unger's Bible Dictionary.* Chicago: Moody Press, 1966.

Williams, Don. *The Apostle Paul and Women in the Church.* Ventura, California: Regal Books, 1977.

Organizations and Publications

Adopted Child: A Newsletter for Parents
Published monthly by
Lois R. Melina
P.O. Box 9362
Moscow, ID 83843

A four-page newsheet.

AMEND
Dian Hoffman
1548 Brenthaven
Floirisant, MO 63031

Peer Support group for parents of handicapped or deceased babies.

ARENA
Adoption Resource Exchange of North America
67 Irving Place
New York, NY 10003

Center for processing available information on adoption in North America; specializes in seeking families for children with special needs.

American Fertility Society
1608 13th Avenue South,
Suite 101
Birmingham, AL 35205
(205) 933–7222

Supplies information on infertility specialists and facilities available in geographical area of inquirer.

Candlelighters Foundation
2025 Eye Street N.W., Suite 1011
Washington, D.C. 20006

Mutual-help group for parents of children with cancer.

The Compassionate Friends
P.O. Box 1347
Oak Brook, IL 60521

Self-help group for those mourning the death of a child.

Families for Children, Inc.
100 Bowling Green
Pointe Clare 720
Quebec, Canada

Provides information about various international adoption possibilities.

Holt Adoption Program
P.O. Box 2420
Eugene, OR 97402

International adoption agency specializing in Korean children.

NON
National Organization for
Non-parents
806 Reistertown Road
Baltimore, MD 20218

Promotes and supports the decision for childfree living.

OURS
Organization for a United
Response
3148 Humboldt Avenue South
Minneapolis, MN 55408
(612) 827–5709

Organization for adoptive parents which publishes an outstanding bimonthly newsletter.

RESOLVE, INC.
P.O. Box 474
Belmont, MA 02178

National nonprofit organization which provides literature, structure for local support groups, telephone counseling, and community education services.

Stepping Stones
Box 11141
Wichita, KS 67211

Bimonthly publication by Stepping Stones Ministry, a nonprofit ministry of Central Christian Church in Wichita. Excellent four-page newsletter for infertile couples.

United Infertility
P.O. Box 23
Scarsdale, NY 10583

Organization which provides information on infertility.

World Family Adoptions, Ltd.
5048 Fairy Chasm Road
West Bend, WI 53095

Agency for international adoption.

3-25-23